GOOD DIRT

GOOD DIRT
Confessions of a Conservationist

Second Edition

DAVID E. MORINE

LYONS PRESS
Guilford, Connecticut
An imprint of Globe Pequot Press

"Professional Courtesy" appeared originally in the May 28, 1990, issue of *Sports Illustrated* under the title "Done In by a Snake in the Mansion." © 1990, The Time Inc. Magazine Company.

"Negotiations" is reprinted from the March/April 1990 issue of *American Forests* magazine of the American Forestry Association, 1516 P St. NW, Washington, DC 20005.

"Divine Intervention" appeared originally in *Small Claims, My Little Trials in Life* by David E. Morine; Camden, ME: Down East Books; 2003.

"The Intern" appeared originally in *Small Claims, My Little Trials in Life* by David E. Morine; Camden, ME: Down East Books; 2003.

"Lt. William Barrett Travers" is reprinted from the December 10, 1990, issue of *Sports Illustrated* under the title "Tale of the Bewildered Bird Dog." It also appeared in *Small Claims, My Little Trials in Life* by David E. Morine; Camden, ME: Down East Books; 2003.

To buy books in quantity for corporate use
or incentives, call **(800) 962-0973**
or e-mail **premiums@GlobePequot.com**.

Lyons Press is an imprint of Globe Pequot Press.

Project editor: Julie Marsh
Layout: Sue Murray

The Library of Congress has cataloged the previous edition as follows:

Morine, David E.
    Good dirt : confessions of a conservationist / by David E. Morine. — 1st ed.
        p. cm.
    ISBN 0-87106-444-8
        1. Nature conservation—United States. 2. Nature Conservancy (U.S.) I. Title.
QH76.M67   1990
333.7'2—dc20

                                        90-43074
                                        CIP

ISBN 978-0-7627-7364-0

Printed in the United States of America
10 9 8 7 6 5 4 3 2 1

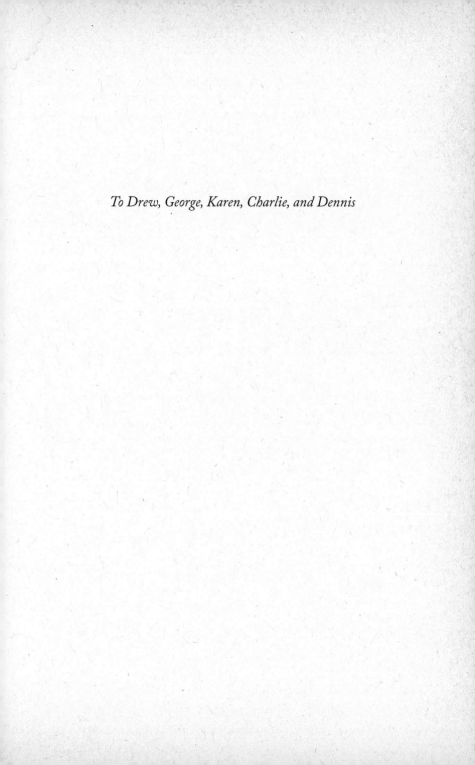

To Drew, George, Karen, Charlie, and Dennis

The reason the eagle can fly so high is because it takes itself so lightly

—MARYANN BASSETT

TABLE OF CONTENTS

Acknowledgments

Thanks to Holly Rubino and Mary Norris the editors at Globe Pequot Press who came up with the idea of republishing *Good Dirt* and Julie Marsh, Melissa Evarts, and Libby Kingsbury who put the book together; Kerry Sparks, my agent at Levine/Greenberg Literary Agency, who has figured out how a contract should read in the digital age and how to keep a coot like me afloat in the turbulent seas of the literary world; Dick Evans and Mark Zenick, two dedicated conservationists in western Mass who provided many insights into local conservation efforts; Spencer Beebe, who let me borrow liberally from his new book *Cache*, which, I might add, is an excellent read; Ruth Morine, whose memory is a lot better than mine and helps keep the facts in line, or at least almost in line; Charlie Taylor, who is always there to solve my computer problems, of which I have many, and to make sure that everything is legal; Jynx Eldridge and Evan Maurer, two great art historians who directed me to the Garden of Eden; Doug Wheeler, who provided sound advice on environmental matters; and of course, Paul Flint, who structures, hones, and enhances everything I write. As I've said before, it's Paul who makes my stories readable. Finally, I want to say how much I appreciated this opportunity to revisit, at least in spirit many of the neat places, great people, and significant natural areas we helped save. There is nothing I enjoy more than saving land.

Introduction

1990

Conservation is my chosen profession. From 1972 through 1987 I was in charge of land acquisition for The Nature Conservancy. During that time we acquired three million acres of land, completed 5,000 projects, and protected 2,000 of America's most significant natural areas. We ran a good business. We raised some money. We saved some land. We had some fun.

When I started with the Conservancy, saving land was a relatively simple business. We'd look around, find some land that we liked, and buy it. Once we had acquired an area, I really believed that it would be protected in perpetuity. I, like most people, had never heard of acid rain, the greenhouse effect, or holes in the ozone layer. We didn't deal in doom and gloom. We bought land.

Today, things are different. Dire predictions seem to be the staple of the conservation movement. Most conservationists are consumed by problems for which there are no simple solutions. What good does it do, for example, to buy a forest unless you can protect it from acid rain? Why save a tidal marsh if it is going to be lost to rising oceans resulting from global warming? Who can worry about a piece of native tall-grass prairie when we are destroying the atmosphere? It is no wonder that many of today's conservationists seem somber. They see so many threats to the environment that they can't enjoy being conservationists. For them, humor has become a rare and endangered species.

During my tenure at The Nature Conservancy, we were generally considered the most businesslike of the conservation organizations. We probably were. But that didn't mean that we didn't have our share of screw-ups. Any time you undertake a major land deal, something is going to go wrong. When that happens, you can do one of two things: you can get upset or you can laugh. More often than not, we laughed.

I believe that a large part of the Conservancy's success has been due to the fact that we never took ourselves too seriously. We never let the big issues get us down. We never spent too much time agonizing over the big picture. We attacked the problem of saving significant natural areas one piece at a time. We weren't naive. We knew we weren't going to save the world, but we thought we could save small and important parts of it. We were focused in our work; we were happy being conservationists.

This collection of stories describes some of my more monumental foul-ups. Most are informative, a few are irreverent, and at least one is totally tasteless. Despite my having been justifiably accused of never letting the facts get in the way of a good story, these stories are, on the whole, true. I hope they will explain a little about land conservation and give conservationists a much-needed lift. With all the doom and gloom in the world today, we could all use a good laugh.

2011

That was then. Now, in 2011, as far as the cause is concerned, nothing has changed. The identification and protection of significant natural areas is still the most important thing land conservation organizations could be doing. What has changed are the organizations. They've gotten too big, they've taken on too much overhead, they've lost their focus. Today, resources that should be going into saving land are being diverted into maintaining the organizations. During the 1960s, the cause of land conservation was a movement run primarily by volunteers. During the seventies and eighties, in large part thanks to The Nature Conservancy, it became a business. Now, people who think they're giving to the cause are for the most part supporting the bureaucracies that have grown up around it. This is a natural progression. It happens to a lot of nonprofits, but that doesn't make it right.

Hopefully the stories in this revised edition of *Good Dirt* will help remind conservationists that the cause is about saving land, not building big organizations, and the fun is getting your hands in the dirt, not sitting in some spiffy office. To that end, I've included a lesson after each story. They're simple and anecdotal, and they might seem like common sense; however, there is an old adage that says, "Common sense comes from experience, but experience often comes from a lack of common sense."

During my time at The Nature Conservancy, we had a lot of experiences that helped us gain a considerable amount of common sense. Use these lessons as you see fit, but never forget, the reason the eagle can fly so high is because it takes itself so lightly.

Wormsloe Plantation

On January 3, 1972, I started with The Nature Conservancy. I was the forty-sixth paid employee. When I walked into TNC's very modest national headquarters in Arlington, Virginia, that first day, the motto embossed on the glass door read Land Conservation Through Private Action. That's what TNC did: it conserved land through private action, and at that time most of that private action was provided by volunteers. It was the volunteers in TNC's thirty-two chapters who found the projects, did the deals, and raised the money. The professional staff's primary role was to keep the books and clean up after the volunteers.

A typical day went as follows. Once Pat Noonan, TNC's bright, energetic, fun-loving director of operations, picked up the mail, a half dozen of us would gather around the coffee table in his office. Pat would dump the mail onto the table and start sorting through it. "Ah, here's a good one for you, Brad," he'd say, picking out a letter and reading it over. Brad Northrup was another young MBA like Pat and me. "That pro bono attorney we have up in Schenectady has a client who just died. The guy left us five acres in his will. It's in the middle of a swamp. The attorney says the guy liked to go out there and look at birds. He wants to know if we'll accept the deed." Pat chucked the letter over to Brad. "You're from upstate New York. Call the Eastern New York Chapter and see if they want us to take it."

While Brad read the letter, Pat resumed fishing through the pile. All of us patiently waited for him to get another bite. "Davis," he said scanning the next letter, "didn't you meet with the guy who runs the San Juan Islands Project? You know, the one who's all excited about the blipty-blip bird?"

Davis Cherington ran the Conservancy's stewardship program. He was not an MBA. He was a naturalist and as such felt obligated to correct Pat's almost total ignorance of the natural world. "Yes, that's Jon Roush, one of our best volunteers. I believe the bird he saw was a blue-throated booby."

Pat flipped the letter to Davis. "Well, this booby needs more money. Roush wants a list of everyone who's ever given to the San Juan Islands. He's going to go back and hit them again."

And so it went. Every morning we'd meet in Pat's office for an hour or so and go through the mail. Then we'd spend the rest of the day working on our assignments. With 18,000-plus members, many of whom were actively involved with one of TNC's preserves, there was always plenty for us to do. As TNC's assistant director of operations, most of my time was spent dealing with chapter chairs trying to make sure the projects they were working on were done in a businesslike manner. Few, if any, of them thought of TNC as a business. All they wanted to do was save land.

I'd only been with the Conservancy a couple of months when Pat handed me a letter postmarked Atlanta, Georgia. The name embossed on the back of the envelope read "Jane Hurt Yarn." I recognized it immediately. Mrs. Yarn was a member of the Conservancy's National Board of Governors and one of the most visible conservationists in the South (not that she had much competition). In 1972 TNC had no chapter and only a handful of members in Georgia. "You'd better plan a trip to Atlanta," Pat said. "Mrs. Yarn is tight with the new governor, some peanut farmer from south Georgia. He's probably asleep at the switch, but Mrs. Yarn says he likes conservation and wants to do something big. Don't ever underestimate Mrs. Yarn. She's as sweet as a Georgia peach, but she thinks big and knows how to get things done."

Mrs. Yarn was waiting for me outside the old Hartsfield terminal. She was a stunningly beautiful woman, sleek and stylish. Her car was an old blue DeSoto badly in need of a paint job. "Chollie keeps gettin aftah me to buy a new cah," she cooed apologetically, "but Ah can't see why as long as this one runs. Isn't that what conservation's all about?"

"Chollie" was Mrs. Yarn's husband, Dr. Charles Yarn, one of the South's foremost plastic surgeons. I could understand his dismay. The

Doc made everything he touched look better so it must have been embarrassing to have his wife, the conservationist, driving around Atlanta in some beat-up old bomb. "We're going to stop to see the Guvnuh," Mrs. Yarn said as we rattled along the maze of interstates that crisscross Atlanta. "Jimmuh's very interested in conservation. I told him we'd be happy to help."

As we breezed through the state capital, everybody said hello to Mrs. Yarn. We hardly had a chance to sit down before the governor himself came out to greet her. "Jane," he said, flashing his toothy grin. "Ah'm delighted you could stop by."

Mrs. Yarn rose gracefully, like she was welcoming the governor into her parlor, and extended her hand. "Why Jimmee, I mean Guvnuh, we're just delighted to be heah." As the governor took her hand, she turned to me and added, "And this heah is Dave Morine. Dave's from the national office of The Nature Conservancy. He knows all about conservation and should be able to give us some good help."

That was a huge exaggeration. At the time, I knew very little about conservation. My specialty was real estate, but coming from Mrs. Yarn, these trumped up credentials sounded perfectly true. The governor smiled at me. "Welcome to Georgia, Dave," he said shaking my hand. "We really appreciate your willingness to come down heah and lend us a hand. We truly are concerned about conservation."

Jimmy Carter didn't seem like your typical glad-handing politician. There was a glint of genuine commitment in his deep blue eyes. "Thank you, Governor," I said. "I just hope that I can live up to Mrs. Yarn's billing."

The governor turned back to Mrs. Yarn. "Jane, why don't you and Dave step into my office? I've got Joe and Chuck in there, and we've been discussing your idea."

Joe was Joe Tanner, the state's director of natural resources. Chuck was Charles Parrish, the head of the Department of Natural Resource's Office of Research and Planning. Joe and Chuck were about my age and were probably just as green. Mrs. Yarn started talking in her sweet, comforting drawl. We all listened. She said given the growth sweeping over Georgia, it was time to save what was left of the state's heritage. She proposed that the governor create a program for Georgia that would identify and protect the state's best remaining historical, recreational, and natural sites. The governor liked the idea. Joe and Chuck liked the idea. I liked the idea. Heritage was big in the South. Preserving it would be popular. If the Conservancy could help Georgia get this type of program going, we could use it as a model for other states in the South. Mrs. Yarn's idea was big, but were Joe, Chuck, and The Nature Conservancy's expert from the national office big enough to pull it off?

All that spring we worked with Bob Friedman, a young Californian just out of Harvard, who was serving an internship with the state before going to law school, on what we labeled the "Georgia Heritage Trust Program." On July 21, 1972, by executive order, Governor Jimmy Carter created the Georgia Heritage Trust Advisory Commission. This group of fifteen prominent Georgians chosen by the governor would direct the Heritage Trust Program. Joe Tanner was chair; Jane Hurt Yarn was the key member.

The commission's charge was to identify the state's most significant historical, recreational, and natural sites and develop a ten-year plan for protecting them. The governor wanted the commission's initial report by the end of the year. Based on that report, he planned to go to the legislature and ask for funding to acquire the sites on the list. It was all very exciting. If this bill passed, it would be the largest appropriation ever for conservation by a state government.

When I reported our progress to Pat, he immediately saw the potential. "Bait the hook to suit the fish," he said. Pat was hopelessly addicted to cornball phrases. "We need a great project to kick this program off. Make sure it's highly visible, that it has historical and cultural as well as natural significance. Work a deal that will show the legislature how we can leverage their funds into other projects. We want to make the governor look good."

At the next meeting with Joe, Chuck, Bob, and Mrs. Yarn, I presented Pat's idea of finding a lead project that would excite the legislature, one that contained all the elements of the Heritage Trust Program. "Well," Mrs. Yarn said, "seems like to me you're talking about Wormsloe."

"Wormsloe?" I said. It sounded like some kind of endangered species. In fact, as we learned later, Wormsloe was an old Scottish word for "silkworm farm."

"Wormsloe Plantation," Joe said. "It's just outside of Savannah, 850 acres of virgin timber and marshland surrounding a beautiful antebellum home, all perfectly preserved. It's been in the same family for 239 years. They have it in a nonprofit foundation, but the real estate is not tax exempt, and the taxes are killing them. The family doesn't know what to do. They can't afford to hold on to the place, but they refuse to sell any of the land. They've asked if we can help."

"Let's do it," I said. "Historical, natural, cultural, just outside of Savannah. It sounds perfect. Who controls the foundation?"

"The Barrows," Mrs. Yarn said. "They still live in the main house. They're a wondahful family. Ah'll be happy to introduce you."

Mrs. Yarn arranged for us to meet with the Barrows at the plantation in mid-September. I flew to Savannah, where Chuck and Mrs. Yarn were waiting for me. We drove south out of Savannah until we came to the Isle of Hope. There we turned through wrought-iron gates under an impressive stone arch. The inscription chiseled into the face of the arch read "1733 Wormsloe." The oyster shell driveway ran for almost a mile. Majestic live oaks lined both sides of it, forming a perfect canopy. Gray strands of Spanish moss fluttered from the twisted branches like tattered remnants of the Confederacy. "Well, Dave, what do you think?" Mrs. Yarn asked, already knowing the answer.

"God, it's beautiful," I said. "Will you look at those trees?"

"You'll never see anything like them again," Chuck said. "These trees were hand-planted by slaves 135 years ago."

We headed down the drive, the sound of shells crunching under the tires, and pulled up in front of a large brick plantation home. Mr. Craig Barrow Jr. and his son, Craig III, were standing at the top of the ballast brick staircase waiting for us. Mr. Barrow came down the stairs to greet us. He opened the car door for Mrs. Yarn. "Welcome to Wormsloe."

"We're so pleeeased to be heah," Mrs. Yarn said, graciously stepping out.

Mr. Barrow was somewhere in his sixties. Craig III was about my age, and like his father, a perfect gentleman. The Barrows ushered us into the sitting room. The room looked out over a huge expanse of verdant marsh. A faint offshore breeze blew through the triple sash windows and with it came the squawks of a great blue heron lumbering over the marsh. They were the only sounds breaking the midafternoon somnolence. The heat dictated that we start with a large glass of iced tea flavored by a sprig of green mint. While we sipped, Mr. Barrow explained his problem. "Wormsloe Plantation," he said, "was stahted in 1733 with a 500-acre grant from George II from which, of coase, we get the name Georgia. The grant went to Noble Jones, an associate of Oglethorpe, the Englishman that founded the colony of Georgia. We, the Barrow family, are the direct descendants of Jones."

That started the history of Wormsloe. It took another two iced teas for Mr. Barrow to explain how an additional 350 acres were received from George III; how both of the original grants were now preserved in the state archives; how the 850 acres owned by the Barrows were prime for development; how the value of coastal property had skyrocketed all through the 1960s; how, based on the success of developments like Hilton Head and Skidaway Island just across the river, Wormsloe was now worth in excess of $3 million; how the county paid no attention to the plantation's natural, historical, and cultural value and kept taxing the property on its development potential; how when the real property taxes reached $25,000 a year, the Barrows could no longer afford to pay them; how in desperation they placed the plantation into a private foundation whose sole purpose was to retain Wormsloe's natural, historical, and cultural significance; how they hoped the foundation would be exempt from real property taxes, but how in early 1972, the state supreme court ruled that the foundation was not exempt from real property taxes and ordered the Barrows either to pay $120,000 in back taxes or lose Wormsloe.

"Developers are coming to us every day with proposals to subdivide the property," Craig said. "They've offered us ungodly amounts of money, but we've always refused. Our family's never sold one acre from the two original grants. Wormsloe is the only plantation in America that has remained in one ownership since 1733."

With the problem in hand, we all adjourned to the Wormsloe Library, a cool musty mausoleum built in 1870 to house the papers of the Confederacy. The building literally reeked with history. Just inside the entrance, a copy of the Articles of the Confederacy was displayed on a tilt-top stand. "When Ah see that," Mr. Barrow said, pointing to the document, "Ah feel like Jefferson Davis. Ah'm fightin a losin battle."

"Not so," I said. "I think I know how we can do this."

"How's that?"

"Why don't you carve out the main house, the library, and some appropriate acreage and then deed the rest of the land with restrictions to the state for a natural and historical park? The state's exempt from taxes and this could be the first project of the new Georgia Heritage Trust Program."

"Ah don't believe Ah know 'bout that program," Mr. Barrow said, somewhat suspiciously.

"It's Mrs. Yarn's idea, so why don't I let her explain it." Mr. Barrow might not trust a carpetbagger like me, but he'd never doubt the word of a Georgia peach like Mrs. Yarn.

We all sat and listened while Mrs. Yarn described how the new Georgia Heritage Trust Program was created to preserve places like Wormsloe. She did a wonderful job stressing how much of the state's natural, historical, and cultural heritage already had been lost; how now it was the time for all true Georgians to pull together and protect what was left; how the Guvnuh was 100 percent behind the program; how Wormsloe, given its great natural, historical, and cultural significance should be the program's first project; and how it would set the standard for projects to come.

Mr. Barrow was not only charmed, he was sold. "By golly," he said, "that sounds too good to be true."

"But what about the back taxes?" Craig said. "We still have to pay them."

"Easy," I said, "the Conservancy will buy a lot from the foundation for $120,000. With that money, the foundation will pay the back taxes. Then when the Heritage Program gets its appropriation from the general assembly, the state can buy the lot back from the Conservancy."

"But that means we'll have to subdivide Wormsloe," Mr. Barrow said, obviously not pleased with the thought of breaking the family's tradition of never selling an acre.

"It'll be just a paper transaction. We won't actually survey out a lot, and when the state buys the land back, the property will be whole again."

"What if the appropriation doesn't go through?" Craig asked.

"That's a risk we'll have to take. I think the Conservancy's willing to bet $120,000 on this project, am I right Mrs. Yarn?"

Mrs. Yarn smiled. "Don't ya'll worry your sweet heads about that appropriation," she said. "Jimmee, I mean the Guvnuh, will get it through."

"The trick's to get the deal done by December 31," I added, "because if the foundation still owns the property on January 1, the county will want another $25,000 in taxes."

"Ah like it in principle," Mr. Barrow nodded, "but how are we going to guarantee that the state won't turn Wormsloe into another Jekyll Island? We don't want a whole buncha pahkin lots and picnic tables out heah."

Jekyll Island was another one of Georgia's Golden Isles. It was just south of Wormsloe. Many people thought the state had destroyed the island's natural significance when they developed it into a state park.

"I can understand your concerns," Chuck said, "but I think we can take care of that problem with restrictions you put into the deed. I'll draw up an initial plan for the park before the transfer and you can base your restrictions on that plan."

Mr. Barrows was thinking it over, but Mrs. Yarn made her move before he had a chance to come up with any more questions. "Ah must say, this has been a most enjoyable aftuhnoon," she said, rising gracefully from her chair. "I know the Guvnuh is going to be very pleased."

The governor was very pleased. He immediately saw how Wormsloe was the perfect project to kick off the Heritage Program and told Chuck to get it done before the end of the year. All through October and November, Chuck and I met with the Barrows regarding the restrictions that would go into the deed, but as Mrs. Yarn had sensed at our first meeting, structuring a deal between the state and the Barrows was not going to be easy. The Barrows loved Wormsloe. They knew every tree and were determined to protect every one. They'd fought for 239 years to keep Wormsloe just the way it was and they weren't about to give up now. If it weren't for the Barrows and their love affair with Wormsloe, the lands granted to Noble Jones by George II and George III would have been covered with golf courses and condominiums long ago.

For Chuck, it was a thankless job. He was supposed to turn Wormsloe into a state park without changing anything. The Barrows dismissed his first plan out of hand. They wanted no parking, no improvements, or anything else that was necessary to accommodate the public, even with very limited access. Chuck, with Bob Friedman's help, drew up plan after plan, only to have them rejected by the Barrows. Meanwhile, the clock was ticking. On December 12, the Barrows finally approved a very passive use of the property that included just a few nature trails leading from a small parking lot set in the far corner of the property.

"Ah think this will work," Mr. Barrow said, studying the plan. "But how do we know these restrictions will run in perpetuity?"

It was a good question, one we couldn't answer. Chuck couldn't agree that the restrictions would last forever, or even beyond Jimmy Carter's administration. The next governor might be another Lester Maddox, someone who was more comfortable with golf courses and condos than with trees and marsh. But we were running out of time. We had to get this deal done. I excused myself and called Pat. "Pat," I said. "We've reached an impasse. What do I do?"

"To the swift belongs the race. Call Mrs. Yarn." Click.

I hung up and called Mrs. Yarn. "Mrs. Yarn," I said, "we've got a problem. We've been having a heck of a time getting the Barrows and the state to agree on restrictions, and now that we've finally reached an agreement, Chuck can't guarantee that the restrictions will run in perpetuity. Nobody can. Pat said I should call you. What are we going to do?"

There was a pause on the other end of the line. Then Mrs. Yarn said in a calm, collected drawl, "Jimmee's going to be in Savannah this weekend. Why don't we have the Guvnuh drop by Wormsloe for brunch with the Barrows on Sunday mawnin? You and Chuck and Joe and Ah will join them. Ah'm sure if we all get togethuh, we can work somethin out."

Sunday morning, December 18, I got up bright and early and headed for National Airport. I was catching Delta's first flight to Atlanta, where I'd meet the state's attorney general, then we'd fly to Savannah in a state plane. Chuck wanted the attorney general there to approve the final document. I didn't see one cloud in the sky all the way to Atlanta. It was going to be a beautiful, crisp, clear fall day, perfect for having brunch with the governor and selling the Barrows on the restrictions. The Delta jet pulled into the gate at 8:16, right on time. I ran out of the terminal and hopped into the first cab. The only hitch in Chuck's plan was that the state plane didn't fly from Hartsfield. The state's hangar was at Fulton County Airport, someplace on the other side of the city. It was 8:30. No problem. The state's plane wasn't leaving until 9:30. It would take an hour to get to Savannah, then another half hour to drive to Wormsloe. Mrs. Yarn had scheduled brunch for 11. "Fulton County Airport," I said to the back of the driver's head.

Judging from the gray, uncombed strands of hair hanging over the seat, the driver was a woman, and she was a mess. A cloud of smoke engulfed her head as we pulled away from the terminal. "Mind if I 'moke?" she said in a slurred voice as the smell of alcohol filled the cab. She was drunk, but what could I do? We'd already pulled from the curb and were heading out of the airport.

What was supposed to be a twenty-minute ride quickly turned into an hour. I kept telling her to pull over and let me out; she kept reassuring me we were almost there. At last she found the airport and pulled up in front of a building that appeared to be deserted. The meter read $52.35. I threw a twenty over the seat and hopped out. She was too drunk to notice.

It was 9:30. I ran up to the building and tried the door. It was locked. I looked around and saw a public phone. Chuck had given me the number where he was staying, just in case of an emergency. This was an emergency. I dialed the number. Chuck answered. When I told him what had happened and where I was, he said, "You're on the wrong side of the airport. The state's hangar's on the other side. Get over there as quick as you can. The attorney general just called. He's about to take off without you. I'll call and tell him you're on your way."

I hung up the phone and looked across the runway. I could see the state plane on the tarmac, its engines running. How was I going to get over there? The runway was easily a mile long. It would take me at least another fifteen minutes to run around it. There was only one answer. I grabbed my briefcase, ran out to the edge of the runway, looked one way, then the other, and darted across. A burly policeman was waiting for me on the other side. The patch on his sleeve identified him as a member of the Fulton Country Sheriff's Office.

"Son," he said rising to his full height of at least six foot three, "do you know it's a federal offense to venture onto an active runway?"

"No, sir," I said. "But I don't think you understand. I'm supposed to be having brunch with the governor."

He was not impressed. "Son, the Guvnuh's down on the coast. Now why don't you just step inside this heah squad car and we'll take us a ride down to the station."

I wasn't about to argue with this guy. "OK," I said, "but first could we stop by the state's hangar? The attorney general's waiting for me there."

When we walked in the attorney general was pacing up and down. He was not happy. He'd been cooling his heels for almost an hour waiting on me. Now I show up having been arrested for running across an active runway. What type of idiot would be running across an active runway? It was 10:30 by the time the attorney general convinced the cop I was there on state business and we were in fact flying to the coast to have brunch with the governor.

We touched down in Savannah at 11:45. Chuck had a state trooper waiting for us. He turned on the siren and we zoomed off to Wormsloe. As we turned down the driveway, we had to pull over to make way for a big, black Continental. Its license plate read "1." As it passed I could see Joe Tanner sitting in the front and Mrs. Yarn and the governor in the back. Mrs. Yarn smiled and waved at me as they passed. Dr. Yarn would have been very proud. The governor's car definitely suited her better than the old blue De Soto. In it Mrs. Yarn looked like the first lady.

When we pulled up in front of the House, Mr. Barrow, Craig, and Chuck were standing at the top of the brick staircase. They were all smiling. Mr. Barrow appeared six inches taller, like a huge weight had been lifted from his shoulders. "What happened?" I said jumping out.

"Everything's fine," Chuck said. "We're just waiting for the attorney general to ratify these here documents." He handed me a sheet of paper.

"What's this?" I said, studying the document. I'd expected a long detailed list of restrictions. What Chuck gave me was just one page. I read it over. It said that Wormsloe Plantation would be held for the benefit of the general public as a historical and ecological nature preserve and would be kept essentially in its current natural state. That was it, only the document wasn't signed by Mr. Barrow and the governor. It was signed by Mr. Barrow and Mrs. Yarn.

"What the heck?" I said. "This agreement says that the Wormsloe Foundation will sell the whole property, less the house and outbuildings, to The Nature Conservancy for $120,000. What happened to the state?"

"Here," Chuck said, handing me a second piece of paper. The restrictive language in this document read exactly like the language in the first one, but this agreement was signed by Mrs. Yarn and the governor.

"Since we couldn't trust the state," Mr. Barrow said, "we agreed to sell all the land with the restrictions to the Conservancy for $120,000 and you agreed to pass it on to the state. That way, if the state ever changes its mind and wants to do something different, it'll have to take on a national conservation group rather than regular folk like us. Mrs. Yarn suggested it. She said having the full faith and credit of The Nature Conservancy behind the deal would give the property an extra layer of protection. The governor liked it and we'ah tickled pink. We get the extra protection and we don't have to carve off some lot. Ah'm surprised you didn't think of it."

Wormsloe was saved. As Pat predicted, the general assembly was impressed. It appropriated $12 million for the first year of the Heritage Trust Program but made it clear that if the program kept doing deals like Wormsloe, there would be more to come. My first big deal in conservation was a huge success, only it wasn't mine. It was Mrs. Yarn who'd made Wormsloe work. She was the one who started the Georgia Heritage Trust Program and gave TNC a model for land conservation that we were able to use not only in the South but all across the country.

Just Like the Library

WHEN PEOPLE ASK ME WHAT'S THE NATURE CONSERVANCY'S BEST preserve, they're sure I'll pick something big and sexy like Wormsloe, the Virginia Barrier Islands, the Pascagoula River, Ordway Native Tall Grass Prairies, or Santa Cruz Island, but while all of these were monumental projects, they are not TNC's best preserve. The best is Mianus River Gorge, a very common hemlock gully carved by the clean, clear waters of the Mianus River just thirty miles north of New York City.

Anybody who knows anything about natural areas would have to question my answer. While scenic and undisturbed, there's nothing rare or unique about Mianus River Gorge. There are hundreds of areas like it all over the Northeast. That's because when the early timber barons cut over this part of the country, there were so many big, beautiful, virgin oak, white pine, chestnut, walnut, ash, elm, beech, and birch that they couldn't be bothered lugging hemlock out of the gullies. So if Mianus River Gorge is not rare and not unique, how can it be TNC's best preserve?

In 1950 The Nature Conservancy was a purely scientific organization modeled after England's Ecological Union. Academics would gather a few times a year to read and discuss papers relating to the natural world. The bulk of these papers were given to documenting areas that were being lost. When the discussion turned to a very attractive piece of the Mianus River Gorge that was about to be developed, someone noted that TNC had $4,000 in the kitty and rather than just sitting around discussing the loss of natural areas, why not do something about it? The seed was planted. "Land Conservation Through Private Action" was born.

Since 1950 there have been fifty-four additions to Mianus River Gorge and three generations of people have taken an active role in creating and managing the preserve. Over that time Mianus River Gorge has become an integral part of the community. Today the preserve is like the library. Whether people around the gorge actively use it or not, they expect it will always be there and they'll do whatever it takes to protect it.

That's the level of protection natural areas should have to be considered real preserves. The problem is very few have it.

With an ever-growing population, ever-increasing pressure is being placed on natural resources. Areas designated as nature preserves are not immune from this pressure. Compounding the threat is the fact that many conservation organizations, especially the large ones, have taken on so much overhead they are no longer able or willing to protect their preserves. Wormsloe, the project that was the basis for TNC's state heritage programs, learned this back in the mid-1990s when a developer bought Pigeon Island, a little barrier island just to the east of Wormsloe.

To get to the island, the developer sought permission from the state to build a causeway over marshland that was part of Wormsloe. Apparently, nobody at the Georgia Department of Transportation knew or cared that this marsh was protected in perpetuity by the restrictions in the deed from the Conservancy to the state. Unbeknownst to the Barrows, a right-of-way was granted to the developer. When Craig Barrow III found out about it, he naturally went ballistic. His first call was to the state. It claimed since the right-of-way already had been granted, there was nothing it could do. Craig's next call was to the national office of The Nature Conservancy. Surely the full faith and credit of TNC would be enough to straighten this out.

"Wormsloe in Georgia, you say? Never heard of it." No one at the national office of TNC knew anything about the restrictions, or Wormsloe for that matter. Craig was referred to TNC's Charlotte office. Craig called, wrote, called, and wrote again, but TNC's full faith and credit was no place to be found. Eventually, Craig threatened to sue. At that point TNC's Georgia state director called and told Craig she'd try to work behind the scenes, but TNC was not going to publicly defend Wormsloe. She was pushing her own projects and didn't want to do anything that might upset the state.

Given this tepid response, Craig did the only thing he could do. He rallied local support for defending Wormsloe. The tide turned, and the Georgia Heritage Trust Commission, aided by a $100,000 grant from the Wormsloe Foundation, bought the developer out. Today, Pigeon Island is part of the Wormsloe Plantation Historic Site, and Craig, like so many committed conservationists, had learned an important lesson: over time organizations change. During that Sunday brunch in 1972, when Mrs. Yarn pledged the full faith and credit of The Nature Conservancy to protecting Wormsloe, none of us could imagine how TNC would evolve over the following twenty-five years. Institutional memory is short. To protect an area in perpetuity, it needs the full commitment of the community. Mianus River Gorge is our oldest preserve, and that's why it is, and always will be, The Nature Conservancy's best.

Welcome to the Family

ALL THROUGH THE 1970S THE NATURE CONSERVANCY WAS A FAMILY. The board of governors were the parents giving us their work, wisdom, and wealth. When Pat Noonan moved up to president, he became the big brother—protective, supportive, understanding, and continually leading the way. Raised in this idyllic atmosphere, it was no wonder that the rest of us grew up as bright, happy, energetic, clean-cut conservationists.

Every Friday afternoon Pat hosted an informal happy hour in our conference room. He'd personally buy a couple of cases of beer, and while attendance wasn't mandatory, everyone who was in town always showed up. These get-togethers would often last far into the evening. Pat would set the tone and direction by highlighting what we'd accomplished during the week and in doing so, make sure each individual knew that he or she was playing an important role in the success of the Conservancy.

"Miriam wrote the check that saved 1,500 acres of environmentally sensitive tidal marsh in Georgia," he'd announce. "Thank you, Miriam." There was enthusiastic applause. Miriam would flush, overcome with the significance of her deed.

"Josephine opened the envelope that contained the donation that allowed Miriam to write the check," Pat would continue. More applause. "What'd we do today, Jo?" he'd ask, knowing the answer.

"Everyone we could, and the good ones twice," Jo would always chime. "We got 122 new members this week." Jo loved opening those envelopes and counting those checks.

"We *can* do 'em twice because Mirdza made the labels for all those new members," Pat would say. Clap, clap, clap.

Mirdza was a very precise Latvian who pounded proudly on the Addressograph for eight hours a day. "Dat vas vun hundert und twenty-eight, Pott, vich is da best vee haff ever done." More clap, clap, clap.

Fitzie, our controller, had known Pat since they were kids. He loved to needle him. "Say, buddy boy," he'd ask accusingly, "do those 122 new members know their hard-earned money is being used to send you and these other bozos all over the country? You guys have already busted the travel budget."

Unfazed, Pat would respond, "Fitzie, I'm sure all of our new members would like to hear this from you directly. In fact, why don't you get on a plane and fly around and tell them." Much laughter. Everyone knew Fitzie got woozy just thinking about getting on a plane.

Pat saved his best for those of us who were doing the deals. "Greg just completed a 120-acre addition to the Blackwater Refuge." With that, he'd hold up the article from a local paper as proof that he wasn't making it up. "He even got his picture in the paper." Pat would circulate the paper. And there would be Greg, accepting a deed from an eleemosynary old couple with some official from the U.S. Fish and Wildlife Service standing in the background flashing his pearly whites. "As usual, Greg's wearing his photo shirt." Much hilarity. Greg always wore the same striped shirt whenever he thought he was going to have his picture taken. He claimed that the stripes showed up better in a photo. "We're going to send this picture down to the *Rocky Mount Observer*," Pat would add. "Let the folks back home know that Greg's not up here sleeping."

The amazing thing was that Pat would actually do it. A few weeks later Greg brought in a copy of the *Observer*. His picture appeared on the front page, captioned, "Local Boy Saves Land in Maryland." The article talked about Greg, his degree from UNC, his parents, his grandparents, the Conservancy, and anything else the *Observer* felt was newsworthy. What the article didn't say was that Pat had thrown Greg a softball, that he'd set the whole deal up. Greg knew it. We all knew it. But it didn't matter. Once you joined the family, Pat, like any good big brother, did his level best to make sure you didn't fail.

Everything was going fine until the board of governors charged the staff with developing our first long-range plan. Pat's summaries of what we'd accomplished each week were no longer sufficient. The board wanted to know what we were going to accomplish over the next five years. We'd still spend Friday evenings sitting around the conference table drinking Pat's beer, but rather than rehashing the glories of the past, we were debating the future. Conviviality began to give way to acrimony. Dr. Robert Jenkins, the Conservancy's chief scientist, had a different vision than the rest of us. He wasn't focused solely on buying land. He maintained that the mission of The Nature Conservancy was the preservation of biotic diversity.

Most of us didn't fully understand, or much care about, the concept of biotic diversity. We were MBAs and lawyers, not scientists. Our diversity was in the deals. This attitude incensed Dr. Bob. "Noah's Ark!" he'd scream, pounding his big fist on the table. "Think Noah's Ark. We need two of every kind. Our mission is the preservation of biotic diversity, not just buying land." We'd look to Pat for guidance. He'd hand us each another beer.

By 1974 we'd managed to develop a long-range plan that we felt would make the Conservancy the preeminent land conservation organization in America. It divided the country into four regions. These regions would be the Conservancy's second generation. Each region was to be a family unto itself. Regional directors in turn were charged with establishing self-funding programs in every state. The state offices would be the third generation. They would carry the Conservancy's philosophy of "conservation through private action" into the 1980s. At Pat's insistence, Dr. Bob wrote the preamble to the plan. It stated boldly that the Conservancy's mission was "the preservation of biotic diversity." Few of us bothered to read the preamble.

Senior staff presented the plan to the board and chapter chairmen at the 1974 annual meeting. The state chapters, which up to now had consisted solely of volunteers, immediately seized upon the idea of having their own full-time, paid directors. They wanted to skip right to the third generation. That posed a major problem. Our idea was to staff the regions first, then have them do the same for the states. That was going to take time, but now with the chapters wanting to hire directors as soon as they could raise the funds, we didn't have time. Our current staff couldn't fill the demand. Pat knew that the only way the national office could retain control was to find some good people, fast. He also knew we had no training program, no job descriptions, and no recruiters, nor were we offering enough money to attract anyone with business experience. We'd have to gamble.

Our first gamble was a Vietnam vet Pat hired as the executive director for one of our oldest and most conservative chapters. This guy made us nervous. He didn't look like us, he didn't act like us, and he didn't seem to know squat about business. But he did have two principal qualifications: he wanted to get close to nature, and he was willing to accept the pittance we were paying state directors.

Pat asked the chapter chairman, a distinguished professor and community leader, to personally meet the new director's plane. The chairman called Pat from the airport. He was not happy. When the vet got off the plane, he had hair down to his shoulders, was wearing fatigues, was barefoot, and was three sheets to the wind. "Give him a chance," urged Pat. "He's had a tough time. I'm sure he'll come around. He wants to get close to nature."

Pat flew out to meet with the new director. The vet reaffirmed his desire to get close to nature. Pat said that was nice. He advised him to get his hair cut, to wear a coat and tie, to buy a pair of shoes, and to drink in moderation, especially around the board members. Pat's advice was ignored. The vet showed up for his first field trip shoeless, disheveled, and carrying a six-pack. The only person who seemed to find him attractive was the comely and somewhat rebellious daughter of one of the wealthier board members. Within a week she had moved in with him. Her family was understandably upset. Pat was summoned to a special meeting of the chapter board. Getting close to nature was one thing, getting close to a board member's daughter was something else. Still shoeless, the vet was sent packing from the Conservancy.

The chapter then proceeded to ignore the national office and hired their own man, a nice young guy from an old and very wealthy local family. He looked right, he acted right, he knew all the right people, but it soon became obvious that he wasn't going to make it. He said he felt awkward asking people he knew for land and money. In less than a year, Pat was summoned to another special meeting of the chapter where he was told to fire the guy.

Contrary to the orderly growth we envisioned in the five-year plan, other chapters and committees began hiring their own people. Most of them looked right, acted right, knew the right people, but couldn't do the job, at least the type of job we expected. When they failed, it created tension within the family. Friday happy hours were spent hashing and rehashing what it took to be a good state director. None of us had an answer. Finally, we drew up six characteristics: a historical perspective, a philosophical outlook, a good financial mind, a lot of common sense, a sense of humor, and a passion for the work. We printed them up and put them in our new employee manual. They didn't mean a thing. These were characteristics everybody wanted in every employee.

In the fall of 1976, Brad Northrup and I were summoned to Pat's office. Brad had started at the Conservancy just before me and was now being groomed for the new position of director of personnel and administration. Pat was his usual jovial self, but from the look in his eyes, we sensed we had a problem. "Good news!" Pat said. "I've got a great trip planned for you guys this weekend." Brad and I looked at each other. Weekend trips normally meant attending an annual chapter meeting.

Sure enough, Pat was sending us to one of our more obscure chapters. There was nothing unusual about that. Annual meetings were our chance to thank the volunteers for all they had done. We would pump them up by giving them a slide show highlighting the major natural areas the Conservancy had saved across the country. What was unusual was that Pat wanted two of us to go to the meeting of this relatively small and inactive group. This sounded like trouble. "Why do you want both of us to go?" Brad asked.

Pat explained why. "This is a very important meeting," he said, looking quite serious. "The state has proposed the creation of a major park surrounding the preserve managed by this chapter. They want our endorsement. I want you guys to make sure they get it. Dr. Bob says getting state governments involved is key to his blueprint for preserving biotic diversity."

"But what do the local people think?" I asked.

"They're wonderful people, long-term supporters, and we have to start paying more attention to them. Some of them might have a slight conflict of interest." Ah, now it was clear. The board was rebelling.

"For example?" Brad asked.

"Well, one of the members owns a beautiful motel," Pat said. "She's afraid that if the state puts in a lot of public campsites, she'll lose business."

"Is that all?" Brad asked.

"That's about it," Pat said matter-of-factly, then added, almost as an afterthought, "But there are a couple of board members who have large tracts of land and don't want the state taking their property. Then, of course, there's our major donor who owns a sawmill and is convinced the park will dry up his supply of timber."

"Pat!" I exclaimed. "There can't be more than half a dozen members on that board. Is anyone in favor of this park?"

"There must be a couple. I'm sure you'll be able to turn them around. And don't worry, their new executive director will be right there with you."

"New executive director?" Brad's voice went up an octave. "What new executive director? Those guys spend half their time recycling paper clips. How can they afford a new director?"

"They're all excited," Pat said. "They've coughed up the dough. He's some young hotshot from Madison Avenue. He wanted out of the rat race. The chairman told me that they were lucky to get him. Help him out. Welcome him into the family."

We got our tickets. Brad called the new director. "He might be OK," he told me. "He's originally from that area. He's going to meet us at the airport."

Our plane got in at five on Friday afternoon. The annual meeting started at six. A field trip through the preserve was scheduled for the next morning, followed by a picnic lunch. Brad and I would have to stay over Saturday night. Fitzie insisted we get the weekend rates.

We scanned the crowd meeting our flight. We were expecting somebody like us, a clean-cut, rosy-cheeked guy wearing a blue blazer, white shirt, chino pants, and Weejuns. He wasn't there. We scoured the airport. We finally found our man in the Hangar Club. He was sitting at the bar sipping a Scotch and water, a cigarette dangling from his lips. His stylishly long hair, tailor-made suit, silk tie, and Gucci loafers were all Madison Avenue. He looked very comfortable.

The new director recognized us immediately. The oak leaf patch on Brad's rucksack must have given us away. He acknowledged our arrival with a wave to the bartender. "Hey, Pete, set these boys up, and how about another one for me."

We normally abstained from drinking before meetings, but the new director hadn't left us much choice. We each ordered a draft, the preferred beverage of Conservancy staff.

The new director was apologetic. "Gee, I'm sorry things look so bleak."

Brad pulled out his notes for the meeting. "No, no, I'm sure we'll be able to turn these people around."

"What people?" the new director said. "This place is dead. It doesn't pick up until happy hour." He checked his Rolex. "It starts at six. Two for one, all drinks. It's a great deal."

Brad looked at me for help. "Ah, we were talking about the annual meeting," I said. "Doesn't that start at six?"

"Don't worry, we've got plenty of time. They'll be flapping their gums over that park issue all night."

"Don't you think we should be there pushing for the park?" Brad asked.

"Naaah," said the new director, lighting up another cigarette. "These meetings are a waste of time. If the state wants a park, they'll make a park. Who cares what we think. I'm not getting paid enough to worry about it."

I looked at Brad. Brad looked at me. We didn't like this guy. "Well, we care," I said. "Let's get to the meeting." We grabbed our rucksacks and headed outside. The new director gulped his drink and followed reluctantly.

The meeting was being held at an old lodge overlooking the lake. The lake was to be the centerpiece of the proposed park. When we walked in, the debate was raging. A couple of dozen people were all clamoring to make their points, for or against the park. The chairman looked relieved to see us. The meeting had gotten out of hand. He banged his gavel. "Ah, at last. Two representatives from headquarters. Let's hear what the Conservancy is up to in other parts of the country."

"Good luck," said the new director. "I'll see you in the tap room."

Brad quickly set up the slide show and took the membership on a tour of our major preserves. He was careful to stress how we were working with state governments. Then I talked about our five-year plan and our effort to leverage our private resources by serving as a catalyst for public funding. As soon as I was through, the chairman opened the floor to questions. There weren't any. Some guy in the back jumped up. "Let's get on with it. I move we vote down this damn park." There was a murmur of agreement.

I leaped to my feet. Pat had instructed us not to come back without an endorsement. "We're not leaving here without a positive resolution," I told the chapter. "The Nature Conservancy strongly favors the creations of state parks. We don't care how you word the resolution, just so long as it's positive."

After another two hours of acrimonious debate, the chapter finally voted begrudgingly in favor of a conditional, contingent resolution supporting the park. It called for strictly limiting public access and acquiring land only from willing sellers; it strongly supported traditional uses such as timbering and mining; and it recommended no more than one motel. But all things considered, it was an endorsement.

The meeting adjourned and the chapter headed for the tap room. By the time Brad and I packed up the slide show, the only seats left were next to the new director. "How'd it go?" he inquired cheerfully.

"Fine, no thanks to you." I was a little short, since we'd just spent two hours doing his job.

The new director sensed our displeasure. "Say, how'd you guys like to go sailing tomorrow? I just got a good deal on a twenty-six-foot O'Day. I'd like to show you the lake."

"We're hiking the preserve with the chapter tomorrow," Brad told him. "Aren't you going?"

"Naaah. I've already seen the preserve."

That did it. I thought Brad was going to pop him. Here we were, giving up our weekends to attend his meeting, and he was going sailing. "Let's get out of here," Brad said.

"Right. That was a long meeting," agreed the director. "Let me take you to the motel. It's not the Plaza, but I got you a room for nothing."

Brad and I didn't have much to say during the ride. The new director did all the talking. He told us all about the deals he had gotten on his boat, suits, shoes, cameras, and watches. He pulled up in front of the motel. "Sure you won't change your minds about sailing? It'll be a lot more fun than tromping through the woods."

"We're not here to have fun," I said self-righteously. "We're here to save some land."

"Yeah, well, if you ever need a Nikon, I can get you a great deal." And off he went.

On Monday morning we presented our patchwork resolution to Pat. We told him it wasn't much, but it was the best we could do. We told him that we'd had to overcome tremendous opposition, that the new director wasn't any help, that he didn't fit the Conservancy's image, that he'd never make it. "Give him a chance," said Pat. "I'm sure he'll come around. He's working on a big project."

A few months later, at the Friday afternoon get-together, the conference room was packed. Pat had indicated that there would be a major announcement. After dutifully acknowledging the good work of Miriam, Jo, Mirdza, and several others, Pat announced the creation of the new state park. He gave Brad and me full credit. "Had Brad and Dave not pushed through this resolution," Pat told the staff, "the state never would have approved the park." Of course that wasn't true, but everybody clapped.

Then Pat announced that the new director had just obtained an easement over 25,000 acres of ponds and streams and virgin forest within the park. The owner had agreed that he, his family, his heirs, and assignees would never develop the property. It was the largest conservation easement we'd ever gotten. This donation had been made by one of the most prominent families in America. Pat held up a copy of the *New York Times*. There was a picture of the new director pumping hands with the landowner. The governor was standing between them, beaming. There was much applause. Even Dr. Bob approved. "Bigger is better," he said. "At last, we're beginning to relate our land acquisition efforts to the preservation of biotic diversity."

Brad grabbed the paper from Pat. We all huddled over the picture. People wanted to know which one was the director. All three appeared far too smooth to work for the Conservancy. Fitzie looked at the picture and said to Greg, "Buddy boy, stuff that striped shirt of yours. Here's a guy with some real threads."

Later, Brad and I took Pat aside. "Pat," I said, "how did you set this guy up? He doesn't look like us, and he doesn't act like us. He won't even hike his own preserve."

"I didn't," said Pat. "He did it on his own. He knows how to get a deal."

"Impossible!" said Brad.

"Diversity, gentlemen; think diversity. Business is like nature. We don't want to grow into an organization where everybody looks alike, acts alike, and thinks alike. That's the first step toward extinction. We have to be able to adapt to different environments. We live on deals, so what we need are people who like to get a good deal." Pat paused and sipped his beer. "You guys should listen to the Doc. You might learn something."

As Good a Reason as Any

PEOPLE ARE ALWAYS ASKING ME HOW I GOT INTO CONSERVATION. THE answer's simple. When I was three, Dad had just gotten back from winning World War II, and we were all living with my mother's parents. While living with Gramma and Grampa was fine for me, it was tough for Mom and Dad. With the war over, they were eager to get on with their lives, but with all the veterans returning home, there was a shortage of housing, at least in our price range. When Dad's first vacation came along, Mom decided we should get away for a couple of weeks. Grampa always had a long list of chores that needed doing, and she realized cutting the lawn, weeding the garden, trimming the hedges, washing the car, painting the steps, and cleaning the cellar wouldn't be much of a vacation for Dad.

Mom had found an ad in the *Boston Herald* for some camps in Frye-burg, Maine. The ad said to write to Rev. Jack Jordan. Mom was a good

Episcopalian and figured if they were run by a man of the cloth, the camps must be nice. Dad hated the thought of dipping into our savings, but at $15 a week, the price was right, so he agreed. It was love at first sight. Jordan's Camps consisted of eight rustic, little green cabins nestled in a stand of majestic white pines on the shores of Lovewell Pond, a rectangular one-by-two-mile spring-fed lake that flowed into the Saco River. We had such a good time that first year we kept going back for the next twenty.

Life at Jordan's was delightfully simple. There was no phone and no TV. Our only form of telecommunication with the outside world was an old radio, and that was permanently set to the Red Sox. My big brother, Ted, and I shared one bedroom, Mom and Dad the other. When I woke up my first look was for rays of light streaming through the pinholes in the old World War II blackout shades Reverend Jordan used as drapes. If I saw the rays, I knew it was going to be a nice day. After a big breakfast of fried bacon, eggs, potatoes, and fish, Ted and I would do our chores. Chores at Jordan's weren't like the chores we had at home. At home we had to take out the garbage, sweep the cellar stairs, and mow the lawn. At Jordan's we had to get wood for the stove, ice for the refrigerator, and drinking water from a spring a good quarter mile back in the woods. Once our chores were done, we were pretty much free to do whatever we wanted.

Most days were spent swimming and fooling around on the beach, but if we got bored, Mary and Sue Jordan, the Reverend's two daughters, would lead us on an adventure. Mary and Sue seldom wore shoes, could swim like fish, run like the wind, handle any boat, and knew everything we'd ever want to know about the out-of-doors. They were our Sacajaweas.

Evenings were spent fishing. After supper Dad would tell Ted and me to grab our poles and the three of us would climb into one of the Reverend's old green wooden boats. Dad would sit in the middle seat working the red oars while Ted and I sat in the stern holding out our lines. Lovewell Pond was loaded with hornpout, pickerel, smallmouth bass, and white and yellow perch, so we always caught lots of fish. With the exception of the yellow perch, which the locals claimed contained worms, they were all good eating.

The real treat was when Old Tom showed up. Old Tom was a resident eagle who had a nest somewhere on Arrowhead Mountain, which ran along the far side of the lake. When we saw Tom dive for a fish, Dad and all the boats on Lovewell would start rowing for the spot. We knew if we could get there in time, we'd end up in a school of perch. One evening Old Tom surprised us by bursting out of a tall pine not thirty yards from where we were fishing. Looking as big as a B-52, he swooped down right in front of us and came up with a fish. Dad pulled on the oars and within seconds we were in the middle of a huge school of white perch. "Quick, get your lines in!" Dad barked. It took something to get Dad that excited and this was really something. For the next twenty minutes, we caught a flurry of fish.

The year I was seven, it was unusually hot when we arrived at Jordan's. After we'd unpacked the car and gone to bed, Ted said, "Dad, we can't sleep. It's too hot."

"You're too excited," he said. "But it is hot. What do you say we all go for a swim?" The change that came over Dad was one of the best things about Jordan's. At home he was always working and worried about money. At Jordan's he was relaxed and full of fun.

"Yeah!" we said, jumping out of bed.

With his big gray Navy surplus lantern, Dad led Mom, Ted, and me through the pitch black night along the rocky path that led to the beach. The pine-scented air was warm and soothing on our bare skin A loon's mournful cry rose from down by the outlet. Across the lake a lone light flickered from Trebor, one of the two girls' camps on Lovewell Pond. Dad turned off the light, and in the total darkness we slipped into the water. "It feels like silk," Mom said, and she was right. It did feel like silk, soft and smooth and inviting. Sitting in Lovewell Pond that night with Mom and Dad and my big brother Ted was the best moment we ever had together.

My friend Bil Gilbert once told me the reason I got into conservation was because I wanted to get back to Jordan's Camps, "and that's as good a reason as any," he added. That *is* the reason. Who wouldn't want to recapture breathing in the pine-scented air, swimming in the clean silky water, fishing with Old Tom, and exploring the wilds with your own Sacajaweas, all in a place where life was simple and everyone was relaxed and happy? We all need more places like Jordan's Camps.

Going for the Touchdown

EVERYONE AT THE NATURE CONSERVANCY HAS A FAVORITE PROJECT. Mine is the Pascagoula. I favor the Pascagoula because it represents a lot of firsts for the Conservancy. It was the first major project we did in Mississippi. It was the largest appropriation we had ever worked through a state government. It was the start of our ongoing effort to preserve a viable system of bottomland hardwoods. It brought the sportsmen of the Deep South into mainline conservation. And most importantly, from my point of view, it was the first time that I was able to emerge from under the long and distinguished, if somewhat stocky, shadow of Pat Noonan.

Pat was the best dealmaker in land conservation. He had single-handedly saved more significant natural areas than anyone. He was the standard against whom everyone in land conservation was judged. When Pat became president of the Conservancy, he recognized his primary responsibility would be to raise money and that he would no longer be personally able to direct major projects. In 1972 he appointed me director of land acquisition. "Your job," he stated, "is to do bigger and better projects than we have ever done before."

Stepping into his shoes was no easy task. He cleaned off his desk by engineering the donation of 50,000 acres in the Great Dismal Swamp from the Union Camp Corporation; buying Parramore Island, the largest of the Virginia barrier islands, for $1.6 million; and working with then-governor Jimmy Carter to protect a large stretch of the Chattahoochee River. "There," Pat said as we were flying home from the dedication ceremony in Atlanta. "Now I can start raising money while you find our next major project."

Over time, thanks to the Doc's system of state natural heritage programs, we identified habitats for just about every endangered species in the United States. We had all of the significant natural areas inventoried. We knew exactly what land we wanted to protect and why. Back in the early 1970s, we didn't have that information. Most of our major projects came in over the transom. We used to profess that "haphazard conservation is no better than haphazard development," but we seldom were able to practice what we preached. If it was big and wet, and we thought we could raise the money, we'd buy it. Common sense and expediency were the two most important criteria in our selection process.

On my first day as director of land acquisition, I was on the phone, calling our contacts in New England. I'm from Massachusetts and knew that there was growing support for conservation in the Northeast. Common sense told me that's where I'd find our next major project. I was hoping for some good news from the Northeast when a retired attorney who was volunteering at the Conservancy told me about a 42,000-acre swamp along the Pascagoula River, in Mississippi.

"It's been owned for years by four families from Laurel," he said. "Some of the kids would rather have money than land. It's one of the last great undisturbed river swamps left in the country. You could probably get the whole thing for around $15 million. You should have a look at it."

Yeah, right, I thought. What were the odds of us doing a major project in Mississippi? We didn't know anybody in Mississippi. We had never done a thing in Mississippi. Of all the states in the Southeast, Mississippi had shown the least interest in acquiring land for conservation. When Governor Carter hosted a seminar to explain the Georgia Heritage Trust Program and to introduce the Conservancy to the conservation agencies in the Southeast, Mississippi was the only state that failed to attend. Mississippi, America's perennially poorest state, was much more interested in development than conservation. There was no chance of me earning my spurs in Mississippi.

I immediately forgot about the Pascagoula and started redialing my contacts in Boston. All they wanted to know was how Pat was doing and when he was going to come up and do a project with them. I told them Pat was no longer directly involved in projects and that they would be dealing with me. Invariably, that was the end of the conversation. After a few weeks I was getting worried.

Then my phone rang. Some guy named Avery Wood was calling from Jackson, Mississippi. He wanted to talk to the person in charge of land acquisition. His accent was so thick I could hardly understand him. I finally figured out he was the new director of the Mississippi Game and Fish Department. He wanted me to come down and meet with him. He claimed he "wanted to create the best wildlife management program in America."

I was skeptical, but I had no place else to go. And finally, someone was willing to talk to me instead of Pat. I went to the dead-project file and retrieved the few notes I had taken on the Pascagoula. All they said were, "42K acres. Finest river swamp in S.E. Kids want $. Pascagoula Hdwd. Co. For sale at $15 million?" This was the sum total of our conservation efforts in Mississippi.

It was a cold November day when I got off the plane in Jackson. The chill in the air surprised me. It had never occurred to me that Mississippi might be cold. My only impressions of Mississippi came from Hollywood and the press. Mississippi was a hot place, a place that didn't like strangers, especially from the North. I smiled nervously at the burly state trooper who was eyeing the passengers coming off the plane. He reminded me of the pictures of troopers in my college yearbook, the ones who were shown pounding my classmates over the head. Amherst had sent a delegation to Mississippi during the civil rights protest. They were lucky to get back alive.

Fortunately, Avery was there to meet me. He was pacing up and down, puffing on a cigarette. His steel-rimmed glasses and shaggy, prematurely gray hair didn't make him look like the self-proclaimed best damn duck hunter in all of Mississippi. He loaded me into an official state vehicle and drove me downtown to his office. The speedometer seldom dipped below ninety. Our conversation kept pace. Avery's country-boy manners camouflaged a very quick mind that was continually popping off ideas. He wanted to learn everything I knew as quickly as he could.

Avery's office was on the eighth floor of the Robert E. Lee Hotel. The state had purchased this ancient edifice and converted it into an office building. The conversion had been minimal. Except for the furniture, Avery's office still looked like an old hotel room.

Avery's dream was to save Mississippi for the sportsmen. He felt that the state, in its frantic efforts to shed its Ku Klux Klan image and attract new industry, was destroying its best business: game and fish. He produced figures showing that out of a population of roughly two million, more than 600,000 Mississippians bought licenses to hunt and fish. He reached into a closet and pulled out a big cardboard graph. One axis was labeled SPORTSMEN; the other, DOLLARS SPENT.

"Just take a look at this here graph," Avery said, waving his cigarette in the air. "Outdoor recreation generates $150 million in bidness every year. That there bidness pumps over $7 million of unsolicited tax revenue into the general fund. If we're gonna be bringin people in from out of state, we oughta be bringin 'em in to enjoy our natural resources, not to destroy 'em. Those boys over in the legislature want to make Mississippi just like everyplace else. Hail, when it comes to outdoor recreation, we're the leader."

I was beginning to regret this trip. What was this guy talking about? Game and fish as a business? I didn't come all the way to Mississippi to talk about the hunting and fishing "bidness." I came to talk about conservation.

"The problem with Mississippi," Avery continued, "is that it takes its natural heritage for granted. We assume we got an infinite supply of land. Well, lemme tell ya, that ain't the case."

By now, Avery seemed to have forgotten that I was even there. He railed at the fact that the state owned a paltry 20,000 acres that were dedicated to game management. The bulk of the game and fish program was run on leased lands. "Them lands ain't gonna be there forever," he exclaimed. "When development comes—and it's gonna come—people ain't gonna let the state use these lands. They're gonna lease 'em to private hunt clubs, or sell 'em for more development. The average guy, the millworker who's been buyin his license and registrin his boat every year, he's gonna be locked out. We gotta set up a system of wildlife management areas that are owned by the state. We gotta protect our best bidness. We gotta save Mississippi for the sportsmen!"

Avery took his graph and, in disgust, scaled it into the bathroom. He collapsed into his chair and studied me.

Finally, it dawned on me that Avery might be on to something. I began to see the connection between the game and fish business and conservation. If you were protecting land for game, you were also protecting it for nongame species. If the Conservancy could tie into the states' game and fish business, we could save a lot of significant natural areas.

Pat had already concluded that the best way to move conservation forward was to get the states more involved. He knew that less than one-half of 1 percent of philanthropic giving went to conservation. It would take conservation years to catch up with more established charities like religion, health, and education. The best natural areas would be long gone by then. Even if we could catch up, it was doubtful that there was enough private money to get the job done.

Under Pat's leadership the Conservancy's new strategy was to use private funds as a catalyst to stimulate public funding for conservation. We had initiated programs with the U.S. Fish and Wildlife Service, the Forest Service, and the Park Service, but many members of our board were hesitant to bet all our chips on the Feds. The Feds were too fickle. We had made some real progress under Nixon, but he was gone, and who knew what Ford would do. Historically, conservation had been an easy target for budget cuts. As lawmakers were quick to say, "Birds don't vote."

The best way to secure public funds for land protection was to buffer our federal program with individual state programs. The big question was, how could we sell conservation to the states? And here was Avery, giving me the answer. The states had to buy land to protect an existing and very profitable business, the game and fish business. This was the genius of Avery's plan. What made it especially attractive to me was that it was coming from Mississippi. Mississippi was perceived as the last in everything. If suddenly it emerged with the best wildlife heritage program, other game and fish departments would have to take notice.

"Avery," I said with genuine awe, "you've got it figured out. Sportsmen should be America's best conservationists. But how do we bridge the gap? How do we start buying natural areas for game and fish?"

Avery sat up. He knew he had me hooked. "Now let me tell ya," he said smiling. "I've set up this here committee, the Wildlife Heritage Committee, and these boys got the wherewithal to make things happen, if ya know what I mean."

I didn't but nodded knowingly.

"Now, these boys, they ain't gonna believe me when I tell 'em we got a problem, 'cause I'm just a country boy. So we'll bring you in, and tell 'em you're the expert."

"Expert?" I protested. "Me? I'm no expert. I'm from Boston. What do I know about hunting and fishing?"

Avery looked at me as if I were a dumb younger brother. "Bubba," he said, "you come in here lookin Ivy League and throwin out all those big words, they gonna believe you. An expert ain't nothin but a regular guy who's a long way from home. With that Boston accent, these boys are gonna know you're a long way from home."

"But what will I tell them?" I asked.

"Just give 'em the same facts that I gave you." He got up and went into the bathroom. "Here," he said, coming back with his graph. "Use this. Make it sound like you learned this stuff at MIT."

"Avery, that's a start, but it's not going to do it. You can talk about conservation until you're blue in the face, but people don't respond until they can get their hands into the dirt. We have to give them a project. What do you know about the Pascagoula?"

Avery's eyes lit up. "That swamp's got some of the best huntin and fishin in the state. But it's owned by some folks in Laurel. It's never been open to the general public."

"What if I told you we could buy it for $15 million?"

"$15 million?" Avery fell back into his seat. "How the hail we gonna raise that much money? You forgettin, this here is Mississippi."

"I thought you said these boys had wherewithal. How are you going to create the best wildlife management system in America if you can't raise $15 million?"

Avery regained his feet and looked at his watch. "Bubba, it's time we had ourselves a drink."

The following Monday, at the Conservancy's weekly staff meeting, I described Avery, the Wildlife Management Committee, the concept of game and fish as a business that could help conservation, and our plan to undertake a major project in Mississippi. Most of the staff thought I was crazy. "Yeah, right," they said. "What are the odds of us doing a major project in Mississippi? Nothing ever gets done in Mississippi. Let's not get sidetracked with these game and fish people. You're wasting your time in Mississippi."

As usual, Pat didn't weigh in until he had heard what everyone else had to say. "Game and fish as a business is an interesting concept. Only a handful of people understand biotic diversity, less than four million people support conservation, but there are more than twenty million sportsmen. If we want to raise some real money, we've got to expand our base of support. Dave, do you really think we have a chance of doing something in Mississippi?"

"Well, Pat, this guy Avery Wood might be crazy enough to pull it off. I'll know more after I meet with this Wildlife Heritage Committee."

"I guess we can afford another plane ticket to Jackson. Go ahead. Just don't tell Fitzie."

I was the guest expert at the next meeting of the Wildlife Heritage Committee. The meeting was held at the old Robert E. Lee Hotel. The conference room consisted of two former hotel rooms that had been joined together. The result was a long, narrow chamber with a bathroom at each end. The carpeting was threadbare and there was a gap in the middle where the wall had been removed. The mismatched chairs around the conference table looked as if they had been picked up at a goodwill sale. The protection of Mississippi's wildlife heritage would have to evolve from these humble origins.

The nine committee members looked like something straight out of Tennessee Williams. They were all middle-aged men. They all brandished big, black cigars. Those with a full head of hair had it slicked back into a modified ducktail. Those without had what was left cropped close, Marine-style. Even though it was winter, their suits were florid. There was much guffawing and backslapping before the meeting. As a guest, I sat demurely in a corner while Avery did his politicking. The room was filled with deep Southern drawls. I couldn't understand most of what was being said.

Three of the members were from the Mississippi State Senate, three were from the House, and three were prominent citizens appointed by the governor. Easily the most prominent was John Vaught, the winningest coach in Ole Miss history. He was a living legend, the man who had brought the Rebels to eighteen consecutive bowls. Not surprisingly, the pre-meeting chatter centered around the coach.

From what I could make of the conversation, he was telling the members about last year's victory over Tennessee. The coach had come out of retirement in 1973 and reclaimed his Rebels from Billy Kinard. Billy had been appointed head coach in 1971 by his brother, Bruiser Kinard, who had taken over as athletic director when Coach Vaught was taken ill. The Bruiser was another of Mississippi's living legends. He had been an All-American at Ole Miss and All-Pro with the Green Bay Packers. With Bruiser and Billy back on the sidelines, Coach Vaught completely reshuffled the 1973 Rebels and marched them up to Knoxville, where they upset Johnny Majors and the Vols, 21–0. "Ol' Johnny, he had us scouted out pretty good," the coach drawled. "He was sure he was gonna stop us cold. So I juggled our lineup, and by the time Johnny figured out who was playin where, the game was over."

The chairman called the committee to order, and after quickly plowing through its routine business, asked Avery to introduce his guest. Avery's introduction was lengthy and inflated. According to Avery, I had been all over the United States carrying the entire conservation movement on my broad shoulders. After looking at the whole country, I had settled on Mississippi as America's best hope for protecting its great natural heritage. "This here Dave Morine has seen it all," Avery concluded. "He comes here from Boston, and he's been to all of them fancy schools up there. Believe me, this boy knows what he's talkin about."

Avery sat down and started puffing nervously. Everyone was puffing. The room was blue with smoke. My eyes were watering; I could hardly see through the haze. I got up, told the committee how honored I was to be in the great state of Mississippi, and began my plea.

"Mississippi is unique because she still has a chance to determine her own destiny. Growth is going to come to Mississippi. She is still rich in natural and human resources, and industry needs those resources. Mississippi is like a pure young woman. Her virtue must be protected. She should be looking for a lasting relationship with industry, one in which she remains an equal partner. She must preserve her dowry of natural resources, rather than allow industry to plunder it." I paused. I could see Avery's eyes flicking nervously around the room. Maybe I was spreading it on too thick with my analogy, but it was too late to change now. "If Mississippi allows herself to be raped by out-of-state industry, she has no one to blame but herself."

There was a brief silence while the members mulled over what I had just said. Coach Vaught was the first to speak. "This boy's made a good point. We've got it pretty good down here. We shouldn't just give the ball to those big bidness boys from out of state." He looked at Avery. Everyone looked at Avery. "What play you callin, Avery?"

"Well, Coach, we gotta put some points on the board. Right now we're way behind. We only got 20,000 acres for game management. Arkansas's got 300,000; Louisiana's got over 250,000; Tennessee's got close to 200,000; Florida's got 120,000; hail, even Alabama's got 40,000." At the mention of Alabama, people straightened up and puffed even harder. Avery knew how to motivate his team. "Dave, why don't you tell the committee about the Pascagoula?"

A week earlier Avery and I had gone down to Pascagoula and toured the swamp. It really was an amazing place. The Pascagoula Hardwood Company owned 42,000 acres of virgin land. It encompassed forty-five miles of the Pascagoula River, more than fifty natural ox-bow lakes, and ten miles of frontage along Black Creek, the state's most popular canoeing stream. There were Indian mounds and thousand-year-old cypress trees, some of them as much as thirty feet in circumference.

"If Mississippi is really serious about preserving her natural heritage," I concluded, "it is doubtful that she'll ever have another opportunity to acquire such an incredibly large, beautiful, and ecologically significant tract of land." I sat down.

The questioning began. The discussion lasted for two hours; it was the toughest grilling I had ever been through, worse than an IRS audit. These guys were not naturalists. All they wanted to know was how the purchase of the Pascagoula lands would enhance the profitability of the state's game and fish business.

"How much timber was on the property? How many sportsmen user days could it accommodate? What was the population within one hour's drive? Two hours' drive? Three hours' drive? How many users would be out-of-staters? What was the price of a nonresident license, and how much could they increase it? How much hunting could the property support? Who hunted it now? Were there any on-site studies of fishing in the Pascagoula River Basin?" And on, and on, and on.

Finally, the chairman moved that the committee request $15 million from the legislature for the purchase of the Pascagoula Hardwood Company's lands. The motion was seconded by Coach Vaught. It passed unanimously. The committee adjourned.

Avery was euphoric. I was drained. "How'd I do?" I asked, fishing for a compliment.

"Hail, you were talkin so fast, they only got about half of what you said, but that was enough. Now it's time to get to work." Avery said it as if we hadn't done a thing so far. "I've got to push this bill through the legislature, and you've got to go get that land."

Avery spent most of the next three months over at the legislature, lobbying. I spent my time in New York, Washington, and Laurel, meeting with various members of the four families. My friend had been right, the younger generation wanted to sell. What he had neglected to tell me was that the younger generation had very little control over the company. The biggest block of stock, close to 25 percent, was controlled by a distinguished old gentleman in Laurel. The patriarch of one of the four families, he was perfectly content to leave things just the way they were. He felt that this land was a good investment. He had no desire to sell. "We've held these lands for close to half a century," he told me on one occasion. "Back when we got 'em, this swamp was worth nothing. If we sold 'em, we'd end up givin half their value away in taxes. Mr. Morine, there's nothin I hate more than payin taxes."

The fact that the lands would be sold for conservation purposes appealed to many members of the other families, but it was clear that nobody was willing to try an end run around the old patriarch. I elected not to pass this information on to Avery. Why upset him when he was so busy trying to get the money, especially when the funding still looked like a long shot? Better for Avery to fail than me.

At two in the morning on March 20, 1975, I was jarred awake by the phone. When I picked up the receiver, it was Avery. His first words were, "Bubba, we done pulled this caper off!"

He was sitting in the governor's office. He described how, in one of the most dramatic sessions in the history of the Mississippi legislature, they had approved $15 million for the purchase of the Pascagoula Hardwood lands. Avery wanted me at the next meeting of the Wildlife Heritage Committee. It was time to present the project.

The governor was planning to sign the bill at a public ceremony early the following week. The committee would meet right after the signing. "You just tell 'em how to sign the check an' we're on our way." Avery could hardly contain himself. He was ecstatic when he hung up. I was petrified. I had exactly five days to figure out what to do.

I was sitting in Pat Noonan's office when he came in the next morning. I'd tossed and turned all night, searching for a solution. I had come up with squat. "Pat. What am I going to do?" I pleaded. "Those guys are going to kill me."

"Dave," he exclaimed incredulously, "you call this a problem? If we can't figure out how to spend $15 million in Mississippi, we're in the wrong business. Get down there and sell them on another project. You're telling me there's only one swamp in all of Mississippi?"

Another project, of course. Why hadn't I thought of that? There were thirty million acres in Mississippi. With $15 million in our pockets, how hard could it be to find another project?

The committee members were aglow when I entered the conference room. They were all rehashing the governor's signing ceremony. It had been a huge success. Avery had engineered press coverage by all of the major papers in the Southeast. Nobody could believe that Mississippi, the poorest state in the Union, had appropriated $15 million for conservation. The chairman immediately waived the reading of the minutes and turned the meeting over to me. "Now that we've got the money, Dave, let's hear about the deal." Everybody settled back to enjoy their cigars and the fruits of their hard-earned victory.

"Mississippi is a state blessed with a great natural heritage," I began. There was much smiling and nodding. "It is a state with many significant natural areas. What Mississippi needs now is a comprehensive natural heritage program that will identify all of these areas and set mechanisms in place for protecting them."

"Dave," said the chairman, "that's all well and good, and we sure are interested in protectin our great natural heritage, but what about the Pascagoula?"

"Well, the Pascagoula's a good project, but it's not the only project we should be considering. Now that the legislature has given you $15 million, it would be foolish to put all our eggs in one basket. We should look at a number of projects across the state."

There was some serious puffing and mumbling. I looked at the coach.

"With all this money, you need to devise a total game plan. The Pascagoula is just one play. And as I'm sure Coach Vaught will agree, you can't go for the touchdown on every play."

Now there was stone silence. The committee realized that I was shifting gears, that after all my hype about the Pascagoula, I couldn't deliver.

The coach stroked his granite chin. His presence filled the room. "Son," he said in his soft, deep drawl. "Down here we go for the touchdown on every play. Now you march on back to Laurel and git us that property." That was the end of the shortest meeting in the history of the Wildlife Heritage Committee. The members filed out.

Avery sat there in shock. "Bubba, what the hail you doin?"

"Avery," I confessed, "the Pascagoula property is not for sale."

"Not for sale? The hail it ain't. I got $15 million that says it is. I got the money, now you get the property. That's the deal."

Avery was right. If we couldn't buy the Pascagoula property, the Conservancy was dead in Mississippi, and probably the entire Southeast. We had to go for the touchdown.

After I got home I sat in my office for two days, wracking my brain, trying to find a solution. The owners had us scouted. They knew our playbook. What would the coach do? He'd juggle the lineup.

I called Avery. "Avery," I said, "if we can't buy the land, let's buy the corporation."

"Bubba," he said, "now you're talkin."

Working with the best legal and financial minds we could find, the Conservancy devised a totally new play. the Conservancy would make a tender offer for 75 percent of the company's stock, implement a tax-free dissolution of the corporation, trade the patriarch 25 percent of the land for his family's stock, and sell the remaining 75 percent of the land to the state. We would use the state's appropriation to pay back the money we had borrowed to buy the stock.

The patriarch approved the plan. It got him his land, tax-free, and got the younger generation out of his hair. The younger generation and the remaining stockholders were very pleased. Not only had they done something good for the state of Mississippi, they had turned a previously dead asset into some real money. Avery and the Wildlife Heritage Committee were jubilant. They had acquired the finest state wildlife management area in the Southeast, laid the foundation for the best wildlife heritage program in America, and best of all, gained some serious yardage on Alabama. The Conservancy was equally pleased. Not only had we helped save a major bottomland hardwood forest, but now we could hold up Mississippi's Wildlife Heritage Program as a challenge to other states. This was the decoy that Pat needed to lure more sportsmen's dollars into the Conservancy.

As for me, I was glad to get out of Mississippi in one piece. Thanks to a kick in the butt from Coach Vaught, I had juggled the lineup and gone for the score. As Avery put it during his remarks at the dedication of the Pascagoula Wildlife Management Area, "Ol' Dave here, he done had us scared for a while, but for a fast-talkin Yankee, he done all right. He done scored a touchdown."

Going Five for Five

DURING MY EIGHTEEN YEARS AS THE HEAD OF LAND ACQUISITION FOR The Nature Conservancy, we completed more than 5,000 individual projects. In the early years we were taking almost anything that came over the transom, but the bigger we got, the more we realized we couldn't waste our time and money on projects that didn't meet our criteria. The problem was, what were our criteria? Fortunately, we were much better determining what it took to have a successful project than we were figuring out what it took to be a successful state rep, and gradually we came up with five criteria. Anybody seeking approval for a project knew that they had to be able to answer these five questions:

One, is it significant? There are more good projects than the time and money to save them so you can't waste your time and money saving land that's not significant. But what is significant? For a local land trust, significant could be a scenic overlook, a piece of farmland, a section of river, or an expanse of open space. For TNC, it came to mean projects that fit into Dr. Bob's system for preserving biotic diversity, but even then there were disagreements. I never saw a piece of land I didn't like, and Pat was always reminding us, "beauty is in the eyes of the beholder." Saving land is an emotional business. It's easy to get attached to a project even if it's something you shouldn't be messing with, so know what you want and stay focused on it.

Two, is it threatened? Know the history of the property. A good owner is often the best protector and steward of the property so there is no need to be investing your time and money into a piece of land that's not threatened. Instead, let the owner know it's significant and that you'd be interested in acquiring the land if the situation ever changed. Just letting an owner know his property is significant and thanking him for taking such good care of it often forms the first layer of protection.

Three, is it the best deal? Remember, you never get a kiss unless you ask for it, so always start your negotiations by asking for a donation. Most people with a lot of money hate to pay taxes. Often somebody who wouldn't write a check to TNC would end up donating all or part of their property if we could show them how the donation could provide a tax deduction. If you do have to raise money for a project, try to have the seller give you an option on the land at the agreed price. Time is money. If you can't get a donation of money, try to get a donation of time. Plus, never forget that raising money for land you already own is a lot harder than raising money for land that you only have under option. In the eyes of many donors, once you own it, it's already protected and the threat is gone.

Four, can it be managed? If we were pre-acquiring land for a governmental agency or some other nonprofit, management was not a problem, but if the land was going to be a TNC preserve, management became a major consideration. Walt Matia, TNC's director of stewardship for much of the time I was there, used to come storming into my office at least once a week raging about some deal we were working on. "Have any of you yahoos ever thought about how this property's going to be managed?" he'd yell at me. Usually, the honest answer was no. As director of land acquisition, my philosophy was to grab as much land as we could while it was still available and worry about how we'd manage it later on. Walt eventually convinced me that having a management plan in place before a property is acquired is an important criterion. Here's where volunteers can play a vital role. Under Walt's direction, stewardship committees staffed by volunteers filled much of TNC's management needs.

Five, will this project lead to something bigger? One-night stands don't lead to lasting relationships. Doing a deal just because it's available doesn't lead to a successful land conservation program. At every Project Review Committee meeting, we were presented with at least one sexy, good-looking project that some state rep was just dying to jump on. Believe me, we all were tempted, but unless the project had the potential to take us on to something bigger, we had to let it go.

There are many considerations that go into picking a project, but these five criteria were the ones that served TNC well. What we learned over time was that if you could demonstrate significance, threat, value, manageability, and potential, you had a winner.

Professional Courtesy

By the mid-1970s, articles about the Conservancy began to point out how it was run by lawyers and MBAs, how it wheeled and dealed, how it focused on the "bottom line." This description was true. The Conservancy's other MBAs and I were constantly developing strategies, crunching numbers, and hammering out deals, while its lawyers trudged through legal descriptions, studied statutes, and agonized over affidavits.

What these articles failed to mention was that the Conservancy's lawyers and MBAs were usually not very good naturalists, that they tended to become babes once they entered the woods. One of the Conservancy's cardinal rules was that we did not mix nature with business. While I greatly appreciated our natural world, my knowledge of it was extremely limited. It was a waste of time for me to evaluate the ecological significance of a piece of land. We had botanists and biologists who were far better qualified than I to do this. Conversely, they'd get out of the way when it came time to make the deal. Mutual respect and professional courtesy dictated that our lawyers and MBAs spend their time communing with money and leave nature to the naturalists. Nonetheless, every now and then a Conservancy lawyer or MBA was forced to meet nature head-on. The result was usually disastrous.

My worst experience came in the spring of 1976. I was working on a little project near Charlottesville, Virginia. This preserve was not one of the Conservancy's more spectacular natural areas. It was 100 acres of second-growth woods and floodplain that protected the watershed of a small creek. I became involved because a very generous donor had committed a substantial amount of money to the acquisition of this area. This donor insisted I personally inspect the property and handle all of the negotiations.

A key tract we hoped to protect was called Hidden Springs. This country estate, which had nearly a mile of frontage on the creek, controlled the upper slopes of the watershed. If it were developed, the resulting siltation and septic runoff would inevitably degrade the natural qualities of our preserve. The estate was owned by a professor emeritus at the University of Virginia and his wife.

Unfortunately, the Professor and his wife, Louise, were not members of the Conservancy. Our research showed that they were well-off, childless, and totally committed to the university. I was sure that Hidden Springs was destined to be willed to UVA. If that happened, the area would be in serious jeopardy. In my opinion, schools, churches, and other nonprofits are among the most callous landowners in the country. To them, land is purely a commodity from which they have a fiduciary duty to squeeze every last nickel. Judging from what had happened to the rest of Charlottesville, the university seemed to have little concern for the preservation of open space. They'd probably have bulldozers grinding over Hidden Springs while the overseers were still chipping the Professor's name onto the Rotunda.

I called the Professor and Louise to set up a meeting. They were most cordial. They had met our generous donor and claimed to be very sympathetic to the Conservancy's objectives. They insisted that I come for dinner. They even implied that I was welcome to spend the night.

My strategy was simple. I was going to ask them to donate a conservation easement over Hidden Springs. A conservation easement seemed like a perfect solution. The Professor and Louise could own Hidden Springs for the rest of their lives, and upon their demise they could leave it to the university, but the property could never be developed without the Conservancy's approval. The Professor and his wife would get a substantial tax write-off, the university could still make a bundle by selling the property as a country estate, and our preserve would be protected in perpetuity. All I had to do was sell the deal to the Professor and Louise.

The evening couldn't have started any better. It was cool and clear, with the scent of new grass and wildflowers wafting from the fields. The Professor, bedecked in a UVA tie and blue blazer with the Cavaliers' crossed swords embroidered in orange on its breast pocket, poured three bourbon and branches into silver UVA cups. He and Louise escorted me to the patio. In the twilight I could see the creek below, and beyond it the Rotunda, the centerpiece of Mr. Jefferson's university. "Ah," I said, sipping my bourbon, "it's a pleasure to be back in Charlottesville. I received a fine education here, at the business school."

They looked at each other and nodded approvingly.

Louise and the Professor were a calm, gracious, dignified couple. The Professor still taught a course on Faulkner. He was surprised when I confessed I'd forgotten "The Bear." He immediately produced a dog-eared copy. "I'm sure that as a conservationist, you'll recognize this passage," he said. "Let me refresh your memory."

The cool of the evening was creeping over Hidden Springs, so Louise suggested that we move inside by the fire. Out of nowhere, an elderly butler in a heavily starched white serving jacket appeared with a bucket of ice, a bottle of Virginia Gentleman, and a silver UVA pitcher filled with good Virginia branch. He recharged our cups as the Professor settled into his UVA captain's chair and began to read aloud.

Then I remembered why I had forgotten "The Bear." The Professor went on and on and on. He didn't finish with Faulkner until we were ready to be seated for dinner. As we walked into the dining room, a full moon could be seen rising through the windows. A Black Angus was lowing at the Milky Way. The three of us took our places at a table as long as one of Faulkner's sentences. Another fire was ablaze. As I watched the flames flicker in my crystal wineglass, the Professor intoned grace. Once the meal had been properly blessed, Louise tinkled a little bell. Out came the soup, and I prepared myself to strike.

It was accepted practice within the Conservancy that you always made your pitch just before the soup. The setup was perfect. I took another sip of wine. My palate was tingling with the taste of success. This deal was as good as done.

I was clearing my throat to speak when a cry came from the kitchen. "Professor! Professor! Come quick, we done got ourselves a snake!" Snake? My mouth suddenly went as dry as dust.

The Professor looked over apologetically. "Please excuse me. Missy seems to be upset about something." He got up from the table and purposefully strode off into the kitchen.

I smiled at Louise. She smiled back. "It's probably nothing," she said. "Missy gets excited over the least little thing. I'm sure my husband can handle it."

I hoped so. I soon heard the professor stomping up the cellar stairs. "Sakes alive! You should see the size of that snake! He must be six feet if he's an inch. I don't believe I've ever seen one quite that big." He stood in the doorway to the dining room with his arms outstretched.

I had read somewhere that the length of a person's outstretched arms equaled his height, which, coincidentally, was roughly the length of a fathom. All I could fathom from this scene was that there was one big snake downstairs. Louise and the Professor looked at me. The message was clear. They didn't have to say it: What luck! We have the biggest snake we've ever seen right in our own cellar, and here's a professional conservationist to remove it!

I felt obliged to say something. "This is really an *excellent* wine." I poured myself another glass as I tried to figure out what to do. "Don't worry about the snake," I said as nonchalantly as I could. "It's probably just come in to get out of the cold. If we leave it alone, I'm sure it will find its way out."

Louise looked at me incredulously. "Leave it alone? We most certainly will not leave it alone. This is my house, and I shall not have a snake upsetting my help. That snake is going out, and it's going out now." With that, she got up and marched toward the cellar. The Professor followed directly.

I had no choice. I fell in behind the Professor. As we passed through the kitchen, I saw Missy and the butler huddled in a corner, their eyes wide with fear. Louise hesitated at the top of the stairs. The Professor manfully assumed the lead. When we reached the bottom step, I could see a light coming from an open door. It was a cellar pantry. We tiptoed toward the light and peeked in.

The Professor pointed to a shelf in the far corner. "There he is," he whispered. "Do you see him?"

I looked at the shelf. I didn't see any snake. Then I rocked back in abject terror as the whole shelf readjusted itself. There was a rattle of glass. The snake was laced around an entire row of preserves. It seemed to be everywhere. My eyes widened as they followed its long black body around and around until they finally reached its head. The snake was staring directly at me. It cocked its head menacingly, its red tongue flitting in and out. I seriously thought I was going to pee my pants. What was a snake doing in the pantry? I prayed that it would slither away. It didn't. It just lay there, as if to say, "OK, Mr. MBA. Come move me."

Louise broke the silence. "Goodness gracious! It *is* the biggest snake I've ever seen." She turned to me. "Be careful it doesn't bite you!"

I fought to keep my composure. I tried to chuckle, but my voice cracked. "It's, ahem, just a black snake. You're lucky to have him. You won't have any mice or rats with this fellow around, ha, ha. I suggest we just ignore him. He'll leave when he's ready."

Louise was firm. "He'll leave right now!" She turned to the Professor. "Isn't that right, dear?"

The Professor was equally firm. "Yes, by all means! It can't stay here. It's upsetting the help."

I knew that if I could walk into that room, grab that snake, and throw it outside, Hidden Springs and our new preserve would be protected in perpetuity. If real conservationists were throwing themselves in front of bulldozers and standing in front of harpoon guns, surely the least I could do was pick up a snake. I took a step. The snake hissed menacingly. I recoiled. I felt a warm trickle down the inside of my thigh. There was no way I was going to walk into that room and grab that snake. They didn't teach snake-grabbing at the business school.

I tried one last retreat. "Black snakes aren't poisonous, but one that size can give you a nasty bite. If you're determined to move him, which I do not recommend, I suggest we find something to grab it."

"The tongs!" exclaimed the Professor. "I'll get the tongs from the fireplace. They should do the trick."

"Good idea," I said. "I'll help you."

"No, no. You stay here and keep an eye on that fellow. We don't want him slipping away."

Louise stood there silently as the Professor bounded up the stairs. The snake didn't move. The only thing slipping away was my deal. The Professor was back in a flash. He was in good shape for a man his age. UVA might have to wait a while before it got its hands on Hidden Springs. That was fortunate. The Conservancy would need all the time it could get to resell the Professor and Louise on the idea of a conservation easement. My credibility was just about shot.

The Professor proffered the tongs, but I was too quick for him. "I'll get the cellar door," I said, looking back over my shoulder. "Try to grab him right behind the head." I opened the door with a flourish. "OK. Any time you're ready."

The Professor entered the pantry. He was a brave man, but then again it was his house. Louise backed away to the foot of the stairs. I could hear the Professor snapping away with the tongs. "Dammit, hold still, you rascal!" A jar shattered as it hit the floor. "Aha, there, now I've got you!" Louise started to run up the stairs as the Professor burst from the pantry. In front of him was the snake, twisting and twirling. I could see its white belly. He must have grabbed it somewhere in the middle, because both ends were thrashing wildly.

I tensed as they came hurtling toward me. Suddenly the Professor let out a shriek. One end of the snaked had wrapped itself around his hand. He dropped the tongs. The snake fell to the floor. It swayed back and forth, trying to get its bearings. It sensed its escape and came wriggling right at me. I stumbled in panic out the cellar door and ran smack into a wall. The impact knocked me off my feet. I started groping my way up the stone steps but froze when I felt all six feet of the snake slither over me and disappear into the darkness.

I got up and tried to dust myself off, but my hands wouldn't stop shaking. Slowly, I followed the light back into the cellar. The Professor had picked up the tongs and was going up the stairs with Louise. I took a deep breath, straightened my tie, and sheepishly followed. I heard the Professor reassuring Missy and the butler as he passed through the kitchen: "No need to worry now. That old snake is back outside where it belongs."

"Thank goodness. We don't need no snakes around here," Missy said with great relief.

"You're absolutely right, Missy, but it's all over now. Let's clean up that broken jar and finish our meal."

I went back to the table and dutifully delivered my pitch. I should have just gone home. The snake had ruined everything. Louise and the Professor were polite but cool for the rest of the evening. They kept looking at me as if they had just caught me cheating on an exam. I could no longer be trusted. Anybody who was afraid to pick up a snake couldn't be much of a conservationist. I wasn't quite through with my pecan pie when Louise pointedly reminded me that it was a long drive back to Washington.

—◦—

When I left the Conservancy in 1990, we still had no conservation easement over Hidden Springs and no guarantee that the creek would be protected in perpetuity.

Every now and then I think of the Professor and Louise and what might have been if I had walked into that room, picked up that snake, and thrown it outside. And then I think of the snake. Why wasn't it down by the creek where it belonged? I was in a house, where I belonged, with silver cups and fine china, communing with money. It was the snake that was wrong. It had broken one of the Conservancy's cardinal rules; it had mixed nature with business. It should have shown some respect and excused itself when it saw that it was blowing my deal. Whatever happened to professional courtesy?

—◦—

Look Out

In 1963 Bob Lemire was a financial consultant living in Lincoln, Massachusetts. Founded well before the American Revolution, Lincoln lies just outside Route 128, the beltway that runs around Boston. Since revolutionary times, Lincoln had been the picture-perfect small New England town, but in the early 1960s that picture began to change. A wave of growth flowing out from the Hub was beginning to swamp little villages surrounding the city, turning them into a sea of suburbia.

At the time, Bob was not active in conservation. He was a young guy with a wife and two young kids who got up in the morning, grabbed the train to the hubbub of Boston, and at night boarded it back to the rustic tranquility of Lincoln. That all changed when Bob stepped onto the train and by chance settled into a seat next to the town moderator. By the time they detrained in Lincoln, Bob, much to his surprise, had been offered and had accepted an appointment to Lincoln's five-year-old Conservation Commission. And so began an ongoing commitment to conservation that, against all odds, resulted in the town of Lincoln retaining its rural character.

I met Bob in 1972 shortly after I'd started with TNC. By then Lincoln was becoming a model for creative land development and Bob was being asked to speak at many conservation meetings. Calm, thoughtful, analytical, and somewhat spiritual, Bob would start off by asking his audience to present him with a problem their community was facing. Then using that problem as a way into the community, he'd work with the audience to create a plan that would save natural, historical, recreational, and scenic lands while at the same time directing development into areas where it would be physically and financially feasible.

One question that always came up at these talks concerned the public ownership of land. Many people saw the management of public lands as a big, expensive problem that included people dumping trash, kids buzzing around on ATVs, hunters poaching wildlife, even flooding caused by beavers building dams. Bob's response to this question was always the same. "You're viewing them through the wrong end of the telescope. Rather than looking in and seeing problems, look out for opportunities, namely how can your land influence the use of the properties around it?" Bob's advice was the reason one of TNC's five criteria for evaluating a project was "Will it lead to something bigger?" He went on to write *Creative Land Development,* which in addition to describing Lincoln's experience, served as a widely used text for conservationists all across the country.

In the spring of 2003, an old friend from business school and I took a canoe trip down the Connecticut River. As part of the trip, a foundation run by Dan Lufkin, the great financier and conservationist, had pledged $50,000 as seed money we could use to seed projects along the river. One project that caught our eye was the Great Meadows just south of Hartford. This 4,500-acre area of bottomland hardwoods and fields is the last major floodplain before the river starts its final run to Long Island Sound and also the most naturally significant and threatened area on the lower half of the Connecticut. The Great Meadows Conservation Trust (or GMCT as it's known) is a little, all-volunteer land trust with about 250 members that had been working for 35 years to save the meadows. During that time GMCT had been able to acquire 33 individual tracts totaling just under 200 acres. These 33 tracts were scattered all through the meadows, and in accordance with Lemire's mantra of always looking out for opportunities, GMCT seemed like the perfect prospect for a grant.

When we got to the Great Meadows, we met with Jim Woodworth, president of GMCT. Jim told us the trust had just received a $45,000 bequest from one of its founding members and asked what we thought they should do with the money. I told Jim that with all the individual tracts GMCT owned, they were in a tremendous position to save a lot of land. Every tract represented an opportunity to reach out to their neighbors and exert a real influence over protecting the Great Meadows. In fact, it was such a great opportunity, I said that if GMCT used that $45,000 to start a land preservation fund, we'd make a grant of $5,000. By aggressively leveraging that money and then rolling it over, GMCT could really start saving land.

In the spring of 2010, I was asked to be the guest speaker at the Annual Meeting of GMCT. The reason for my invitation was that *Two Coots in a Canoe,* a book I'd written describing our trip down the Connecticut, had just been released, and the board of GMCT was hoping I could entertain the general membership with humorous anecdotes from this great adventure. While waiting to speak I was listening to the treasurer give his report. He was proudly describing how the Land

Preservation Fund had increased for the seventh straight year and was now up to $145,215. That sounded good until I looked at the annual report for 2009 and saw that during the whole year, GMCT spent absolutely nothing on land acquisition. The trust had fallen into a common trap. Rather than being a means to the end, its Land Preservation Fund had become the end. Instead of using it as a revolving fund, GMCT was viewing it as endowment. Watching it grow was more comfortable than spending it to save land.

So much for humorous anecdotes. When I got up on my soapbox, I was all fire and brimstone. I told the membership that this was the best time since the Great Depression to buy land; that they had to start looking out; that they should make a map showing all the Great Meadows properties they already owned; that they should go to each of their neighbors and tell them that if they ever thought of getting rid of their property, GMCT would be interested in acquiring it; that it was time to stir the pot; that they had to start using that money to save land!

I just received the 2011 Annual Report from GMCT. In the year since my speech, the Land Preservation Fund has grown to $157,157 while the total spending on land acquisition was $800. Telling people how to save land is easy; getting them to actually do it is tough.

Bagging the Limit

My FIRST INVITATION TO GO DUCK HUNTING CAME IN THE FALL OF 1978. It wasn't just any invitation. I was asked to shoot at Long Point, arguably the most prestigious hunt club in North America.

The club was in Canada but was controlled by a group of Americans, all of whom had been born into the Social Register. Despite the members' uniformly deep pockets, operating expenses had become a burden for the club. After much thought the members came up with an idea. Since they only hunted ducks in the marsh, why not give all of the club's high ground to the Canadian government as a new national wildlife refuge? This disposition would cut their operating costs, and, hopefully, give them a whopping tax deduction.

That's when I received a call from the minister of natural resources of Canada. He explained the problem. The Canadian government wanted to acquire the club's land as a gift for a new national wildlife refuge, but the Americans would not make the donation unless they could be assured that the gift would qualify for a U.S. tax deduction and that the land would in fact be managed in perpetuity as a refuge.

"We've been eyeing this tract for years," the minister told me. "It's one of the premier natural areas in all of Canada. We'll do anything we can to get it, but these damn tax laws are a real bugger. Would you chaps mind having a go at it?"

I had been director of land acquisition for TNC for six years. During that time we had done some innovative deals, and one of our lawyers, Mike Wright, was becoming an expert on using the U.S. tax code internationally. I thought that we might be able to figure something out. I knew that we wanted to meet the members of the oldest hunt club in North

America, any one of whom could become a major supporter of the Conservancy. "We'd be happy to have a go at it," I told the minister.

The next week I flew to New York to have lunch with the president of the hunt club. In real life he was the president and CEO of one of New York's major banks. We met in the president's private dining room. He was very affable; we got along right from the start.

I listened carefully as he outlined the situation. As expected, the deal hinged on our ability to answer two questions. First, how could the club donate the land so that the individual members would get a tax deduction, and second, how could the club be sure that the Canadian government would be obligated to manage the land as a national wildlife refuge? Thanks to a plan devised by Mike Wright, I had answers to both of those questions.

Most of the old hunt clubs are stock corporations. The robber barons who formed these clubs back in the 1800s did not like partnerships; they liked corporations, especially when they controlled the stock.

Fortunately for the robber barons, they didn't have to deal with the Internal Revenue Service of 1978. The IRS looked upon the club as a separate corporation. Unlike a partnership, a corporation cannot pass tax benefits through to the individual shareholders. Thus, the members of the club would not get a deduction if the club gave the land away. The only way that the members could claim a deduction was to give some of their stock in the corporation to a qualified U.S. charity.

Our solution was that the individual members would donate to the Conservancy shares of stock in the club equal in value to the appraised fair market value of the land that the Canadian government wanted for the refuge. After an appropriate holding period, the Conservancy would redeem its stock in the club for the land. This gift-and-redemption would take care of the first problem.

After we had redeemed the stock, we could transfer the land to the Canadian government subject to restrictions that would require the Canadian government to manage the land as a national wildlife refuge. Mike Wright had dug out some IRS rulings that indicated that this transfer would be a separate transaction and would have no adverse impact on the value of the individual members' donations. That would take care of the second problem.

Mike Wright's plan was pure genius. I finished my presentation and smugly settled back into the rich leather chair. I fully expected the president to jump up and gratefully pump my hand. Instead, he frowned. He had detected a flaw. The land that the club wanted to give away represented the bulk of the club's value. That would make The Nature Conservancy the majority stockholder of the oldest and most prestigious hunt club in North America. The flaw in the plan was The Nature Conservancy. *Who* was The Nature Conservancy?

"Surely you have another alternative?" he asked, hopefully.

"No," I said, fidgeting in my chair. "We see no other alternative. This is it."

"If we accept your plan, you'll control the club. How do you propose we limit your control?"

"You can't," I confessed. "The members will have to give their stock with no strings attached. Otherwise, they can't claim a deduction."

"How long would you have to hold our stock?"

"A minimum of two years," I replied.

"Two years!" exclaimed the president. He stared at me as if I had just asked him for a big loan with no collateral.

I smiled weakly. "I'm afraid so. If the club wants to do this deal, they'll just have to trust us. We're not a bunch of tree-huggers. We take a businesslike approach to conservation, and some of us actually enjoy hunting."

"Hmm. Hunting." He stroked his chin in contemplation. "That's a thought. Do you think that you could come up to the club, meet the members, and explain your plan—and, of course, do a little shooting?" It wasn't a question. It was an order. I was being summoned before the loan committee.

"Well, maybe," I hedged. Legally and financially, our plan would pass muster. What the committee wanted to review was The Nature Conservancy's social acceptability.

"Fine," said the president. "We'll expect you this weekend."

We were in trouble. I had never shot anything in my life. I am not opposed to hunting. I had just never had the opportunity to hunt.

Back at the office, Mike Wright was aghast. "You mean to say that our deal depends on your ability to shoot some ducks? When did you ever shoot anything?"

Good point, Mike Wright. "Relax, Mike," I said with a certain bravado. "I've got Cabela's, Bean's, and the Orvis catalogs. Let's pick out some duds. I'll do just fine."

We spent the next hour poring over the catalogs. Cabela's stuff looked the most practical, but it was too common. I'd fit right in drinking with Beebo and Bubba, but definitely be out of place at the classiest hunt club in North America. Bean's was a step up when it came to boots, but the rest of the catalog was too preppy. True to L.L.'s philosophy, Bean's was following the market. It no longer catered to just the hunter.

Orvis looked like just the ticket. I pictured myself arriving at the club bedecked in Orvis's moleskin slacks, shotshell belt, mallard-colored chamois shirt, Thornproof Gamekeeper jacket, and Outback Chukka shoes, toting a Battenkill duffel. Then we checked the prices. Even Cabela's was out of our range. Attention Kmart shoppers!

"Now that you're gonna look like hell, what about a gun?" Mike Wright asked.

"Gun? Do you think I'll need a gun?"

Mike groaned. "How else do you propose to shoot a duck?"

"We'll have to borrow one," I reasoned. "Who do we know that has a gun?"

"Ray has a gun, and it might even be a shotgun," Mike said.

Ray was the head of designing preserves and unlike the rest of us, actually went out into the field once in a while. Sure enough, Ray had an old 12-gauge Remington 870 Wingmaster. It was pretty beat-up, but that was all right. It might even give me some credibility.

My first view of the club came as the launch weaved its way through acres upon acres of prime marshland. I had expected to see a grand old building with weathered shingles and massive stone chimneys, similar to the legendary clubs that once dominated the Carolina marshlands. Instead, we pulled up to a series of little cottages on stilts, connected by wooden walkways. They were almost hidden by the marsh grass, like some shantytown tucked away in a Louisiana bayou. Maybe my Kmart wardrobe would be all right after all.

The president was waiting on the dock. He looked concerned. I surmised that our plan had encountered some opposition. "Welcome to Canada," he said, extending his hand.

"Thank you, it's nice to be here." His grip was firm as he pulled me onto the dock. The pilot passed up my $9.95 Naugahyde overnighter with a look of contempt. The president studied it inquisitively. "Interesting bag," he commented. "I've never seen one quite like it."

"Thank you," I replied. "Could you please hand me my gun?" The pilot produced the Remington with the same look of contempt.

"Ah. Brought your own gun, I see," said the president.

"Yes," I said proudly. "The Wingmaster and I go back quite a way."

"Oh, dear, a 12-gauge? I'm sorry, I should have told you. We only shoot 20s here. Club rules, you know. I'll lend you one of mine."

So much for Ray's Wingmaster. "I'd appreciate that. I should have thought to bring my 20."

"No problem," he said. "We'll leave the Wingmaster right here in the boathouse." I watched as he shoved it under a pile of old life jackets. "Be sure not to forget it," he added.

The president showed me to my cabin. Each member had his own cabin, and each cabin was named after some part of a duck. I was staying in Widgeon Wings. It belonged to a legendary Wall Street financier who was now too old to use it. Widgeon Wings would pass to his oldest son when he died, but, as the president told me, "He'll be damned if his son is going to use it while he's still alive."

The interior of Widgeon Wings looked like an advertisement for Ducks Unlimited. The lampshades, the rugs, the glasses, and even the ashtrays were all covered with images of ducks. Some were flying, some were swimming, some were landing, some were taking off. In the painting over the head, two were flying united.

We spent the afternoon walking some of the land that the Canadian government wanted for the refuge. The refuge would encompass most of a sixteen-mile-long peninsula that jutted into Lake Ontario. It was easy to see why the government was so eager to acquire it. The peninsula provided the last resting place for migrating birds before they crossed the lake. It was totally wild and loaded with all types of birds and animals. During our walk we flushed duck, geese, deer, fox, and even a moose.

I was exhilarated as I washed up for dinner. The crisp, clear Canadian air had heightened my senses. Now that I had seen the area, I knew that it had to be protected.

I rummaged through my Naugahyde overnighter and cut the price tags off a pair of khakis, Docksiders, a checked tattersall shirt, and a lime green 100 percent cotton sweater. It wasn't Orvis, but I felt sure that I could pass as one of the boys.

I was wrong. When I got to Pintails, the main lodge and dining hall, I politely tapped the mallard-head knocker. A middle-aged aristocrat opened the door. I couldn't believe it. He was wearing a cashmere blazer and club tie. I heard the conversation behind him fade to a murmur. "Oh, my," he said. "No one is allowed in Pintails after five without jacket and tie. Club rules, you know."

"I don't have a coat and tie," I confessed. "I thought I was going hunting."

The president quickly came to my rescue. "Not to worry," he said reassuringly. "We've got everything you need down at Greenhead." Things were not going well. I didn't have the bearing of a majority stockholder.

When I reentered Pintails in the nicest jacket and tie I had ever worn, the president wasted no time getting into the presentation. The mechanics of our plan withstood all of the members' legal and financial questions. The only unanswered question was the Conservancy's social acceptability. Their man talked a good game, but it remained to be seen whether he could shoot. They would find that out in the morning.

After a hearty breakfast of poached eggs, kippers, and fried tomatoes, we donned our hunting gear and assembled at the dock. That was where we would meet our punts. Long, flat-bottomed boats are commonly called punts, but at the oldest and most prestigious hunt club in North America, a punt was both the boat *and* the guide who poled it through the marshes. Each member was assigned a punt for life. Your punt became part of your family. Like it or not, you were stuck with him and he with you.

The punts were all attired in well-worn but handsomely tailored hand-me-downs from the members. They looked like British game-keepers. Several were calmly sucking on briarwood pipes as they poled their punts up to the dock. I was getting more and more nervous. Not a word was spoken. Everyone knew exactly what he was doing except me. I turned to a portly industrialist from Cleveland who was seated next to me. "Say," I inquired, "how far do you lead them up here?"

His eyebrows rose. "I beg your pardon?"

"You know," I stumbled on. "How far do you lead them up here?" I swung my gun, a beautiful little Beretta, to illustrate my question.

"Oh, I see," he said, somewhat condescendingly. "I suspect that you lead them up here the same as you lead them down there. Wherever that may be."

The president came over. He wanted to introduce me to my punt, a very old and very distinguished gentleman named Percy. Percy had been the punt for Widgeon Wings all his adult life. He eventually would punt for my absent host's son, provided, of course, that Percy outlived my absent host. "Nice to meet you, Percy," I said.

"My pleasure, sir." Percy had a pronounced English accent. He looked like he wasn't averse to a little nip before breakfast. "What say we push off."

I gingerly settled into the front of the punt. The president handed me my gun. "Be sure to bag the limit," he admonished.

"Stoke up the oven," I replied confidently. "We'll be having duck for lunch." My optimism rose as Percy poled the punt to our assigned section of the marsh. Ducks were everywhere. They looked like softballs as they floated by. I was sure that I could hit them.

Percy became more and more garrulous as we glided along. At first I assumed that he was just an old gentleman that liked to talk. Then I noticed the flask he kept in his waders. Percy was getting sloshed.

After a while he stopped poling, got out, and pushed our punt into the high grass. He took out a pocket knife, cut some long reeds, and began to camouflage the punt. It was a clear, cold day, and a stiff breeze from the lake beat hard against my face. Percy's bare hands should have been frozen, but by now he was fortified with antifreeze.

Once satisfied with our cover, Percy flopped back into the punt and handed me a box of shells. "Here you go, lad," he mumbled. "Now get yourself ready. They should be coming in shortly."

As I loaded up, I was startled to hear a loud quacking right behind me. It was Percy. He sounded more like a duck than a duck did. Two curious greenheads immediately swooped in for a look. I was transfixed by their graceful motions as they set their wings and glided toward us, swaying back and forth into the wind. "Shoot, man, shoot!" Percy shouted.

I raised the Beretta, took aim, and pulled the trigger. Nothing happened. The ducks veered off and retreated over the marsh. "What the hell?" I exclaimed, studying the gun.

"The safety, lad, you must remove the safety."

Not to worry. Within a few minutes, four canvasbacks responded to Percy's calls. *Bang. Bang.* I squeezed off two shots. Nothing fell. Percy groaned. "Too low, lad. Block them out with your barrel. Reload, quick!" *Bang. Bang.* "Behind him! You're way behind him! Follow through, lad. You must follow through. Quick, reload!" *Quack, quack. Bang, bang.* Nothing. "Swing, man! Swing! Swing with the bird!" *Bang, bang.* Nothing. "By Jove, don't shoot at the lot of them! Pick one bird and stay on him!" *Bang, bang.* Nothing. *Bang, bang. Quack, quack. Bang, bang.* Nothing. The Beretta was steaming. I reached for more shells. The box was empty. "Percy, I need more shells."

Percy slipped the flask back into his waders, reached into his finely tailored jacket, and produced another box. "Here you go, lad, but mind you, this is it."

"What?"

"Two boxes is all you get. Club rules, you know."

"No sweat," I assured him. "I was just warming up. Get ready to jump into that marsh. They're going to be dropping like flies."

Fifteen shots later, I was still cold. "Percy," I said. "How many birds do I need to bag the limit?"

Percy thought for a minute. Clearly his flask was getting the better of him. "It depends on what you shoot, and when you shoot them. But ten birds is generally the limit." I could see that he thought it a foolish question. There was no way I was going to get ten birds. I'd be lucky to get one.

"Percy," I said. "You ever shoot one of these things?"

Percy smiled smugly. "Yes, sir. I've been known to take a duck."

"Do you think you can shoot my limit?"

Percy cocked his head proudly. "Your limit, sir, is in the bag."

I was taking a gamble. I knew that Percy was in the bag, but what choice did I have? "Remember," I cautioned, "we only have ten shells."

"That should be enough. Here, move to the rear, if you please." I thought for sure that Percy was going to tip us over as he wobbled to the front of the punt. Somehow we managed to exchange places.

A lone pintail was the first to test Percy. He dropped him cleanly. Next, a pair of widgeons came winging by. Percy took both with a couple of beautifully executed passing shots. I watched in amazement as a flock of blue-winged teal dropped in flawless formation in response to Percy's call. I could hardly follow them as they whooshed over our little blind. Percy raised and fired. Nothing. He scowled at the Beretta. "Bloody Eye-talians."

Two stragglers wheeled into the wind for another look. They were coming in low and fast. Percy lined them up and fired. They both dropped with one shot. Percy looked very pleased with himself. "There," he said, "that evens us up."

He then took a redhead, a pair of canvasbacks, and finished up with two drakes. He had bagged the limit.

The president was waiting for us at the dock. We were late. I could see that he was worried. I turned to Percy, who had, of course, reclaimed his position in the rear. "Percy, my good friend Andrew Jackson would like to make your acquaintance, and I think it would be wise if we kept my shooting prowess to ourselves." Percy took my $20 bill and discreetly slipped it into his waders. "Mum's the word," he said.

"How'd you do?" shouted the president. Proudly, I held up a sampling of my limit. Relief swept over his face. "Wonderful. Wonderful. I'm sure the members will be interested to hear about your hunt."

Over roast duck I described each of Percy's shots as if they were my own. The members were particularly interested in how I had doubled up on the teal. "That's one hell of a shot," the portly industrialist from Cleveland said. "I'm glad you figured out your lead."

That afternoon the club voted unanimously to accept Mike Wright's plan. Today, Long Point is one of the crown jewels in the Canadian Wildlife Refuge System. The refuge itself is named after one of Canada's great sportsmen and conservationists. Only I know that it should be named after Mike Wright and Percy. It was Mike Wright's plan and Percy's shooting that saved it.

~~~

Walking the Maze

After our serendipitous success at Long Point, we thought it would be a good idea to write down the steps to evaluate how best to protect a piece of land. Dusting off our MBAs, we decided to create a Project Evaluation and Review Technique (PERT) chart that would allow us to employ the Critical Path Method (CPM) for evaluating TNC deals. The chart started with the "physical property," then listed each step, and every alternative that had to be considered in order to protect it. The chart was divided into four parts: Dissolution, Reorganization, Planning, and Implementation (DRPI). If properly followed, PERT would plot the CP through DRPI for each project.

For all our efforts, three people, at most, ever bothered to look at the chart, and one of them was Samantha Black, TNC's project review coordinator, whom I asked to type it up. To the best of my knowledge, nobody, including me, has ever used PERT to plot the CP through DRPI for a TNC project. Who can blame them? Saving land isn't about CPMs, PERTs, and DRPI. It's about people dealing with people in a patient and thoughtful manner and experiencing the give and take that goes into figuring out the best way to save a piece of land. However, looking at the chart wasn't a complete waste of time. What it showed was that saving land was like walking through a maze. There were lots of wrong turns and dead ends, but finding the answers was the fun of it.

After reviewing thousands of projects, I could lead anybody through almost any maze in about ten minutes. In the for-profit world, that knowledge would be a huge asset. In conservation it was a tremendous liability. Most people who are thinking of giving or selling their property for conservation don't want to be told how to get through the maze. Instead, they want to explore every possible route and experience for themselves why certain options turned into dead ends. What they want is somebody to hold their hand while they figure it out.

Diplomatic Immunity

In the fall of 1975, Dr. Robert Jenkins, the Conservancy's top scientist and most vocal proponent of the preservation of biotic diversity, made an unexpected pronouncement. "Henceforth," said the Doc, "the Conservancy will no longer haphazardly acquire little lifeboats of diversity. We shall protect entire biological systems."

This change of focus resulted in a major turn for the Conservancy. Originally, the Doc envisioned building our Ark from the scraps of natural areas left lying around after development: a hemlock gully here, a desert spring there, a patch of prairie in between. Now he'd decided that saving these little lifeboats of diversity was not the answer. Eventually they would be swamped by the ever-surging waves of human population growth. What we needed were luxury liners.

This change in course by the Doc undoubtedly was influenced by the work of his contemporaries, most notably Professor Paul Ehrlich. Professor Ehrlich was quickly emerging as a principal defender of the environment. His books covered the entire spectrum of environmental issues: *The Population Bomb; The Race Bomb; How to Survive Affluence; Ark II; Population, Resources, Environment;* and *Ecoscience* were just a sampling of his numerous publications. His shingle hung conspicuously near the top of Stanford's ivory tower. Yet unlike most scientists, Ehrlich could explain the dangers facing the environment to the man on the street. He had an easy, outgoing style that worked well on TV. He was becoming a regular on Johnny Carson. No one could yuk up the environment like Ehrlich.

In contrast the Doc's style was more dogmatic, authoritarian, and territorial. He often had trouble articulating why it was important to preserve biotic diversity, even to members of the Conservancy. It was predictable that he would be taken aback when the board invited Professor Ehrlich to speak at one of our meetings. Worse yet, the professor took that particular opportunity to lecture the Conservancy on the proper way to preserve biotic diversity. Ehrlich warned that his studies at Stanford had proven conclusively that most small, isolated biological communities, both plant and animal, had little chance for survival without the support of surrounding ecosystems. Moreover, if one species in a small community were lost through either a natural calamity or human intervention, it could lead to the loss of dependent populations. "A cascading series of extinctions could quickly reduce the diversity in any small preserve plot," the professor intoned. "If the goal is to save biological diversity, the major focus must be on conserving entire ecosystems!"

The Doc, like any good Harvard man, was quick to expand on a competitor's research. It was not long after our meeting with Ehrlich that the Doc recruited a whole new crew of specialists. He gave them the rank of "preserve designer" and ordered them to identify the best remaining natural systems left in America. "Forget the scraps. Bigger is better!"

Soon these young eager-beaver biologists were drawing lines around millions of acres. The Doc installed a bank of computers whose sole function was to spit out reams of biological information. Biological scorecards were set up for each state. "No Conservancy project," he warned, "will be approved by the science department unless it is part of a pre-identified biological system."

Those of us involved in land acquisition were shocked. We were having enough trouble trying to buy the lifeboats. How were we ever going to pay for luxury liners? After many heated debates and a realistic review of our resources, we settled on a course of action. We would focus on the protection of relatively undeveloped islands. Consequently, almost all of the Virginia Barrier Islands, most of the Golden Isles of Georgia, Little Travers Island in Lake Michigan, more than three dozen islands off the coast of Maine, Dog Island in Apalachicola Bay, and large parts of the San Juan Islands in Puget Sound were protected by the Conservancy in the late 1970s. Most of these preserves were more than lifeboats; a few, like Parramore and Ossabaw, were legitimate luxury liners. Then in early 1978 we were presented with the *Queen Mary* of natural areas: Santa Cruz Island.

The Doc was ecstatic. Santa Cruz, the largest of the Channel Islands, was practically within the shadow of Stanford's ivory tower and just fifty miles from Burbank, home of *The Tonight Show*. Except for a small ranch house and some jeep trails, the island was totally undeveloped. Fortunately, the family who owned more than 90 percent of Santa Cruz was conservation minded, wanted to see the island preserved, and, due to a death in the family, had to sell. The National Park Service was interested, but the family did not want the island to go into public ownership. They were afraid that, being so close to Los Angeles, the island would be overrun with tourists if it were turned into a national park. The family wanted to see Santa Cruz forever managed as a natural preserve, a living remnant of what Southern California must have been like before the white man arrived bearing freeways and tinsel.

Henry Little, director of The Nature Conservancy's western regional office, was captain of the Santa Cruz project. It was his job to put the deal together and steer it through our board of governors. After long and complex negotiations, the family finally agreed to sell the island to the Conservancy for the bargain price of $2.5 million. That was already more money than we had ever raised privately for an acquisition, but $2.5 million was just the start. Henry estimated that we would need another $1.5 million as an endowment to manage the preserve. The reason that we needed to raise such a large endowment was that we would have to eradicate 30,000 feral sheep.

During the 1950s the family had started a hunt club as a way of generating some extra income for Santa Cruz. The club's membership was composed of well-heeled sportsmen from Los Angeles who would pay a fat fee to motor out to the island and pop a few feral sheep. The club worked fine for a while; but as the membership got older, it became obvious that the rugged terrain of Santa Cruz was more suited to the sheep than to the elderly hunters. The club members did less and less hunting. The only sheep that were shot were the ones too old or too stupid to stay away from the ranch house. The young, smart, virile sheep were free to reproduce to their hearts' content.

Sheep are frequent fornicators. By 1978 there were 30,000 feral sheep industriously munching away on our biotic diversity. That number was growing exponentially. If left unchecked, the sheep would soon have Santa Cruz, this last remnant of native Southern California, looking like the surface of the moon.

The Doc had undertaken an exhaustive study of the sheep problem. Ecologically, there was no question that the sheep had to go. Here was a classic case of one very common animal threatening to destroy a treasure trove of endangered species. The Doc's study showed that there were forty-two plant species on Santa Cruz that were found only on the Channel Islands. These plants had been evolving for centuries, and since there were no grazing animals indigenous to the Channel Islands, they had never developed natural defense systems. Unlike plants of the same genus on the mainland, Santa Cruz's flora have no spines, stickers, poisons, coarse textures, bad tastes, or any of the other defenses characteristic of their mainland cousins. The sheep loved them. Biologists labeled them the "ice cream plants." "So what?" the man on the street might ask. "The sheep are just doing what comes naturally. Too bad for the plants. Isn't that nature—survival of the fittest? Besides, sheep are warm and cuddly. What good are these plants?"

The answer, of course, is, "What good are you?" No species can survive by itself. Our world is dependent on biotic diversity. Who knows how these forty-two plants might help us in the future? Agronomists had already discovered that plants on Santa Cruz were far more drought resistant than similar plants on the mainland. This characteristic might become extremely important, especially as our planet enters a new warming cycle. It was entirely conceivable that a plant from Santa Cruz might make it possible to save millions of people in Africa from starvation.

Removing the sheep from Santa Cruz was going to be a very sensitive issue. We had looked at everything from Scottish sheepdogs to Navajo shepherds. All were prohibitively expensive, and none guaranteed satisfactory results. In fact, we discovered a humane society that had offered to remove the sheep at an exorbitant price actually had a contract with a dog food company. The only feasible alternative was to pick the very best of the Conservancy's land stewards, arm them with high-powered rifles, and have them put down the sheep as quickly and painlessly as possible.

It was a hard decision for the staff. Raising $4 million was one thing; that's what nonprofit organizations were supposed to do. Slaughtering 30,000 feral sheep was something else. What conservation organization engaged in genocide? But if the goal was to preserve an entire, unique biological system, it was senseless to buy the island unless we were committed to getting rid of the sheep.

The Santa Cruz project was scheduled to be presented to our board at the May 1978 meeting. It was such an important project that Henry suggested to Pat we should hold the meeting on the island. That was a huge risk. Mother Nature didn't always cooperate with meetings on islands. Getting caught in a storm or a fog coming off the Pacific would be a disaster, but after much discussion, we thought it was worth the gamble. Once we got the board members onboard the *Queen Mary*, we hoped that its sheer size would overshadow the issues of money and sheep. Overshadowed or not, these issues were still going to be problems.

To make the project work, we figured we'd need a lead grant of at least $1 million if we hoped to receive approval from the board. That seemed impossible. There was little interest in conservation in Southern California. Big money in L.A. went to Palm Springs and Vegas, not to conservation. Northern Californians were the ones who gave to conservation, but they didn't like Southern California. They considered everything south of Santa Barbara a materialistic wasteland that was frittering away its water on swimming pools and golf courses. Northern Californians would have liked to turn off the tap and watch Southern California wither into desert.

Fortunately, Henry Little had unearthed an heiress from New England who had recently migrated to San Francisco. This heiress was a very interesting young woman. She had graduated with honors from the Yale School of Forestry and was committed to conservation. Despite her conservative upbringing, she was a free spirit who found the Northeast physically overdeveloped and mentally confining. She liked the openness of the West and had indicated that she would like to do something significant for California. Henry enthusiastically described the enormous potential of Santa Cruz. He gave her a copy of the Doc's report. She was intrigued. Eradicating the sheep didn't bother her. She understood the concept of biotic diversity, and just as important, she didn't care that people from Northern California did not ordinarily give to projects in Southern California. She was her own person. She would do what she damn well pleased.

Henry invited the Heiress to accompany the board to the island. He assigned Spencer Beebe as her escort. Spencer was one of the Conservancy's best deal makers and fund-raisers. Unlike most Conservancy deal makers, Spencer actually knew something about nature. More important, he could use nature to excite donors. Spencer was forever picking up snakes and finding baby birds. I once saw him present a potential donor with a young raptor. While the bird froze the donor with an icy glare, Spencer pounced on his pockets. Together, they plucked the donor clean. But like any of us, Spencer wasn't perfect. He liked to raise money for anything having to do with conservation. He might start asking a donor for $100,000 for a prairie in eastern Oregon and end up with $500,000 for a study of brown bears in Alaska, so Henry assigned me to chaperone Spencer and keep him focused on Santa Cruz. If Spencer could get a million-dollar lead grant from the Heiress, that would take care of our immediate money problem.

As for the sheep, we all knew that the approval of our plan would hinge on one vote: the Ambassador's. The Ambassador was a very proper career diplomat, a longtime board member, and the self-appointed chief of protocol for the Conservancy. He had one approach to every issue: Would it affect TNC's image? If we could persuade the Ambassador that the sheep must go, he would persuade the rest of the board. After all, what were ambassadors for if not to explain difficult situations? We figured the Ambassador would want to take an in-depth tour of the island before casting his vote. He liked to know all the facts and wouldn't be intimidated by the rugged terrain. He had spent a good deal of time hiking through the Swiss Alps.

Henry assigned his old friend Tom Macy to guide the Ambassador. Tom was a former Marine officer who had served in Vietnam with Henry and, like the Ambassador, was in tremendous shape. Henry instructed Tom to show the Ambassador the damage the sheep were doing, even if it meant chasing them through every ravine and crevice on Santa Cruz. Tom's mission was to so prejudice the Ambassador against the sheep that he would vote to do what was right rather than what seemed socially correct. If the Ambassador supported annihilation, that would take care of our sheep problem.

Mother Nature was smiling on us as we boarded the boat to the island. It was a beautiful May day, sunny but pleasant thanks to an offshore breeze. Spencer started working on the Heiress right away. It was not a tough assignment. Just as we expected, she was bright and sincerely interested in nature. She was also extremely attractive and very informal. She wrote down the birds that Spencer identified. I interrupted only once, when a pod of whales swam by. Spencer immediately took a new tack and started talking about a friend who had a plan to save the whales, if only he could find a few million. Fortunately, the whales sounded and I was able to get Spencer back on course.

Henry had arranged a sumptuous picnic lunch at the ranch. Local treats like abalone and calamari were washed down with fine California wine. After lunch Henry made a detailed presentation of the financial and management problems we faced. Then the Doc rose to exhort the board. "If our goal is to save biological diversity, the major focus must be on saving entire ecosystems. Bigger is better; and once the sheep are gone, we will have saved nothing bigger and better than Santa Cruz."

Henry encouraged us all to explore the island before the board took its final vote. Most of the board members and staff were content to sit in the warm sun with a glass of fine California wine and watch some old sheep nibble on the flora. A few, like the Ambassador and Macy, set out in pursuit of nature. I would have preferred to stay behind, but I dutifully tagged along when Spencer invited the Heiress to go for a hike. Spencer guided us up a jeep trail that led to the highest ridge on the island. It was a tough walk but well worth the effort. From the top, we could see all of

Santa Cruz and the distant haze of L.A. A flock of sheep came scampering over the next ridge. The Ambassador and Macy were close on their heels. The Ambassador, striding purposefully, gave us a hearty hello and headed down into the adjacent ravine. Macy looked at us, shook his head, mopped his brow, and tromped off in pursuit.

We could see the Pacific lapping the shore below. After our heavy exertion under a hot sun, it looked cool and refreshing. "Let's go for a swim," said Spencer.

"Great idea," echoed the Heiress.

"I don't know," I said. "It could be quite a hike. This trail seems to wind all over the island."

"We'll go straight down this ravine," Spencer said. He kicked off his shoes and sprinted down the grassy slope. The Heiress immediately followed. I reluctantly tailed after them.

Descending the ravine proved to be a mistake. The grassy slope soon steepened and led to jagged rocks. It was heavy going. Spencer would never have admitted it, but he shouldn't have left his shoes. The sheep had denuded all the vegetation, the soil had eroded, and the protruding rocks were cutting his feet. We kept pushing on. The lower we got, the hotter it got. There was no breeze in the ravine and no cover from the midday sun. We were glad to find a little pool of water. We stopped to splash our faces and let Spencer soak his feet.

I was startled when the Heiress took off her blouse, dipped it into the pool, and tied it around her head. Then she slipped out of her slacks, soaked them in the water, and tied them around her waist. Spencer looked equally startled. "Um, let's keep moving," he stammered. "We're almost to the beach." He hobbled forward while the Heiress, clad only in her bra and panties, strode behind. I brought up the rear. And what a rear! I actually was disappointed when we finally reached the beach. Following the Heiress had given me the inspiration to carry on. "Quick, over here!" Spencer yelled over the pounding surf. Ever alert, he had spotted a bird washed up on the beach. "Let's catch it!" He took off down the sand. I ran after him. The bird saw us coming. Though it waddled awkwardly toward the sea, it was too slow. Spencer grabbed it.

"It's a surf scoter," he told me as he flipped it over. "See, its feet are so far back on its body that it can't take off on land." I must have looked confused. "Like a loon," he continued. "Good for swimming but terrible on land. This guy must have gotten washed up by a big wave."

We turned to look at the waves, but our eyes never reached the water. They froze on the Heiress. She was walking toward us, stark naked. "Oh, no. Now what?" I heard Spencer mumble under his breath.

Obviously the Heiress had shed her New England heritage. She was now a free-spirited Californian. "Hey," Spencer said, trying to act nonchalant, "here's a surf scoter for you." It was the old "give the donor the bird" trick, only this donor had no pockets for Spencer to pick clean. The Heiress fondled the little fellow. "I was just showing Dave how its feet are so far back on its body that it can't walk on land." Spencer started to reach for the bird, but then pulled back his hand. "Ahh," he said awkwardly, "if you flip it over, you can see its feet." The Heiress did as she was instructed. I tried to focus on the scoter but her ample assets got in the way.

I felt a strong need to get in the water. "Let's go for a swim," I suggested. "Yeah," Spencer quickly concurred. Conservancy employees wear Patagonia shorts instead of underwear when they go into the field. Experience has shown that Patagonia shorts can get you through almost anything. You can run in them, swim in them, hike in them, climb in them, or even sleep in them. The preferred color is oak-leaf green.

Spencer and I dove through the surf trying not to stare at the Heiress as she assisted the scoter over the waves. We all paddled out beyond the surf and watched as the scoter flapped its way to freedom. The cool blue Pacific felt good. It revitalized us and soothed our battered bodies.

We were surprised to see Macy and the Ambassador come swimming along the shore toward us. They were both using the modified Australian crawl, a popular stroke for serious long-distance swimmers. The Ambassador had to be crowding sixty, but he was still plenty game and was keeping up with Macy. The Ambassador swam right into us. He pulled up with a start. "Say, pleasant day for a dip, isn't it?"

We all treaded water and chatted for a while. The Ambassador was entertaining the Heiress with tales of his hike. I wondered what he would say if he knew that the attractive young woman bobbing in the water a few yards from him was totally naked. I hoped I would never find out. Swimming with a nude major donor could not possibly fit the Conservancy's image.

Macy swam in to shore and began prying mussels from the rocks. "Anybody hungry?" he hollered, holding up a handful.

"Say, Pacific mussels on the half shell. They're the best. Have you ever tried them?" the Ambassador asked the Heiress.

"Oh, we prefer clams in New England, but Pacific mussels do sound special," she replied.

Spencer and I looked at each other. Here was more trouble. If the Heiress got out of the water, she probably would throw the Ambassador for such a loop that he'd never again want to hear the words "Santa Cruz." The Ambassador was anything but "California casual." The only way that we could cover her nudity was to keep the Heiress in the water until the Ambassador left.

"Gee," said Spencer, "we were just about to swim out to, uh, to, uh . . ." Spencer gazed at the empty sea. "To those rocks over there," I interjected, pointing to a promontory far down the beach. "Right," Spencer added. "That's where we're sure to see some sea lions."

"Nonsense," the Ambassador scoffed. "We just came from there. There are no sea lions. The Conservancy staff are such kidders," he said knowingly to the Heiress. "Let's sample the local delicacies."

"Come and get 'em!" yelled Macy. He was holding up another handful of mollusks. I could have killed him. Obviously, he had no idea of our predicament.

That was all it took. The Ambassador and the Heiress turned toward shore. Spencer and I looked at each other again. We were sunk. We braced for what we knew was about to be one of the most embarrassing moments in the history of The Nature Conservancy.

They caught the same wave and came popping out of the surf like a couple of penguins. "Oh, my God!" exclaimed Spencer. I rubbed my eyes in disbelief. There was the Ambassador, emerging from the water, looking quite proper but totally in the buff. Where was his bathing suit? Macy, draped in the standard Patagonia shorts, was so stunned that he dropped his mussels.

As usual, Spencer was quick to recover. "Come on," he said, "it's time to sell the island."

"What about our suits?" I asked.

"Leave them on," said Spencer. "The Ambassador is covered by diplomatic immunity."

When we emerged, the Ambassador, the Heiress, and Macy were leaning on the rocks eating mussels. The Ambassador was telling old war stories. Were it not for his attire, he could have been at a lawn party at the embassy.

The Ambassador borrowed Macy's Swiss Army knife, expertly shucked a mussel, and offered it to the Heiress. She lapped it from its shell. I shuffled from foot to foot and discretely glanced at the Ambassador. Miraculously, he was maintaining his composure.

It was getting late. Spencer was right; it was time to sell the island. "So, what about the sheep?" I asked the Ambassador. "Do you think we can handle that problem?"

"They've got to go!" he said unequivocally. "They are destroying the island. I intend to make that recommendation most emphatically."

"That's great, but we still need a lead grant of at least a million if we hope to exercise the option," stated Spencer. He looked directly at the Heiress. "Can you help?"

She took another mussel, arched her neck, and let it slide slowly down her throat. "I'll commit $500,000 up front and another $500,000 to finish it off. That ought to give you enough to start and a strong challenge to raise the balance."

With that, she bounded back into the surf. "Hear, hear," exclaimed the Ambassador. "It seems we have a project. Nice work, gentlemen."

There was an awkward silence. "Ah, just one question, Ambassador," I asked. "What happened to your suit?"

The Ambassador assumed his most diplomatic stance. *"Honi soit qui mal y pense,"* he said, throwing open his arms to emphasize his nudity. He dove through the surf and began crawling his way back down the shore.

Spencer shook his head. "What does that mean?"

That evening, the Ambassador, immaculately garbed in a monogrammed blue blazer and club tie, stood before the full board of The Nature Conservancy and pronounced sentence on the sheep. The Heiress, attired sedately in a green-and-white cotton dress, formalized her pledge to Santa Cruz. The vote was unanimous. Henry, thanks in large part to a major grant from Arco, raised the rest of the money, and the island was purchased. Today the sheep are gone, the native flora and fauna are flourishing, and Santa Cruz is becoming the Queen Mary of natural areas. The Doc was right: bigger is better!

*Historical note: In 1349 King Edward III was dancing with the Countess of Salisbury at a great court ball. Quite unexpectedly, the countess lost her garter. As the king, always the gentleman, bent over to pick it up, he saw several persons smile and indulge in snide remarks. This made the king angry, and he exclaimed, *"Honi soit qui mal y pense."* (Evil be to him who thinks evil.) The king slipped the garter onto his own leg and went on to say, presumably in English, that he would "make the garter so glorious that everyone would wish to wear it." He thus founded the Order of the Garter, which is the highest and the oldest order of knighthood in Great Britain. Its emblem is a dark blue garter, edged in gold, on which is printed HONI SOIT QUI MAL Y PENSE, the expression I heard for the first time from the Ambassador on that successful day in May.

The Stink Test

BACK IN THE 1970S AND '80S, EVERY PROJECT OF THE NATURE CONservancy had to be approved by the National Board of Governors. These approvals came at the board's quarterly meetings. It was a three-step process. On the Wednesday and Thursday before a board meeting, the senior staff at the national office, the four regional directors, and any state reps that had an unusual or potentially controversial project would meet in TNC's modest conference room. It is a well-established fact that the simpler a project the better, so for two days we'd go over every project with

Occam's razor, breaking them down into their simplest components, then putting them back together.

These meeting were raucous affairs. Everyone was free to comment and no question was too stupid, though many were labeled as such. Ideas were free flowing, discussions lively, sacred cows gored, egos deflated, egos inflated, compromises made, and through it all, projects were improved. For anyone wanting to know how to save land, it was the ultimate learning process. By Thursday evening we'd be drained, but we'd have the projects ready to take to the next step: their presentation to the Project Review Committee of the board.

The Project Review Committee met on Friday afternoons and consisted of five members. One was usually a scientist, one a philanthropist, one from the board of a chapter, one a businessman, and one a lawyer. Through the late 1970s and 1980s, the committee was chaired by a series of high-powered lawyers: David Harrison from Colorado, Frank Boren from California, Mason Walsh from Pennsylvania, and Charlie Deaton from Mississippi. We were always pushing the envelope looking for new ways to put deals together, and since major land owners tended to be wealthy and hated paying taxes, playing with the U.S. Tax Code was a large part of our business.

Let me tell you that there's nothing wrong playing with the tax code. Our job was to find the resources we needed to protect America's finest remaining natural areas, and the tax code was where we could generate the most resources for doing that. Tax evasion is illegal. Tax avoidance is good business. Sometimes there's a fine line between the two. Having a high-powered lawyer as chairman of the Project Review Committee was the board's way of making sure we didn't cross the line. Another was having Leonard Silverstein, the lawyer most responsible for drafting the 1964 Tax Code, on the board. With Leonard as the final arbitrator, TNC always knew where it stood.

By the time the committee finished its review of the projects, they were ready to be presented to the full board at its meeting on Saturday morning. This approval usually consisted of a single resolution presented by the chairman of the committee, but every now and then there would be a project that warranted individual discussion by the full board. It could be a big project like Santa Cruz Island where we were proposing to shoot 30,000 feral sheep, or a little project where we'd been asked to grant a septic easement that would permit the development of an abutting lot.

More often than not, it was projects where we were trying to mix conservation with development that ended up in front of the full board: letting an owner retain a few house sites, permitting selective timbering, granting a gas or oil pipeline easement, anything that might appear contrary to TNC's stated mission of saving land. Due to these types of projects, Charlie Deaton came up with something he called the "stink test." We'd present the project to the committee, there would be a discussion, and finally Charlie would lean back, take a puff on his ever-present panatela, and say, "Boys, I'm afraid this one don't pass the stink test."

That was it, the project was dead.

For the record, there is no such thing as "limited development." You can't have it both ways. You're either saving land or you're developing it. There's no middle ground. Every time we tried to find some, we got ourselves in trouble. Being part of a development, any development, was like having a piece of dog shit stuck to the bottom of your shoe. It would never pass the "stink test."

This fact became painfully obvious in 2002 when the *Washington Post* ran a three-part exposé on The Nature Conservancy. One part focused on inside deals TNC was doing with board members and big-time supporters. These deals sounded like they crossed the line. At times tax avoidance was smelling a lot like tax evasion. According to the *Post*, "one Conservancy trustee who benefited from such tax breaks described the transactions as 'not illegal' but was reluctant to discuss the details because he said he wanted to avoid alerting the IRS. 'I don't want to attract any attention to this in any way,'" was his quote. That didn't sound good, and it sure didn't smell good. What happened to the project review process? Why wasn't the board checking the bottom of TNC's shoes?

Negotiations

DURING THE LATE 1970S THE NATURE CONSERVANCY DID SOME OF THE biggest land deals in the history of conservation. There was no secret to our success. We knew what we wanted, had the financial ability to acquire it, and always tried to be nice to people.

We seldom publicized our deals. We were in the real estate business. The less people knew where we were going, the better. Plus, some of our best projects were supported by donors who preferred to remain anonymous. They didn't want to be hounded by other nonprofits, and they didn't want their names associated with the conservation movement. This necessary low profile puzzled many within the environmental community. People assumed we knew things that they didn't, or that we were withholding vital information, information that was the key to success.

As the vice president for land acquisition, I began to receive invitations to conferences and workshops hosted by other conservation groups. They billed me as an expert and hoped I'd reveal TNC's secrets. I politely declined. I knew I was no expert, and I told them that I honestly didn't think I had much to offer. These refusals only added to the Conservancy's mystique.

In September of 1979 I finally got caught. Jon Roush, a good friend and member of the Conservancy's national board of governors, asked me to attend a workshop in Jackson Hole. It was being hosted by a new nonprofit organization that Jon had helped form to assist citizen groups involved in the natural-resource issues confronting the environmental integrity of this pristine area. The workshop was titled "Negotiations." When I told Jon that I honestly didn't think I had much to offer, his response was, "You'll be surprised."

I've never liked Jackson Hole. It's a very phony place. Everyone walks like a cowboy, talks like a cowboy, looks like a cowboy, but nobody is a cowboy. No real cowboy could afford to live in Jackson Hole. Land prices have skyrocketed. The real cowboys have been stampeded by dudes in designer jeans and Tony Lama boots who clip coupons from bonds. Big bonds.

Even the famous Jackson Hole Elk Hunt is a sham. When the valley floor was taken over by urban cowboys, the U.S. Fish and Wildlife Service had to set up a refuge for the elk. The Jackson Hole National Elk Refuge, encompassing less than a thousand acres, is all that is left of the herd's winter range. Once they leave the high country, the majestic elk go on welfare. They mill around their little refuge waiting for the Fish and Wildlife Service to hand out bales of hay. When the herd gets too large, the service authorizes another famous Jackson Hole Elk Hunt. A "hunter" lucky enough to win the lottery is issued a permit that allows him to ride out on the feeding sled and pop an elk. This is about as sporting as shooting a barnyard cow. Cowboys, elk refuges, hunters; nothing is real in Jackson Hole.

The workshop was being held at the Triple X, a well-known dude ranch some forty miles north of town. I was surprised that there was no one to meet me when I arrived at the airport. A cab would have destroyed Fitzie's travel budget, so I walked out to the John D. Rockefeller Jr. Memorial Parkway and stuck out my thumb. Two guys in a shiny new pickup stopped. They were wearing crisp, clean ten-gallon hats and had the standard high-powered rifle hanging in the gun rack. "Where ya headin?" they asked.

"A placed called the Triple X," I said. The driver nodded and pointed to the back of the truck.

There was a nip in the air, but I was warmed by the midday sun. As I lay in the bed of the truck, I looked up at the Tetons, ablaze with golden aspen and adorned with crystal-clear streams sparkling in the light like tinsel on a Christmas tree. Even the caravans of motor homes going to and from Grand Teton National Park could not detract from the natural beauty all around me. If ever a place deserved protection, it was the Grand Teton Valley. I was disappointed when the pickup pulled up to the entrance of the

Triple X. I wanted to keep going. It was too nice a day to be inside talking about the environment when I could have been outside experiencing it.

I climbed out of the truck, grabbed my bag, dusted off my sport jacket, and looked up at the entrance to the Triple X. It was the classic two log posts with a crossing beam from which hung the XXX brand. I could see what looked like the main ranch house half a mile or so up the dirt road. I started walking.

The reception desk was deserted. I heard a lot of yelling coming from behind a door marked "Conference Room." Evidently the workshop had started without me. True to my Conservancy training, I decided to avoid the controversy and moseyed out to the stables.

I had a reason. That very night Larry Holmes was defending his WBC heavyweight championship against Ken Norton, and I wanted to find a TV. I figured that the rest of the workshop would have little interest in the fight. Most environmentalists, while continually seeking confrontation on complex issues, have no time for something as simple and straightforward as a fight for the heavyweight championship of the world. A ranch hand who mucked out the stables wouldn't be burdened by the natural-resource issues confronting the northern Rockies. He'd be a fight fan for sure.

I was wrong. The guy I found down at the stables was leaning back in a chair, his well-worn boots propped up on a bale of hay. He was sucking on a piece of grass. His dirty ten-gallon hat was tilted down over his dirty, unshaven face. His eyes moved contemptuously from my Weejuns to my argyle socks, up my corduroys to my gold-buttoned blue blazer. "How ya doin?" I asked.

He slowly withdrew the grass from his mouth. "What can I do for ya, podner?" He looked and sounded like a real cowboy, an endangered species in Jackson Hole.

"You got a TV in this place?"

He sat up in his chair, pointed the piece of grass at me and scowled accusingly. "Podner, yew want tennis courts, a golf course, and a swimmin pool, you've come to the wrong place. This here's a ranch."

Ranch? Who did this guy think he was kidding? There hadn't been a real steer at the Triple X since John D. Rockefeller Jr. was in his prime.

"Yeah, and you're the Lone Ranger."

The piece of grass fell from his hand as he clenched it into a fist. Fortunately, he remained seated.

"I didn't ask for tennis courts, a golf course, or a pool." I continued. "All I asked for was one lousy TV so I could watch the heavyweight championship of the world along with forty million other Americans."

He looked me hard in the eye. "Well, podner, we ain't got that either."

So much for Holmes versus Norton.

The workshop was breaking up when I got back to the main house. Someone called out, "Hey, Dave, where have you been?" It was Jon Roush.

I told him about my altercation with the real cowboy. "Don't worry," he said. "You won't have time for any fights. We'll be working all night."

He then introduced me to the conference facilitator, an intense young man who looked far too preoccupied with natural-resource issues to worry about meeting somebody at the airport. "Oh. So glad you finally got here," he said, as if being late was my fault. "You missed the first session, but no harm. We're just getting ready to introduce the resource people."

"That's wonderful," I replied, "Only I have no idea what I'm supposed to do."

"Oh. Didn't you get a packet describing the workshop?"

"No," I said, a little testily. After flying two thousand miles, bumming in from the airport, and arguing with the Lone Ranger, I was starting to get upset. "I've gotten nothing."

"Oh. Here, take my copy." He handed me a tacky little brochure entitled *Negotiating Resource Policy* and then yelled, "Everybody back in the conference room."

I was swept up in a wave of eager environmentalists. Soon the room was packed. Most of the guys had beards; the women had long, straight hair. Their dress could best be described as Western casual: boots, Levis, chamois shirts, heavy wool sweaters, and down vests. No loafers, ties, or blazers—this group looked even less businesslike than I had expected. I tried to hide myself in a corner.

The conference facilitator clanged an old cowbell and called for order. It took him a while to settle everyone down. They were charged for action.

The first session must have been a barnburner. I wondered what they had been talking about. I glanced at my brochure—there was no agenda.

"Now, it gives me great pleasure to introduce our resource people," the facilitator told the crowd. "These are the experts. These are the people who have the knowledge we need. Listen to them and learn! After we hear from our resource people, it will be time to play The Game!" The facilitator announced "The Game" as if it were Christmas morning. Someone gave a loud "yahoo!" I couldn't believe it.

The facilitator gestured for silence. He introduced the first resource person, an old codger from the American Arbitration Association. He was pretty spry for an ancient arbitrator. He sprang to his feet and launched into a harangue on how "ours is a culture of confrontation. Good guys finish last. Winning is what counts." Yadda, yadda, yadda. "But to be a winner, a skillful negotiator has to look for opportunities to compromise. . . ."

Finally he wound down: "Through consensus, one achieves better solutions! Give a little, but get a lot!" He sat down. There was polite applause. I disagreed with his emphasis on confrontation, but what else could be expected from the American Arbitration Association?

The facilitator thanked the ancient arbitrator and then introduced a short, dumpy, unhappy-looking woman. She was the founding president of some group having to do with women in labor. I looked down at my brochure. It noted that her work emphasized "the common issues of the feminist, conservation, and labor movements." I wondered what issues feminists, conservationists, and unionists possibly could have in common. She wasted no time in letting me know.

"I am in total disagreement with compromise! Women have always been compromised! Conservation has always been compromised! And labor has always been compromised!" Yadda, yadda, yadda. "Struggle is the essence of life! We must struggle and fight for our existence! We must struggle and fight for our very lives! We are all adversaries at the bargaining table." Et cetera.

"Our enemies change, but the battle is ongoing! Feminists, conservationists, and the labor movement must keep fighting until we have won an unconditional *vic-tooor-y!!* We must *never* compromise!" The woman threw her hands into the air with her fingers spread in a V. She resembled a short, dumpy, unhappy Richard Nixon. There was a thunderclap of applause.

What have I gotten myself into? One more speech like that, and the FBI would round us all up. The facilitator was clanging his cowbell. The air was charged with anticipation. And with good reason. The next resource person was a militant young labor organizer. He had a ponytail, a flowing moustache, and a motorcycle jacket. He was trouble.

"I have come here to praise conflict, not to bury it," he intoned in a sepulchral chant. "I believe that conflict is inevitable and healthy. It is a fact that in our society, power is unequally distributed." Yadda, yadda, yadda. "In our society, there are the have's and the have-not's." His voice started to rise. "For the have-not's to achieve power, they must alter their relationship with those in power. That involves conflict!" There was a scattering of applause. "We must not be afraid to break the rules! Rules are made by those in power to protect their power! Once we have the power, we will make the rules!" I started wondering whether I was in the Rockies or the Urals.

"If there is to be a successful revolution, we must be willing to break the self-serving rules of those who seek to keep us disenfranchised, those who seek to keep us enslaved to their power!" He paused for the spirited applause he knew was coming. He was a real pro. *"I am not concerned with the right solution!!"* he screamed, thrusting a clenched fist into the air. *"I am concerned with power!"* The crowd went wild. They rose to their feet, waving their fists and chanting, "Power! Power! Power!"

This guy deserved the Order of Lenin. I looked toward the door. Where was Jon Roush? We had to get out of here. This was no place for The Nature Conservancy. The facilitator was clanging his cowbell in a frenzy. "Please! Please! Please sit down! Please, may I have your attention! The best is yet to come!" People began to settle back into their seats.

"And now, our final expert!" the facilitator stated with great excitement. "Here is a warrior who's actually done it, a warrior who's gone toe to toe with the captains of industry, a warrior who has faced power and seized it for conservation! Representing The Nature Conservancy, from Washington, D.C., the capital of power, David Morine!"

The crowd started turning in their seats. Where was this mythic hero, this David who had taken on the Goliath of corporate America? I stood in the corner, twiddling the gold buttons on my blazer. What could I conceivably say to these fanatics?

"Gee, it sure is nice to be here," I mumbled. "I am pleased to have this opportunity to meet with all of you." I recognized my voice, but I couldn't believe it was me talking. "I'm afraid that at The Nature Conservancy we approach our business a little differently. We don't like conflict. We don't like confrontation. We always try to be nice to people, especially people in power. We think that most of them are basically OK, that they want to do what's right. We always try to be ethical, we try to understand their positions, we look for reasonable alternatives. We work for the best possible solutions."

I could feel the electricity draining from the room. "The concept of environmental warriors battling captains of industry is not valid for the Conservancy. We find we save a lot more land working with industry than by fighting with it. We use the tax code to forge partnerships with corporations and individuals who have the power to make decisions affecting significant natural areas.

"We have learned that to save our natural resources, we must deal ethically and effectively with the people who control them. That's the secret to the Natural Conservancy's success."

I expected at least a businesslike round of applause. There was nothing. People were staring at me as though I came from another planet.

The facilitator came to my rescue. "Thank you, Dave," he said somewhat condescendingly. "The Conservancy certainly has a novel approach to conservation." Then to the crowd, "Let's take a ten-minute break before the game."

At the mention of the game, the participants forgot about me altogether. They buzzed excitedly as they moved into the corridor. I was totally ignored except for Jon Roush. He came over looking very much amused.

"See, I told you you'd be surprised," he said gleefully.

"I can't wait for the game. What is it, a public lynching?"

"You'll see," said Jon, still smiling.

The game was called "Operation Wilderness: The Ultimate in Environmental Conflicts." The participants were divided into four groups: the

Forest Service, a local timber company, residents of the town, and the environmentalists. The object of "Operation Wilderness" was to hammer out an agreement satisfactory to all parties regarding the use of 800,000 acres of timberland located just sixty miles from an urban area of one million people. Historically it provided hunting and fishing opportunities for the townspeople, recreational land for city people, and logs for the local timber company. Now the demands for more recreational land for people from the city and more timber for the local mill were causing a conflict. The Forest Service, which managed the land for the federal government, had to adopt a long-term management plan for the area. It hoped to bring all the interested parties together and have them work out an agreement.

The final agreement had to allow:

- the local timber company to remain prosperous
- the Forest Service to carry out its mandate of multiple use
- the townspeople to remain employed, yet still have enough land for hunting and fishing
- the environmentalists to preserve as much land as possible for wilderness and passive outdoor recreation

Each group was given "negotiating units" consisting of deeds to certain plots of land, money, and political influence, but they were not divided equally, and no group knew what the others had. A resource person had been assigned to coach each group. Naturally, I got the environmentalists. Given my introductory remarks, the environmentalists saw little need for my coaching.

I watched with great interest as each group staked out a corner of the conference room and busily went to work. A young warrior soon emerged as the leader of the environmentalists. "Power," he intoned in the now popular chant. "We must seize power."

"How can we seize power before we know who has it?" inquired an elderly gentleman in a Pendleton shirt, string tie, and Hush Puppies. "We seem to have some political influence," he continued, thumbing through his material, "but what is that worth?"

No one had an answer. Nobody looked to me for guidance, but I saw this as a chance to volunteer my resources. "Why don't you walk around and ask the other groups what they've got?" I interjected. "You're all in the same boat. They might be willing to swap some information. At the very least you'll get a feel for who's got what."

"Ask?" The young buck glared at me. "Warriors don't ask. They take."

No one came to my defense. It was obvious the group was upset that they had pulled such a dud for a resource. Even the ancient arbitrator would have been better.

"Maybe we should consider some type of compromise," suggested a professorial pipe-smoking fellow.

"Compromise?" snorted the gray-haired mate of the elderly gentleman. "We must never compromise."

"Women, labor, and conservation have always been compromised," reiterated an aging hippie with large breasts hanging untethered beneath her turtleneck. "We must fight for an unconditional victory."

"But how much power do we have?" bleated a roly-poly little guy with Coke-bottle glasses and a toupee. "We could very well end up with nothing."

"That's true," reasoned the pipe-smoking professor. "We have little money and no land. We should at least consider a compromise."

The young buck wasn't about to be compromised. "Power. We must seize power."

"But how?" demanded the elderly gentleman.

"You'd be the last to know," snapped his wife.

Yadda, yadda, yadda. I had never seen so much wasted energy. The group wrangled back and forth all afternoon. They hashed and rehashed their negotiating units. Who had the power? Was it the timber company, which was being advised by the union organizer and probably had the money? The Forest Service, which was under the benign eye of the ancient arbitrator? They definitely had the land. Or the townspeople, who were being exhorted by the unhappy little woman? What did they have? Where was the power? To compromise, or not to compromise?

The other groups were starting to break for dinner. The timber company came lumbering by. They were all smiles. It was obvious they thought they had us stumped. The Forest Service looked hungry but content. They couldn't lose under their multiple-use mandate. The townspeople were actually chuckling; what Nixonian plot had they hatched? Only we, the environmentalists, were deadlocked.

Finally the room went silent. Everyone except us had already gone to dinner. The roly-poly little guy's stomach rumbled. "What do you think?" he asked, turning to me in desperation.

Finally, I had a chance to coach. "Seems to me that you can't develop a realistic strategy because you don't have enough information. You want to seize the power, but you can't even find it. All you have is some political influence, whatever that's worth. If you overreach, you could lose everything. The only way you can be sure of saving the maximum amount of wilderness is to know what chits the other groups control."

"That's obvious," countered the young warrior. "So what would Mr. Nature Conservancy do?"

It was time to put these warriors to the test. "I don't see why you're arguing. You need information. Well, there it is." I pointed around the room. "Everyone's gone. Go over and look at their notes. Find out what they have, then you can figure out exactly what to do. You'll blow their socks off."

Again, everyone looked at me as if I had come from another planet.

"Look," I continued in my best locker-room style. "In the real world, you try to get as much information as you can before you negotiate. Information is power. You've got the field to yourself. There's no rule that says you can't look at somebody else's notes if they're dumb enough to leave them lying around. Here's your chance. Go for it!"

The young warrior jumped to his feet. "Just who do you think you are?"

"Yeah," said the elderly gentleman.

"What are you trying to do?" demanded the buxom hippie, thrusting her breasts forward with great indignation. "That would wreck the game!"

Everyone else immediately agreed. It was the first time they had agreed on anything all afternoon. Apparently I had molded them into a team.

"Hey," I insisted, "don't you want to seize the power? Crush your opponents? Win the game?"

"Sure we want to win," protested the young warrior. "But we want to win fair and square."

"Frankly, I'm somewhat disappointed in The Nature Conservancy," said the pipe-smoking professor. "I thought you were an ethical organization that tried to be nice to people. This is not very ethical or very nice."

"Let's eat," said the roly-poly little guy. Again, there was unanimity.

I didn't bother to stay for dinner. I grabbed my bag and hitched a ride back down the Parkway. I just made the last flight to Denver. The world heavyweight championship fight was on when I landed. I watched Larry Holmes knock out Ken Norton in the eighth and caught the red-eye back to D.C.

I was able to sleep the whole way home. Conservation in the northern Rockies was going to be all right. The environmentalists had passed their test. They weren't crazed warriors, after all. They were ethical conservationists who wanted to do right. And eventually, they might even learn to be nice to people.

— ∙ —

Be Nice to People

IN THE EARLY YEARS OF TNC, BEFORE E-MAIL, BLOGS, TWITTER, AND way too much information, we had a simple way of keeping up with what was going on. It was called the dailies and consisted of a folder in which everybody would put a copy of every letter they'd written that day. This folder was passed around the office. By leafing through it, you could get a feel for what everybody was doing.

Because Pat refused to acknowledge unpleasantness, his letters were a constant lesson on being nice to people: always positive, upbeat, and complimentary—no matter what. For example, in 1973, right after we'd transferred Union Camp's 50,000-acre donation in the Great Dismal Swamp to the Fish and Wildlife Service for a new national wildlife refuge, the service asked us if we could help them acquire a key tract abutting the Union Camp gift. It was a 14,000-acre parcel owned by a tough old swamp rat named "Bull" Headley. Bull's nickname was well deserved. He was a hard-headed, hard-charging businessman who'd been timbering in the swamp all his life and had no use for the Fish and Wildlife Service and its new refuge.

Pat and I met with Bull in the double-wide trailer at the edge of the swamp that served as his office. Bull was a big man with a leathery face and hands like meat hooks. After a less than cordial introduction, he asked us what we wanted. Pat told him we were wondering if he'd care to donate his land to The Nature Conservancy so we could add it to the wildlife refuge. No matter how slim the odds, the cardinal rule at the Conservancy was you always started off by asking for a donation.

Bull nearly swallowed his cigar. He faced turned red and he jumped to his feet. "You damn leaf-lickers want me to give you my land? What, are you crazy? Hell, I was timbering this swamp before you pups were born, and let me tell you something, I have no intention of ever giving, selling, leasing, or doing anything with my land that will make it part of that refuge. Do I make myself clear?" He did, especially when he threw us "leaf-lickers" out. Bull might have been as tough as nails, but I had to admit he had a way with words.

The next day I was going through the dailies and saw Pat's letter to "Mr. Headley." It told him how much we enjoyed meeting him, how insightful we found his views on the new refuge, and how if he ever thought about disposing of his land, we'd be interested in meeting with him. There wasn't a hint that we'd been thrown out. Over the next few months, there were more letters from Pat to Mr. Headley. They all were positive, upbeat, complimentary, and contained news about the refuge. Eventually, Bull wrote back. He addressed his letter "Dear Pat," thanked him for keeping him up-to-date on the refuge, and signed it "Bull." And so it went, Pat and Bull became pen pals. Within a year Bull called Pat and told him he might be interested in selling his land. Rather than meet in the trailer, he invited Pat and his family to come stay with him at his home in Bermuda. Pat accepted this kind invitation, the deal was done, and Bull actually ended up donating some of the land to the refuge. It really does pay to be nice to people.

Roscoe Hobbs's Will

ON MY FIRST DAY OF BUSINESS SCHOOL, THE PROFESSOR OF MARKETING walked into the room and without saying a word drew a picture of a screw on the chalkboard. "Anybody know what this is?" he asked. Fifty of us were in the class, and none of us knew where he was going with this. "Well," he said, obviously not expecting an answer, "I'm going to tell you. This is the screw. It represents any deal you'll ever get into, and the first thing you have to do is to figure out where you are on it." Then he drew a stick figure of a guy lying on his back with the tip of the screw going into his stomach. In the bubble coming out of the guy's mouth, he wrote "Ouch."

"If this is you," he said, pointing to the stick figure, "what you have to do is figure out how you're going to get from there to here," whereupon he drew another stick figure standing upright on the top of the screw. The bubble coming from its mouth said, "Yea."

As we soon learned, "on top of the screw" is a popular business term. In negotiating for land, the first thing you have to do is realistically figure out where you are on the screw. What do you have? What do they have? What do you want? What do they want? What's really driving this deal? Once you've figured out the answers to these questions, where are you on the screw? If you're on the top, great. If you're not, what do you have to do to get there? Witness Roscoe Hobbs's will.

Roscoe Hobbs was a self-made man and did a good job of it. Born of modest means in Bentonville, Arkansas, in 1881, there weren't a lot of opportunities open to Roscoe when he was growing up. He was going nowhere slowly until 1908, when, at the age of twenty-seven, he signed on as an entry-level brakeman with the newly formed Arkansas, Oklahoma &

Western Railroad, a small sixty-one-mile feeder line serving fruit growers in south-central Benton County. The railroad business suited Roscoe. He literally jumped onto the fast track, such as it was in northwest Arkansas in the early 1900s, and over the next several years rose to locomotive fireman, depot agent, and ultimately traffic manager for the line. On the side, Roscoe soon began speculating on timber land and saw a niche that once filled would make him a millionaire many times over.

Realizing the need for lumber to make railroad ties, Roscoe, together with four partners, formed Ozark Land and Lumber Company. In 1912 these local boys climbed out on a limb and bought 12,000 acres and a lumber mill from the Van Winkle family, who, at the time, were the major landowners in northwest Arkansas. With lumber from the mill, Roscoe and his partners constructed a railroad bridge over the White River and laid eight miles of track from Monte Ne to War Eagle. Then they leased the track to the Arkansas, Oklahoma & Western Railroad, which by then had been renamed the Kansas City & Memphis Railway. Roscoe had bought his ticket to ride, but then his train got derailed.

In 1914 the Kansas City & Memphis Railway declared bankruptcy, which ended its lease payments to the Ozark Land and Lumber Company, which triggered a foreclosure on the Van Winkle land and mill. For Roscoe, all was not lost. In 1915 the bankruptcy court appointed him as the receiver and general manager of the Kansas City & Memphis Railway, which meant he was still employed, still in the railroad business, and still thinking about the money to be made in railroad ties.

With the railway bankruptcy settled in 1917, Roscoe and five partners formed the Ozark Tie Company in Rogers, Arkansas, and began filling the niche. By 1922 Roscoe was ready to make his next move. He dissolved the Ozark Tie Company, moved to St. Louis, and formed the Hobbs Tie and Timber Company, which soon became the leading supplier of railroad ties in America. Roscoe was quickly becoming one of the richest men in America, but through it all, he never forgot about the Van Winkle land he'd lost. In 1928, fourteen years after the foreclosure, Hobbs Tie and Timber reacquired the mortgage and note, and Roscoe became the sole owner of the entire 12,000-acre tract.

Unlike most of the early timber barons, Roscoe didn't cut and run. He was a dedicated sportsman with roots set deep into the Ozarks. Preserving the natural beauty of this area was important to him, so important that when he died in 1965, he stated in his will that if his heirs ever sold any of his land, the state of Arkansas should have the first option to buy it for a park. In the spring of 1978, Roscoe's heirs decided to put the 12,000 acres on the market. The land, covered with fine stands of upland hardwoods mixed with shortleaf pine, was the largest undeveloped tract left in northwest Arkansas. But what really made this property unique was that it contained twenty-two miles of undisturbed frontage on Beaver Lake, one of the most scenic lakes in the state. With its natural significance and recreational potential, there was nothing else like it in Arkansas, and according to Roscoe's will, the state had the first option to buy it. How could the Razorbacks not jump on this once-in-a-lifetime opportunity?

In many ways Arkansas was the mirror image of Mississippi. Each state had a population of just over two million, each relied on an agricultural economy, and each had a culture that considered hunting and fishing a way of life. But once you crossed the Big River, there was a difference. Arkansas had more of a frontier feel to it. It wasn't as insular as Mississippi. New people and new ideas didn't bother Arkansas. If something was going to change, the Razorbacks were more prone to get with it than to fight it. That was especially true when it came to creating a statewide system of wildlife management areas. Unlike Mississippi, Arkansas didn't have to be sold on the idea. By 1978 the Arkansas Game and Fish Commission had acquired more than 300,000 acres of land for wildlife management and had what was generally recognized as the finest system in the Southeast. But therein lay the problem. In the spring of 1978, Game and Fish was out of money. Two recent acquisitions had left it with payments of over a million dollars a year and there was no guarantee that the legislature would come up with any more. To buy the Hobbs tract, they'd need more . . . a lot more. A state appraisal had placed the value of the Hobbs tract conservatively at $4 million. Game and Fish would have to pass.

At that point I got a call from Bill Gaines, head of real estate for Game and Fish. Bill was a calmer, more controlled version of Mississippi's Avery Wood, but like Avery, he had a passion for saving land and was the principal reason why Arkansas had been able to acquire 300,000 acres for wildlife management. Bill wasn't about to sit back and watch the Hobbs tract be sold to some developer. We'd never done a project with Bill because he'd never needed our help, but now he wanted me to meet with the Game and Fish Commission and explore ways in which we might assist the state in acquiring the Hobbs tract.

At that meeting the commission was unanimous in its desire to buy the land, but there was no guarantee it could find the funding. It was only April and the legislature wasn't scheduled to meet until the following January. We were stuck. Without some guarantee from the state that it would repurchase the land from TNC, we wouldn't put out the money to buy it. The Game and Fish Commission said they'd keep working on it. I said, "Fine, give me a call if you come up with anything."

In early June I got a call from Senator Kaneaster Hodges. Kaneaster had come to Washington when Senator John McClellan died the previous winter and Governor David Pryor had appointed him to fill the seat. I'd gotten to know Kaneaster when he was on the Arkansas Game and Fish Commission and I liked him. He knew the ropes, was a straight shooter, and could close a deal. The senator confirmed that the whole state was behind the purchase and that Governor Pryor had personally taken over the effort to find the funding. He told me the governor had just asked him to go to Cecil Andrus, secretary of the interior, and see if the state could get a grant from the secretary's discretionary fund. In addition, the governor hoped TNC would handle the negotiations. Senator Hodges told me I was to call Ray Scott, the governor's executive secretary, and that Ray would be the point man on this project. When I called Ray, he was quick, smart, and easy to work with. He said he'd help us any way he could with the negotiations and hoped we'd do the same for him when it came to finding the funding.

I went in to see John Flicker. John was TNC's general counsel. Since we'd be dealing with Roscoe's heirs, there undoubtedly would be a lot of legal issues. John and I agreed that the first thing we had to do was to fig-ure out who actually controlled the land. Once we had that information, we could determine where we were on the screw and what leverage, if any, the provision in Roscoe's will that the state should have a first option to buy the property might give us. To do that, we needed a copy of Roscoe's will. We called Ray Scott and he said he'd get the state's attorney general, Bill Clinton, right on it.

It turned out that in 1965 when Roscoe died, the entire property was left in a trust to be administered by the trust department of a prominent St. Louis bank. A one-quarter undivided interest subsequently had been transferred out of the trust to David Cordell, Roscoe's grandson by his daughter Sara, who had died. Another one-quarter undivided interest had been transferred to Roscoe's other daughter, Warrene G. Schlapp, who was alive and living in St. Louis. The remaining one-half interest was still held by the bank in trust.

Up until now, the state had been dealing with a broker in Rogers, Arkansas, who held an exclusive listing on the land. If possible, we didn't want to work through any broker. Dealing with a broker would only add another layer of complexity to a project that already was looking complex enough. We wanted to deal directly with the principals, and since the trust department of the bank controlled a half interest, that seemed like the place to start. I called Timon Primm, one of TNC's national board members. Timon came from an old St. Louis family, and when I asked him if he knew anyone at the bank, he said, "No problem. The president's a good friend of mine. I'll tell him you're going to be in touch."

What we would have liked was an option on the property at below the appraised market value that the governor could take to the legislature in January. That would be the perfect solution, but it wasn't going to happen. Trust departments aren't in the business of making charitable donations and our analysis of Roscoe's will indicated that Arkansas's first option to buy was more of a wish than a legal obligation. We, of course, would ask the bank for an option at below the fair market value, but knowing that was a long shot, it would be nice if we had some funding in place when we went to meet with the bank.

When we closed on the Pascagoula land in Mississippi, we were able to borrow $13.5 million at a below-market rate from two local banks who saw their participation in the project as a public service to the people of Mississippi. With this in mind, we asked Ray Scott if there were any banks in Arkansas that would be willing to lend TNC the money needed to purchase the Hobbs tract and secure the loan with a non-recourse mortgage. Having a non-recourse mortgage meant that if the legislature failed to appropriate the money, the bank's only recourse would be to take the land. Ray said he'd look into it.

Given that we were not very high up on the screw, it would be important we had Governor Pryor with us at this first meeting with the bank. The governor, knowing he was our biggest gun, said he'd be pleased to attend. Ray set up the meeting for the morning of June 28 in St. Louis, but asked John and me if we could come to Little Rock a day early. He'd talked to some bankers about the possibility of granting TNC a non-recourse mortgage and they were interested. Ray wanted us to meet with the bankers, the governor, Bill Clinton, and Jodi Mahony, who was head of appropriations for the Arkansas House of Representatives.

There were no old fogies running Arkansas. John Lewis, chairman of the First National Bank of Fayetteville, Jim Walton, chairman of the Bank of Pea Ridge, Jodi Mahony, Ray Scott, and Bill Clinton were all in their early thirties. The only person over forty in the room was Governor Pryor, and he was just forty-four. Youth didn't seem to hold anyone back in Arkansas. In fact, Bill Clinton had announced he was running for governor, and he was only thirty-one.

John Lewis and Jim Walton were a couple of can-do guys. They'd come up with a politically ingenious way of doing the non-recourse loan. Instead of having just a couple of banks assume all of the risk, they'd put together a consortium of twenty-two banks in northwest Arkansas who were willing to be part of the loan. With the First National Bank of Fayetteville serving as leader, each of the banks would finance a pro rata share of the loan according to their size.

"With all these banks on the hook," John Lewis said, "it's gonna be real tough for the legislature to say no. But heck, even if they do, some of these boys wouldn't mind ownin a piece of that land. I've gotta tell ya, it's somethin special." That was it. We were on top of the screw. We could go to St. Louis with our big gun loaded.

The governor of Arkansas didn't have his own plane, so the next morning, John Flicker, Ray Scott, the governor, and I climbed into a twin-engine Cessna Ray had borrowed from somebody and headed north. When we landed in St. Louis, there was a Missouri state trooper parked on the tarmac waiting for us. "Wow," I said, "this sure beats a cab."

"It's a courtesy the governors extend to each other," Governor Pryor explained. "Anytime you're in another state, they assign you a trooper, but let me tell you, it can be a problem. A few years back, the governor of Kentucky had a place in the Ozarks where he liked to go to unwind. Every time he showed up, we'd have to assign him a trooper whose main job was to keep him in booze. The head of the state police wasn't too happy about that."

When we pulled up to the bank with our lights flashing, there was the president standing on the curb waiting for us. Timon Primm must have told him to lay out the red carpet, and he did. Even the governor was impressed. The president ushered us into the bank and introduced us to the head of the trust department, who in turn introduced us to the trust officer in charge of Roscoe Hobbs's estate. He was a little cock on the walk with a patronizing manner. We weren't comfortable with him from the start and the farther we got into the negotiations, the more things didn't feel right.

What was the problem? We had the money, Roscoe wanted the state to have the property, so let's make the deal. "No, no," said Cocky, "we can't do that. Roscoe Hobbs's wish that the state should have the property is very commendable, but under our fiduciary capacity, the bank is obligated to consider all offers, and the broker who is handling this property for us just informed me he has a very interested party who is willing to pay significantly more than $4 million. In fact, he expects to receive a firm offer within the next couple of days."

"Well, that's all well and good," I said, "but you only control half of the property. What do the other two owners think? They don't have to worry about any fiduciary capacity. They can do whatever they want, and maybe they'd like to honor Roscoe's wish."

"The bank represents Mrs. Schlapp," Cocky said, now getting a little testy, "and she is in full agreement with our position to accept the highest offer."

"What about the grandson?" the governor asked. "What does he say?"

"The bank does not represent Mr. Hobbs's grandson, and for good reason. If the truth be known, Mr. Hobbs never much liked the boy. He considered him something of a wastrel. The bank has nothing to do with him, and I strongly recommend you do the same. We're confident he'll go along with whatever we decide. All he cares about is getting his money."

That was it. We sat there stunned while Cocky told us he'd let us know when he received the other offer, but he doubted we'd be able to match it. What had happened? Somehow we'd gone from thinking we were on the top of the screw to the bottom. On the flight back to Little Rock, the governor said, "Let me see that copy of the will." After poring over it he broke into a smile. "Listen to this. 'And to my grandson, David Cordell of Norman, Oklahoma, I leave my two hunting dogs. May they give him as much pleasure as they have always given me.'" The governor paused, letting those words sink in. "Let me tell you boys something, you don't leave your hunting dogs to some kid you don't like. Hunting dogs are special. If you're leaving them to somebody, you want to make sure they're special too. Ray, when we get back to Little Rock, call Cordell and invite him up to the mansion for lunch with us tomorrow. I think we're going to like this guy."

We did like David Cordell. He and his attorney were a couple of good old boys who had no use for the trust department of the bank and were suspicious of the trust officer. "That little weasel's just looking for fees," David said. "My bet is he and that broker got something going with a developer who wants to chop the property up into a bunch of vacation lots and sell 'em to suckers dreaming about having a place in the Ozarks. A little money down, a few dollars a month, the broker gets his commissions, the bank gets the mortgages, and the property's gone forever. That's not what Roscoe wanted. Governor, how can I help?"

"You can give TNC an option for your quarter interest," John Flicker said. "That way, we'll have a seat at the table when this other offer comes in."

David looked as his lawyer. "We can do that," the lawyer said. "What's the price?"

"Well," I said, "since the state has appraised the property for $4 million, your quarter interest would be worth a million. But you know, if you'd really like to honor your grandfather, you could donate your quarter interest to the state and take the million as a charitable donation."

David Cordell laughed. "Hell, I don't have that kind of money, but I'll tell you what, if you name it after Roscoe, I'll knock off $250,000."

"Thanks to Roscoe's dogs, I think we've got ourselves a deal," the governor said. "Let's eat."

With David Cordell's quarter interest, we were moving up the screw, but we still had a way to go. At our first meeting with the bank, we'd learned that the other trustees for the half interest held by the bank were Warrene's husband Henry Schlapp and W. J. McAfee, Roscoe's old attorney. When we got back to Washington, I called Timon Primm to see if he knew them. "I know of them," Timon said, "but not well enough to be of much help. I suggest you call Warren Lammert. Warren's chairman of TNC's Missouri chapter and a good friend of McAfee."

After I explained to Warren what we were trying to do and the trouble we were having, he said, "Heck, McAfee and I have lunch together every Wednesday. Let me talk to him and see what I can find out."

What Warren found out was that neither McAfee nor the Schlapps knew about our interest in the property, and they were scheduled to meet the next day to approve an offer from a developer in California. We called Cocky and told him we'd like to attend the meeting so we could present our offer directly to the trustees. Cocky told us not to bother unless we were fully prepared to beat the developer's offer, which was substantially higher than $4 million. John and I hopped on a plane for St. Louis. When we came into the meeting, Cocky was not pleased. He was even less pleased when John demanded to see the developer's offer. "I beg your pardon," Cocky said, puffing up with rightful indignation. "You have no right to see someone else's offer."

"I think we do," John said, dropping the option we'd gotten from David Cordell onto the table. "We now hold a legal right to one quarter of the property."

Now it was Cocky's turn to be stunned. We were back on top of the screw. We asked him to wait outside while we talked the situation over with our co-owners.

As David Cordell had predicted, the developer's offer was all smoke and mirrors: a little money down with future payments tied to the sale of lots. After we'd explained to the Schlapps and McAfee that the state really wanted the land for a state park and that our offer was all cash with no contingencies, we told them how David Cordell had agreed to make a $250,000 donation to the project provided the park would be named after his grandfather. Would they be willing to do the same? Roscoe's daughter was delighted and said this is just what her father would have wanted. All McAfee said was, "Hell, I don't have a choice. Lammert told me if I didn't sell this property to you guys, he wasn't going to have lunch with me anymore, and at my age, finding somebody to have lunch with isn't easy."

Using the non-recourse loan, TNC took title to the Hobbs tract on January 4, 1979. In February the legislature overwhelmingly approved the funding necessary for the state to repurchase the property. In March, at a grand celebration in Rogers, Arkansas, former governor David Pryor, Senator Kaneaster Hodges, representative Jodi Mahony, Ray Scott, Bill Gaines, members of the Game and Fish Commission, and a host of very happy bankers were part of the enthusiastic crowd that watched newly inaugurated governor Bill Clinton accept the deed for the Hobbs tract from The Nature Conservancy. Today, Roscoe Hobbs would be pleased that in accordance with his wishes, this 12,000-acre tract that was so much a part of his life is now recognized as one of the largest and finest state parks in all of America. Better yet, he'd take great pleasure knowing that it was his hunting dogs that made it all happen.

~~~

Reveille for Conservation

Volunteers have always been the heart and soul of the conservation movement. I learned that lesson early on. I'd just started with TNC when I drew the short straw and was sent to Iowa to speak at the annual meeting of a fledgling chapter we had in Ames. Getting to Ames was a three-flight, all-day ordeal. I arrived at the Holiday Inn just as the meeting was starting. About twenty people were in attendance. After my slideshow highlighting TNC projects from around the country, we all adjourned to the bar.

I was sipping a beer when a middle-aged member came up to meet me. The white embroidery on the pocket of his green work shirt spelled "Don." "Mr. Morine," Don said, "if you need a ride to the airport tomorrow morning, I'll be happy to take you."

I'm always embarrassed when older people call me Mr. Morine. I guess Don felt he owed me that courtesy because I was wearing a coat and tie and he wasn't. "Gee, Don," I said, "that's awful nice of you, but my plane leaves at six in the morning so it'd probably be easier if I just caught a cab."

"Mr. Morine," Don said, "a cab will cost The Nature Conservancy $10, and that's money you should be using to save land. I can't afford to give $10 to the Conservancy, but I sure as heck can get up in the morning and drive you to the airport." That kind of attitude is what makes volunteers the heart and soul of the movement.

On the first day of spring 1970, twenty million Americans peacefully demonstrated for the environment. That was the birth of Earth Day. Senator Gaylord Nelson, the man who started Earth Day, attributed this tremendous outpouring to "the millions of volunteers working for conservation at the grassroots level." Back then conservation was a movement run by volunteers. Now it's a big business run by professionals.

In retrospect, having the cause of conservation directed by professionals rather than volunteers was not a good thing. Professionals are expensive and to meet their expenses, they've turned much of the support generated for the cause into support for the organizations. With some organizations, it's not unusual to have nine of those ten dollars Don saved by driving me to the airport going to overhead. Now we have to get those dollars flowing back into saving land and the best way to do that is for volunteers to take back the cause.

With roughly 78 million baby boomers heading into retirement, there is no shortage of qualified people looking for things to do. Historically, there have been two levels where volunteers played a major role in land conservation. At the top they were board members who gave their work, wisdom, and wealth. At the bottom they were stewards who helped manage preserves. Today, it's time for volunteers to start filling in the middle level, which is the management of nonprofit organizations.

At three o'clock on a Tuesday afternoon at any country club in America, there are former chairmen, presidents, chief executive officers, chief financial officers, chief operating officers, and general counsels sitting around the nineteenth hole lamenting the fact that if they hadn't triple-bogeyed the seventeenth, they would have broken a hundred. Who cares? What many of these former high-powered execs are really lamenting is that they don't want to spend the last twenty years of their lives just sitting around taking up space. What they'd like to be doing, and should be doing, is running something, especially something fun like an organization that's all about saving land. These are potential $1-per-year people who've seen it all, done it all, and hopefully have learned from it all. With all this talent available, why are nonprofit conservation organizations paying hundreds of thousands of dollars to professional managers when they could walk into any country club on a Tuesday afternoon, blow the bugle, and announce, "Anyone here who'd like to volunteer to do something meaningful and fun for the next few years?"

That's not saying the whole table's going to jump up, but then again you don't need a whole table. All you need is one Mrs. Yarn or Bob Lemire who believes in the cause and can also lead, do the books, handle the legal work, or help with communications, and you've just cut a bunch of overhead. Don't get me wrong, volunteers can be tough to manage. They're often opinionated, like doing things their own way, and can quit at the drop of a dime. However, you can't beat the price, and every now and then it's good to have someone who's not afraid to stir things up. Just be sure that all volunteers know that when you're working for a nonprofit, you check your ego at the door. Other than feeling good and having fun, there are no perks that come with these jobs. The first thing the president of any well-run nonprofit does in the morning is make the coffee. Remember: "The reason the eagle can fly so high is because it takes itself so lightly."

I Give Joy to Women

IN THE SUMMER OF 1980, PAT NOONAN ANNOUNCED THAT HE WAS GOING to step down as president of The Nature Conservancy. His resignation caught most people, including me, by surprise. Pat said he had done what he wanted to do as president, and he felt it was time for him to move on to a new challenge. Nobody could argue with that. During his six years at the helm, the Conservancy had become a major force in land conservation, forged a unique relationship with the corporate community, completed its first capital campaign by raising $23 million, which exceeded all goals, and thanks to Pat's charisma, had drawn exceptionally qualified people into the organization.

"So, what are you going to do?" I asked him.

"I've found a big foundation that wants to become active in conservation," he told me. "The trustees aren't your typical conservationists. They're hard-nosed businessmen. Their interest in the out-of-doors comes from hunting and fishing. They want to save land, but they don't want to deal with a bunch of fuzzy-faced idealists and aren't comfortable with most of the people in the conservation movement."

Pat had mentioned these trustees to me before when they'd made what for them was a modest grant of $250,000 to the capital campaign. For these guys, conservation was just another business. As they saw it, if conservationists wanted to see an area protected, they shouldn't throw themselves in front of bulldozers and haul developers into court. They should compete in the open market with the timber companies, oil companies, mining companies, and developers. They should step up, put their money on the line, and buy it. "Not-for-profits don't pay taxes!" the trustees were quick to point out. "What more of an advantage do they want?"

"I think these guys are ready to make a real commitment to conservation," Pat said. "They like the way we've courted industry. They like our style. They've indicated that they want to see a major proposal from the Conservancy."

"Then, Pat," I asked, "if these guys are coming onboard, why are you resigning?"

"Simple," he told me. "To get them involved, we're going to have to concentrate on a few major projects. I can't work on projects if I'm running the organization." As usual, Pat was right on the money. "What we need now is a major project, so think big. If you could do any project, what would it be?"

"Easy," I said. "Bottomland hardwoods. They're almost all gone, but if we start right now, we might be able to save some of what's left."

"Great. Write it up," Pat concluded.

I sharpened my pencil and went to work. My proposal focused on five relatively undisturbed rivers that flowed into the Gulf of Mexico: the Pearl, the Mobile/Tensaw, the Choctawhatchee, the Apalachicola, and the Suwannee. These five rivers, along with the Pascagoula, were the lifeblood for the eastern half of the Gulf. My introduction waxed eloquently on how, in 1803, when Jefferson made the Louisiana Purchase, there were fifty million acres of bottomland hardwoods covering the Southeast; how by 1980 this system had been reduced to a mere 3.5 million acres; how these remaining forests were being cleared and planted for soybeans at the rate of 300,000 acres a year; how bottomland hardwoods played a vital role in controlling floods and reducing water pollution; how over a million sportsmen hunted and fished along these rivers; how rare and endangered species like the sawback turtle, the Florida panther, the swallow-tailed kite, and maybe even an ivory-billed woodpecker were hiding out, fugitives from development, in these bottomland hardwoods. Given the fact that I knew next to nothing about timbering, farming, hunting, fishing, and biology, I thought it sounded pretty good.

What I proposed was a million dollars of seed money for each river. With a $5 million grant, I figured we could convince the Fish and Wildlife Service to create five new wildlife refuges along these rivers. If we could save 150,000 acres of bottomland hardwoods, it would be by far the biggest land conservation program the Conservancy had ever undertaken.

Pat quickly scanned my proposal. "Hmm. Five rivers. Five new refuges. Seed money. Acreage. It's a start." He looked up. "Not bad. Scrap all this nature stuff in the introduction and throw in a couple of pictures of ducks. These guys know all they want to know about nature. What they want to see are pro formas. Show 'em how their money's going to work. There're only two questions they're going to ask: Where's the leverage, where's the rollover."

I resharpened my pencil and put together five pro formas, one for each river. Leverage and rollover flowed through my figures. We'd take a grant of $5 million over five years and use it as down payments on lands worth $15 million. That would be the leverage: three to one. Then we'd sell these lands to the Fish and Wildlife Service at our cost, recapture our $5 million, and roll it over into more down payments on another $15 million worth of land. Using this method, I projected that we'd save $30 million worth of land. At an average cost of $200 an acre, we could protect 150,000 acres over ten years. It would be a good deal for the foundation because we would be leveraging their grant six to one. It would be a good deal for the Fish and Wildlife Service because we'd be helping them set up five new refuges. It would be a good deal for the Conservancy because we'd be protecting bottomland hardwoods, an endangered system. Not bad, I thought. I was thinking big.

"Not big enough," said Pat. He took his pen and started scribbling. He kept mumbling figures to himself. "Fifteen million dollars. Roll their money twice, sounds good," Mumble. Mumble. "Three million dollars a year for five years. Times six to one. Ninety million. That's it," he pronounced happily. "You do good work."

"Pat," I asked, studying the chicken tracks all over my proposal. "What did I say?"

"Simple. Instead of asking for a grant of five million dollars over five years, you're going to ask for fifteen million dollars over five years. That means . . .," Pat did another quick calculation. "We'll be saving 450,000 acres of bottomland hardwoods. That should be big enough."

"Big enough! That's impossible! Where are we ever going to find that much land and that much money?"

Pat was unfazed. "To the swift belongs the race."

On November 4, 1980, the foundation's trustees approved a grant of $15 million to the Conservancy's new Rivers of the Deep South program. It was the largest single grant ever made in the history of conservation. A check for $3 million was attached to the letter approving our proposal. On November 6, 1980, Ronald Wilson Reagan was elected the fortieth president of these United States. In January 1981 he appointed James G. Watt as the forty-third secretary of the interior. Secretary Watt soon made it clear that he had no interest in protecting any more of the interior. In fact, he was a strong backer of the Sagebrush Rebellion, which would have turned millions of acres over to his fat-cat political cronies. Watt was adamant that the Department of the Interior would be buying no more land. So much for our five new Fish and Wildlife Refuges. I parked our recently attained $3 million in high-interest CDs and waited to see what was going to happen.

Things got worse. By February Watt had not only refused to consider buying any more land, he had welshed on all of the prior commitments that had been made to TNC by his predecessor, Pat's good friend Cecil Andrus. We were left holding $20 million worth of natural areas that we had pre-acquired. By reneging on these promises, Watt had single-handedly wiped out the strong base Pat had built for the Conservancy with the capital campaign.

The final blow came in March when Watt abolished the Bureau of Outdoor Recreation, the federal agency that helped states purchase land with 50 percent matching federal funds. According to my pro formas, Florida, Alabama, and Mississippi were going to use some of these matching funds to buy bottomland hardwoods along the rivers. It now became painfully obvious that there wouldn't be federal funds of any kind flowing into the rivers of the Deep South.

"Now what?" I asked. By this time Pat was serving as a consultant to the Conservancy and an adviser to the foundation. This was a unique relationship, especially suited to Pat. Both the Conservancy and the foundation trusted his judgment, respected his ability to get things done, and knew that they would be done right.

"You'd better come up with something," he told me. "The foundation's general counsel wants to make a trip south in April to see what's happening with their $3 million. He's only going to ask two questions."

"I know," I replied glumly. "Where's the leverage? Where's the rollover?"

This was not good news. Mason Walsh, the general counsel, was the trustee who'd promoted the foundation's relationship with the Conservancy. As such, he felt personally responsible for making sure that we got the biggest bang for the foundation's buck. On the surface Mason was a very pleasant man: calm, affable, and consistently polite. Underneath, this Harvard-trained lawyer was as hard as steel and one of the most focused individuals I'd ever met. Once he decided to do something, it got done. There was no excuse for failure. If our proposal said that we were going to save 450,000 acres over ten years, we were going to save 450,000 acres. The fact that the Feds had dropped out was irrelevant. The foundation had delivered their $3 million six months ago, so where was the first project?

I didn't have it. I had found some land, a 17,000-acre tract along the Pearl River in Mississippi that St. Regis was willing to sell for $3 million. The property had been appraised for $4.5 million, but St. Regis had agreed to take the difference as a charitable donation. That was when Watt screwed us. Without the Feds' money, there was no leverage and no rollover. My last hope was to convince the state of Mississippi to buy this tract as a state wildlife management area.

I called Charlie Deaton. Charlie had been chairman of the House Appropriations Committee for Mississippi and a member of the Wildlife Heritage Committee when we'd preserved the Pascagoula. Now he was the special counsel to the governor of Mississippi and a member of the Conservancy's national board.

"Charlie," I said, "we've got a problem." I could hear him chewing on his big cigar as I explained the situation. "St. Regis is willing to donate a million and a half. Do you think you can get the legislature to appropriate three million dollars? We'll use the foundation's grant to provide the interim financing at no cost to the state."

There was a long pause. "Now let me tell ya, it don't look good," he drawled. "Reagan's cut back on a lot moah than just land. He's hit education, health, you name it. Moah land's the last thang people down heah are thinkin' about."

"Charlie," I pleaded, "according to Pat, this foundation can carry land conservation through the eighties. But they're going to drop us like a rock if we can't perform. We've got to come up with a project."

More chewing noises accompanied another long pause. Charlie used his cigar the way a professor uses a pipe. Chewing on it gave him time to think. "Y'all come on down," he finally said. "We'll get the govnuh to meet with Mason and see what we can do."

This was good news. Charlie, in his own way, was as focused as Mason. He wasn't going to wheel out the "govnuh" unless he thought the state was interested in acquiring the land, and I was sure he liked the idea of introducing the governor to a trustee of one of the largest foundations in America. It would be a real coup for Mississippi to take the lead in the Rivers of the Deep South program.

"We'll have the governor sell Mason on Mississippi," I told Pat, "and Mason sell the governor on conservation. If they hit it off, we're golden. If not, we're dead."

Pat twiddled his fingers. "Hmm." He obviously didn't like the odds. "It's too bad they don't know each other. If only we could think of some way to break the ice."

"They're both lawyers. They're both about the same age. They both like hunting. I'll put them both in the same boat when we tour the property. What more can we do?"

"Hmm." Pat was still thinking. "That might be enough."

Our plan was for Pat, Mason, and me to meet Charlie, the governor, and the rest of the governor's entourage at a little airport in Bogalusa, Louisiana, the only town with a landing strip on the Pearl River. From there, Mississippi Game and Fish officers would drive us to the river, where we'd link up with the St. Regis people for the tour.

Despite all that they did for the public, the trustees were very private people. They preferred to stay out of the limelight and direct publicity toward the organizations they supported. They tended to be very reserved with people they didn't know, and it was tough to break the ice. Mason was even more reserved than usual as we waited for the governor's plane to arrive. I thought he liked the deal we had structured with St. Regis but was skeptical about the state of Mississippi coughing up $3 million for conservation. He knew that the state had appropriated $15 million for the Pascagoula project, but that had been before Reagan's cutbacks. Meeting the governor in Bogalusa, Louisiana, didn't help. As we watched the governor's plane circle the airport, Mason noted, "You know that Bogalusa is the home of the Ku Klux Klan."

Mason sounded cold. Pat raised his eyebrows. So far, we'd broken no ice.

Charlie Deaton was the first out of the plane. His swept-back silver hair blew in the breeze from the props as he stopped, squinted into the sun, put on his mirrored sunglasses, and lit up his ubiquitous big cigar. He filled the bill of a Southern politician. The line of reporters that trailed after him was a sure sign that Charlie was using the tour to help sell the project.

Then came the governor. He didn't look like a Southern politician. He had short, dark hair, tortoise-shell glasses, and didn't smoke. He looked a lot like Mason. Maybe there was hope.

The press flocked around Mason. Having a representative of a major northeastern foundation come to invest money in Mississippi was news. I was sure that Mason would direct all questions to Pat and me, but Pat had slipped away. He had seized this moment to collar the governor. "Governor," he asked, "do you have a gift for Mason?"

The governor didn't know what to make of this question. He was used to getting gifts, not giving them. "Why, er, of course we have something, don't we, Charlie?"

Charlie fiddled with his cigar. "Govanuh, we'll get him an ashtray from the plane. It's got the state seal on it."

"That would be nice," Pat said, handing the governor a small gift-wrapped package, "but here, give him this, and really build him up, the guy's got a big ego." What was Pat up to? Nothing could have been further from the truth. Mason was modest almost to the point of seeming shy.

The governor took the package and turned it over, looking for a clue. Before he could say anything, Mason walked up to meet him. "Welcome to the great state of Mississippi," the governor proclaimed, pumping Mason's hand. "Today is a historic day for Mississippi." The press gathered around, cameras clicking. "Today, private enterprise is extending a hand to help government. Today, a great foundation from Pennsylvania has come to join Mississippi in a program for conservation."

As instructed, the governor was spreading it on pretty thick. I glanced at Pat. He was all smiles.

"We are pleased," the governor continued, "that The Nature Conservancy and the St. Regis Paper Company have been able to work out a deal that will give Mississippi an opportunity to purchase a much-needed game and fish area on the Pearl River. We are honored that a representative of this great foundation has come to our state to see this property firsthand. We hope you will encourage the Conservancy to invest the first $3 million of your grant"—here the governor paused for effect—"the largest private grant in the history of conservation, to help protect one of the finest natural areas left in all of Mississippi, if not the entire United States."

The reporters crowded in closer. The governor was doing great. Charlie had given him an excellent briefing. "And now," he concluded, "as a token of our appreciation, we would like to give you this gift for all you have done for conservation. We hope that each time you look at this little memento, you'll remember this day and your visit to the great state of Mississippi."

We all applauded dutifully as the governor handed Pat's package to Mason. Mason graciously accepted the gift, but the governor's remarks obviously had not cracked his veneer. Then he opened the package. Out came a leather belt with a brass buckle as big as a fist, like something only a real redneck would wear. The governor was visibly taken aback. Charlie Deaton nearly swallowed his cigar. The reporters pressed in for a closer look. There was a collective gasp. Engraved on the buckle were the words "I Give Joy to Women." All heads swiveled toward the governor. The governor's head swiveled toward Pat.

"Obviously, you two must have met," Pat said impishly. Mason began to laugh. The governor began to laugh. Everybody began to laugh. The ice was broken.

We did the deal with St. Regis. The governor and Charlie got the $3 million from the legislature. We rolled over the foundation's first installment into our next project. The Rivers of the Deep South program was becoming a reality.

As hoped, the foundation did carry conservation through the eighties. During that time the trustees gave away over $100 million to thirty-two conservation organizations. Most of it, $55 million, went to Conservancy projects. Through managing that money, I've gotten to know Mason. He remains calm, affable, and consistently polite on the surface, but still has a core of steel. After our trip to Mississippi, that no longer worries me. When things get too tight, I know how to loosen him up. I just suggest he unbuckle "I Give Joy to Women" a notch.

The Ivory-Billed Woodpecker

IMPISH WAS A GOOD WORD TO DESCRIBE PAT, ESPECIALLY AFTER HE'D HAD a few drinks, and following every board meeting, we all had a few drinks. In the early 1970s board meetings at the Conservancy were extremely intense. We had no endowment and no reserves. Just about every dollar we had was put into saving land. We were always right on the edge. After every meeting it seemed like one bad deal could put us under. The reception held after meetings gave the staff and the board a chance to sit back and relax for a moment.

In 1972 Mrs. David Rockefeller joined the Conservancy's national board. Having Mrs. Rockefeller on the board immediately gave what was then a small and relatively unknown conservation organization instant credibility. Landowners who didn't know the Conservancy's name sure knew Mrs. David Rockefeller's. They also knew that the Rockefellers would never lend their name to some fly-by-night organization. But Mrs.

Rockefeller brought a lot more to TNC than just her name. She was a good board member who was easy to work with. There was nothing pretentious about her, and behind a pair of simple, schoolmarm glasses, there was a twinkle in her eye that suggested while it was nice being a Rockefeller, she was definitely her own person.

At one of Mrs. Rockefeller's early meetings, I made a pitch for the Pascagoula project. In it I mentioned that if there was an ivory-billed woodpecker left in North America, it could very well be hidden in this spectacular bottomland hardwood forest. Later that evening at the reception, Mrs. Rockefeller, who proved to be a competent naturalist, asked me if I really thought there might be an ivory-billed somewhere in the Pascagoula. Before I could answer, Pat said, "That's an excellent question, Mrs. Rockefeller." Then, turning to me with a twinkle in his Irish eyes, added, "Dave, tell Mrs. Rockefeller your story about rediscovering the ivory-billed woodpecker."

I knew where Pat was going with this. He often had me tell a joke as a way of loosening things up. As luck would have it, Mrs. Rockefeller's question was the perfect lead-in to one of my better stories. Without thinking twice about it, which was a huge mistake, I put down my drink and dove in. "Obviously," I said, "rediscovering the ivory-billed woodpecker caused much excitement within the conservation community, but what is little known is that it was also cause for great rejoicing within the forest community. You see, historically, the ivory-billed woodpecker had been the grand arbitrator of all forest disputes. Since its disappearance, there had been nobody to settle the everyday problems that arise in all biotic communities: Who gets what territory, who has the rights to which roost, who's on top in the sunny spots, who's stuck at the bottom? Without someone to arbitrate these disputes, there was much disharmony within the forest.

"Well, no sooner had the ivory-billed woodpecker been reinstalled in his judicial role when a gentle breeze rippled through the woods. When it came to the beech tree, the beech fluttered its leaves and announced in a proud voice, 'Members of the forest community, it gives me great pleasure to introduce my heir, for I have sired this young sapling you see before you. I trust you'll share my pride watching it grow into a mighty beech.'

"All the forest seemed genuinely pleased for the beech tree, but when the breeze reached a birch tree, which happened to be exactly equidistant from the little sapling, the birch fluttered its leaves and said, 'I'm sorry to disagree with my old friend the beech, but it is I who has sired this young sapling, and hope you'll share my pride in watching it grow into a mighty birch.'

"Oh boy, this was very bad," I continued. "Sides immediately began to form within the forest as to whether the sapling was a beech or a birch, but before things could get out of hand, the owl, in its infinite wisdom, told everyone to settle down, that this was a job for the ivory-billed woodpecker.

"Bringing in the ivory-billed woodpecker to settle the dispute was, of course, the right thing to do, but there was some concern within the forest community. After all, it had been twenty-eight years since the ivory-billed made its last decision. What if it was no longer up to the job?

"There was hushed anticipation as the ivory-billed came swooping through the trees. First, it landed on the beech, studied its leaves, tested its branches, and checked its bark. Then it flew over the little sapling to the birch, where it performed the same examination. With its red and black crest, trademark ivory bill, and large white-tipped wings, there was no question the ivory-billed looked good, but what about its mind? Did it still have it?

"When the ivory-billed had finished with the birch, it carefully paced off the distance between the sapling and eac of the trees. Finding them exactly equidistant, it then undertook a detailed study of the sapling's leaves, branches, and bark. Finally, much to everyone's surprise, the ivory-billed slid down the trunk of the little sapling and with a ferocious *ratta-tat-tat* pecked a huge hole in it."

At this point I paused. A number of board members and staff had gathered around. Pat was wearing his impish grin and tapping his fingertips together, a habit he exhibited when he was excited. It was time for the punch line. I assumed the stance of the ivory-billed woodpecker so as to better mimic his movement of removing a tasty sliver from his bill, then said judiciously, "'Members of the forest community, I have reached my decision. This young sapling is neither a son of a beech nor a son of a birch, but I've got to tell you, it's the nicest piece of ash I've ever stuck my pecker into.'"

There was a *clunk* as a very conservative CEO from Cincinnati dropped his drink. Other than that, there wasn't a sound. I stood there dumbfounded. I'd been so engrossed in the telling of the story, I hadn't thought through the real meaning of the punch line. I'd forgotten it was completely off color. Now, having just delivered it to Mrs. Rockefeller, it seemed positively pornographic.

Everyone was staring at Mrs. Rockefeller wondering how she'd react. She paused for a moment, then broke into a surprised smile. "Oh, I see," she said. "It's a play on words. Quite clever."

Quite clever, indeed. After the initial pause, everybody started laughing, but we were lucky. In loosening things up we'd stepped over the line. Fortunately, we'd been saved by a grand lady. The lesson I learned that day was know where you are at all times and act accordingly. Forty years later I still break into a sweat whenever I hear mention of the ivory-billed woodpecker.

The *87th Day*

MASON WALSH HAD SUCH A GOOD TIME IN MISSISSIPPI HE WANTED ALL of the trustees to go down with him to see a project. "I don't believe it," I said to Pat when he gave me the news. "How many rabbits do these guys think we have in our hat? We were lucky to pull out the Pearl River deal. I don't have an encore."

"You'd better find one," Pat said. "The trustees want to see something this fall, just before they make their next distribution."

Distribution. He had said the magic word. If getting a grant from the foundation was difficult, performing on it was next to impossible. The trustees never just wrote a check for the full amount and said "best of luck." They stretched their grants out over time and liked to make their distributions in December. That way, they could hold your feet to the fire while they collected more interest on their money. "Leverage and rollover, leverage and rollover," that's all I ever heard from them, but now that Secretary of the Interior James Watt had garroted the federal land acquisition budget, I had to find new sources of funding.

If there were another rabbit anywhere in my hat, it had to be Florida. The state had just launched its Save Our Rivers program. The program was funded by an innovative transfer tax that the state levied on real estate. Five cents was added to the state's documentary stamp tax so that the Save Our Rivers program got a nickel each time a hundred dollars' worth of real estate was sold. Five cents didn't sound like much, but an awful lot of property was sold in Florida. Income to the Save Our Rivers program over the first five years was projected to exceed $100 million. That money was divided among five newly created water management districts.

In 1981 the Suwannee River watershed comprised the most rural section of Florida. Rising in southeast Georgia's Okefenokee Swamp, the Suwannee curls into Florida halfway between Jacksonville and Tallahassee. From there, it winds its way 263 miles south through north-central Florida before flowing into the Gulf of Mexico at the little town of Cedar Key. The river was mostly undeveloped, and much of the land around it was owned by large timber companies like St. Regis, Continental Can, Buckeye, and Owens Illinois. Thanks to Dick Ludington, TNC's Florida rep, we had good relations with all of these companies, many of whom were anxious to sell their slow-growing bottomland hardwoods and reinvest the proceeds into super trees: plantation pines, which could be harvested after twenty years.

With the help of the timber companies, we already had protected both ends of the Suwannee River. The Union Camp Corporation had given us 16,000 acres in the Okefenokee Swamp, and Dick had worked a 50 percent bargain sale with Brunswick Pulp & Paper and Buckeye for another 15,000 acres on the Lower Suwannee National Wildlife Refuge. I was confident that if we could find the funds, we could buy more big blocks of land at bargain sale prices from the timber companies. Our best hope was to tap into the Save Our Rivers program by convincing the water management districts that the best way to manage Florida's rivers was to acquire the land around them, and who better to do that than The Nature Conservancy?

The problem was the Suwannee Water Management District had never heard of The Nature Conservancy, and its idea of water management was rooted in a Corps of Engineers' mentality. Its staff, like the staffs of most water management districts, was made up of engineers who knew more about ditches, dikes, and dams than conservation. For more than 200 years, engineers had been taught that waterways should be straight and clean and that wetlands should be filled and reclaimed. Reeducating them to think that leaving a natural system intact was the best way to control a river was going to be a long, slow process, and I didn't have the luxury of time. I needed a project now.

The Suwannee District was the most contentious, parochial group that I had ever encountered. The board was a strange mixture of academics, timbermen, businessmen, farmers, and one school bus driver. They were a throwback to an earlier era, like a pack of gators. Everybody knew everybody, but nobody seemed to agree with anybody. Board meetings often turned into genealogical debates over who said what to whom four generations ago. Outsiders were fresh meat when thrown in front of the board. As Don Morgan, the executive director, told me after I'd been chewed over, "We treat all our guests the same: crummy."

The Suwannee's board was skeptical of me and leery of my intentions. Who was this Yankee with a Boston accent telling them how to buy land? What is this Natural Conservatory? Where do they get their money? How do we know they aren't some Mafia front? And who is this big foundation that wants to save the Suwannee? Even some Yankee foundation's not dumb enough to be putting hard money into swamplands. Nobody'd fallen for that scam in years.

The board would not agree to do anything until they knew us, and at their pace, that could take decades. I decided to use the old Mississippi trick. I'd have the Mellon trustees sell the board of the water management district, and the board of the district sell the trustees. It'd worked before; maybe it would work again. And what choice did I have? I had to do something.

I arranged a trip along the lower Suwannee. One of the timber companies owned a nice bottomland hardwood tract just north of the Suwannee National Wildlife Refuge. The company was willing to sell the land to the Conservancy for 70 percent of its fair market value. It would be a perfect kickoff project for the district.

I borrowed a plane from a friendly bank in Mobile. It was large enough so we could pick up the four trustees in Atlanta, yet small enough so that we could land right at Cedar Key. I rented a boat at Cedar Key that would take us twenty miles up the river to the tract. There we would meet the board of the district for a barbecue. We would spend the afternoon eating, drinking, touring the property, and getting to know one another. Afterwards the trustees, Pat, and I would get back in the boat and cruise back down to Cedar Key, where I had reserved rooms at a neat old inn. We'd have a nice dinner, discuss leverage and rollover, and be on our way bright and early the next morning. Heck, if he was still with us, I would have had Stephen Foster come in and sing a few verses of "Way Down Upon the Suwannee River" for us. Yes, I was that desperate.

Everything looked good, except for the boat. Cedar Key was not Palm Beach. There were very few charters, and I couldn't dump the trustees into some old tub. I needed something nice. The best I could find was a 24-footer called the *87th Day*. The boat was OK. The captain wasn't.

He was a big blowhard, probably pushing sixty. He wore a thick gold chain with a gold medallion that looked suspiciously phallic. He had a Playboy bunny tattooed on his right forearm and a T-shirt that proclaimed, "Love Me or Leave Me." He'd just brought the *87th Day* up from Key West. "Key West has gone to hell," he told me. "Ya can't tell the girls from the guys anymore, not that it matters. Most of them guys bat left-handed, if you get my drift." The word around Cedar Key was that the captain was mixed up running dope. That didn't bother me. The locals suspected that every outsider who showed up in Cedar Key was running dope, including me. What did bother me was the way the captain ran his mouth. He was bound to aggravate the trustees. They didn't like blow-hards. But what choice did I have?

The bank's plane landed at Cedar Key right on time. The weather was perfect. It was a two-minute walk to the *87th Day*. The big diesels were purring as we came onboard. The captain was slouched over the wheel fiddling with the controls. He stood up when we came into the cabin. "You boys are right on time," he said, slapping Mason on the back. "I thought you might stop for a little piece in Atlanta. Haw. Haw." I could see the trustees stiffen as they studied his tattoo and gold chain. We were not off to a good start.

I ushered them to the stern, as far from the captain as possible, as we chugged out of the harbor. The president, the treasurer, the secretary, and Mason, the general counsel, seemed content to sit in their deck chairs, absorbing the scenery and the warm Florida sun. A great blue heron, the standard bearer for conservation in Florida, broke from a tree, swooped across the bow, and flapped upriver ahead of us, squawking our arrival. The president delighted in the water snakes basking in the branches along the bank. The treasurer chortled as a row of turtles looked up, hesitated, then plopped off a log one by one into the water. The secretary pointed excitedly as a family of mallards burst from the marsh. Mason trained his Leica camera on a half-submerged log, sure he'd spotted a gator.

The *87th Day* wasn't as fast as the captain had promised, and the novelty of the river started to wear off after about ten miles. It was getting hot and the trustees were getting bored. Pat began to look edgy. "Would anybody care for a drink?" I said. We all moved into the galley.

The galley of the *87th Day* was a monument to Ernest Hemingway. A picture, in color, of the Sacred Heart of Jesus hung over one bunk. The Virgin of Cobre blessed the other. A copy of *The Old Man and the Sea* lay on the table. A faded photograph of Papa himself was mounted over the door to the head. The picture was signed, but the writing was illegible. "What's that inscription on Hemingway's picture?" the treasurer asked the captain when we moved back on deck.

That was a mistake. Asking the captain a question was like lighting a fire under a hot-air balloon. He puffed himself up and said, "Oh, me'n Papa, we was fishin buddies. I was the guy who got'm his first marlin." I glanced at the president. His eyebrows were raised. The president's father had founded the foundation. The president had been trained since childhood to smell out bullshit. He had just picked up a scent. "So you fished with Hemingway?" he asked.

"Oh yeah," the captain bragged. "Me'n Papa go back a long ways. He wrote that *Old Man and the Sea* right after I got'm his marlin." If the captain had just shut up then, the president might have ignored him. But he didn't. He puffed up even more. "He got all that stuff about fightin the fish from me. I practically wrote that book for'm."

"So the fish in *The Old Man and the Sea* is a blue marlin?" the president asked.

"Sure, had t'be. I got Papa that fish back in '50, brought it right into Havana. Santiago, the old man, he was our deckhand. We was drunk for a week after we landed that one."

"You and Hemingway used to drink together?"

"All'a time," the captain said. "He knew I was the best fisherman in the Keys. He wouldn't go out with no one but me. We fished together, we drank together, even had a few women together."

This notion was so absurd it left the president speechless. He turned away and walked to the stern. My worst fears were coming true. I wanted to tell the captain to shut the hell up, but what do you say to some idiot who's just claimed to be Ernest Hemingway's fishing, drinking, and screwing buddy?

We rounded a bend in the river, and there was the dock. A haze of smoke from the barbecue pit hung over a modest little hunt camp. The Board of the Suwannee Water Management District came down to the dock to greet us.

The barbecue couldn't have gone better. The trustees probed the board, and the board probed the trustees. By the end of the afternoon, they both liked what they saw. They agreed to go ahead with the deal. The Conservancy would buy the land from the timber company for 70 percent of its fair market value. We would finance the purchase with funds from the foundation's next distribution. Then we'd resell the land at our cost to the district when it had accumulated enough Save Our Rivers money. By purchasing this tract and leaving it in its natural state, the district would be committing itself to a policy of water management through natural area protection.

I was euphoric. I practically skipped back onto the *87th Day*. A few drinks, a nice dinner, a good night's sleep, and we were home free.

The trustees, Pat, and I spent the return trip rehashing our meeting with the district's board and going over the details of the purchase from the timber company. The trustees liked the leverage and liked the rollover, and thanks to the Suwannee's current, the trip downstream went much faster. We were back at Cedar Key ahead of time. As the captain pulled up to the dock, I briefed the trustees on the rest of our schedule. I had everything planned to the minute.

Then it happened. As he tied up to the dock and we prepared to get out of the boat, the captain started to pop off. "Too bad you boys are in such a hurry. Ya'll oughta slow down a bit. That's the trouble with you Yankees. Ya don't know how to enjoy y'selves. Y'always thinkin bout some schedule when y'oughta be thinkin about catchin fish and chasin women. Now, if ya'll stuck with me, ya'd have plenty of both."

I looked at the president. He was giving the captain a long, hard look. This was not good.

"You big-time Yankees are so tight-assed, ya don't leave no time for fun," the captain continued. "What's the sense comin to the Gulf if ya don't know how to fish?"

Little did the captain know that he had just delivered the ultimate insult. Not only had the president been trained to smell out bullshit, he had been groomed to be one of the finest sportsmen in the world. The president sighed, like a professional gunfighter who had just been called out by some dumb sodbuster. He straightened up. "There ought to be some pretty good flats at the end of this river," the president said.

I prayed that the captain had enough sense to go for his gun, but like all blowhards, he kept talking. "You can bet your ass on that. Best in the world. This river spreads out into a bed a grass."

"Should be good for specks and redfish," the president said.

"Catch 'em alla time," the captain boasted, shutting down the engines.

"Let's catch one now!" the president commanded.

"Ah, gee," I interrupted desperately. "It's time for cocktails. Remember the schedule. Don't you think we should settle in and get ready for dinner?"

"Nonsense," the president stated. "It will only take a few minutes. I don't want to fill the bait box. I just want to catch one fish. That shouldn't take too long, should it, Captain?"

"Well, I dunno," the captain hedged, obviously surprised at this turn of events. "It's kinda late and the tide's runnin out. Them fish don't bite good when the tide's goin out."

"Surely Papa's old fishing buddy could find us just one fish," the president taunted.

I slumped onto the bait box next to Pat as we chugged out of the harbor. We were so close to making it. Now, I had no idea what was going to happen. Everyone threw in a line, but no one was getting so much as a nibble. The captain had a tackle box full of excuses. "They feed at night on a full moon." "That cold spell we had last week must have sent 'em South." "They don't bite when the tide's goin out." He kept the *87th Day* moving, searching for new grass beds. We were in real shallow water.

Thunk! We hit bottom just as the president got a bite.

"Damn," said the captain.

The president reeled in a little speckled trout. "Well, what do you know," he said, holding up his fish. "OK, Captain, let's head for home."

The captain revved up the *87th Day*'s diesels, but we weren't going anywhere. We were stuck. I looked toward shore. There must have been two miles of water between us and Cedar Key. If only the stupid captain had kept his mouth shut.

"Seems like we're stuck," he groused, easing back on the throttles. "You boys will have to jump over and try to push us free. That tide ain't gonna turn for a while yet, and we can't afford to lose no more water."

"You want us to jump overboard and push this thing home?" I asked.

"No, not all the way home," the captain scoffed. "Just till we find some water. It's either that or spend the night." I looked at Pat. He was already stripping down. We were not going to spend the night out here with the captain.

Pat and I were both wearing our standard oak-leaf green Patagonia shorts. We jumped overboard. The water was just deep enough and cold enough to suit a soprano. We started pushing. The captain revved the diesels. The *87th Day* didn't budge.

Reluctantly, the secretary, treasurer, and general counsel began stripping down. Each was clad in white boxer shorts, undoubtedly Brooks Brothers. They plopped over the side, one by one, like turtles. As the captain revved the engines, mud and pieces of slimy eelgrass chewed up by the props spewed over us. The trustees looked like they had been mud wrestling. This had to be a low point for conservation.

"Push harder," the captain yelled. We did, but the *87th Day* failed to budge.

"More help," we pleaded, wiping mud and grass from our eyes.

"You'd better get in there too," the captain told the president.

"You get in," the president said. "I'll drive."

"You can't drive the *87th Day*," the captain protested.

"The hell I can't," the president said, seizing the throttles.

"What? I can't go overboard. I'm the captain."

"Not any more. Get in there and push while we still have some water," the president ordered. "We're not paying you to spend the night."

When the president told you to do something, you did it. Despite the mud, the grass, the cold, and the ignominy of our situation, we all started to laugh as the captain began to undress. A pair of skimpy red bikini shorts hinged his skinny white thighs to his bloated white belly. I looked enviously at the ample bulge in the front of his shorts. Maybe he wasn't such a blowhard after all. He grumbled to himself and lumbered over the side.

The president expertly began playing the throttles, rocking the *87th Day* back and forth. On his signal we all gave a mighty heave. The *87th Day* broke free. The president quickly found a channel and we scrambled to get back onboard.

The captain couldn't make it. His skinny little arms couldn't hoist his big belly over the side. He clung to the rail thrashing his spaghetti legs. Pat picked up the gaff. "Here, grab this," he said, offering the round end to the captain.

Once the captain had hold of the hook, Pat braced his feet on the gunnel and pulled him in. The captain lay on the deck gasping like a big fish out of water. His little red shorts had slipped down over his bottom; bits of eel grass clung to his hair. It was tough to believe that this was the same guy who claimed to have been chasing women with Papa.

The president had the *87th Day* almost to Cedar Key before the captain caught his breath, went into the galley, changed his pants, and reclaimed the controls. We steamed into the harbor. This time there was no talk about Yankees being too busy to enjoy life. This time the captain couldn't wait to get rid of us.

Pat regaled us at dinner with a recap of the mutiny. As a finale, he produced the captain's red bikini shorts. When the captain was changing, he'd managed to swipe them. He presented them to me. "Dave," he said, "given the success of the Rivers program, you might be man enough to fill these."

"Thank you, Pat," I said, accepting the shorts with exaggerated dignity. They were still wet and covered with mud and grass. I stuck my fist into the pouch, held them up, and offered a toast. "Gentlemen. To the Rivers of the Deep South. May its pockets be filled to overflowing."

I stole a look at the president. He was contemplating the captain's undies. "My," he said. "That sure would be some endowment."

~~~

On the High Wire without a Net

IN THE FALL OF 1976, THE NATIONAL BOARD OF TNC WAS HOLDING ITS quarterly meeting in San Francisco. The principal topic on the agenda was launching a $20 million capital campaign. The reason for the campaign was that the board felt it was time to give TNC some permanence. During the 1970s we were emerging as the number-one private land conservation organization in the world. Not a month went by that TNC wasn't knocking down some new major project: VCR, Wormsloe, Great Dismal Swamp, Santee Coastal Reserve, the Pascagoula, Long Point, Santa Cruz, Ordway Prairie, Silver Creek, Sycan Marsh, Great Wass Island, just to name a few. While $20 million was a lot of money, the board was sure they could raise it. At the meeting Wally Dayton of the Dayton-Hudson department store family pledged a million dollars to kick off the campaign. Other members were quick to follow. The room was charged with energy. Then Alf Heller stood up.

For the board of TNC, Alf was something of an odd duck. His family had made a fortune in San Francisco real estate and was very charitable, especially when it pertained to land-use decisions in California. Alf was a free thinker who didn't hesitate to speak his mind, even if it went against the prevailing tide. In this case he was totally opposed to creating what would amount to an endowment for TNC. "Look," he said, "this organization is running hard and lean. When the staff gets up in the morning, they know they're walking on the high wire without a net. That's what keeps them sharp. If we put a net under them, they'll get too comfortable, they'll lose their edge. Creating an endowment is the worst thing we can do for The Nature Conservancy."

At the time, everyone thought Alf was nuts. In retrospect he was absolutely right. Colleges, hospitals, churches, museums, and other nonprofits with permanent structures need endowments. For organizations without permanent structures, an endowment is nothing but fat. It makes them soft and slows them down. Instead of being out pushing the cause, they're sitting back watching the endowment throw off income. The Red Cross, which may be the most poorly managed major charity in the world, is a perfect example. In the weeks following 9/11, more than a billion dollars came flowing into the Red Cross's coffers. The intended use of this money couldn't have been clearer: distribute it to the families of the victims. While waiting for the list of victims to be finalized, I suspect the powers that be at the Red Cross became mesmerized by the interest building up on the billion dollars. It was easy money and a simple way to help cover the organization's ever-expanding overhead. When time came to write what amounted to humongous checks to the families, the Red Cross couldn't bring themselves to let go. Instead it decided it would pay out some of the money, which was still a lot, and put the rest into a fund it could use to help cover future tragedies. In other words the Red Cross was taking money that was given to the families of the victims of 9/11 and turning it into an endowment. Talk about soft and slow.

Many land conservation organizations have fallen into the same trap. Funds that are meant to save land actually are being used as endowments. If a group's running hard and fast, it doesn't need a net. A good formula for running the finances of a land conservation organization is as follows: membership dues should cover operating costs, special appeals should go to finance individual projects, and bequests should be put into a general fund, or project revolving fund, or land preservation fund, or whatever you want to call it. This fund should be used to seed new projects. In the beginning it will, but over time it will morph into some form of endowment. Organizations can't resist the comfort that comes from being well endowed. However, having big chunks of money sitting in the bank inevitably turns them soft and slow. Better to keep them on the high wire with no net. Alf Heller knew that, but nobody listened.

Mother Nature

DURING THE LATE 1970S MY FRIEND BIL GILBERT, THE WRITER THE *Washington Post* once called "our best full-time environmental journalist," came up with an interesting theory. "Up until the fifties," Bil maintained, "just about everyone was scared to death of Mother Nature. They thought she was something right out of the Old Testament: a mean old bitch who delighted in floods, fires, droughts, and swarms of locusts. Most people wanted nothing to do with her. They wanted to live in nice, safe, urban environments where Mother Nature could be controlled with things like air-conditioning and DDT.

"Today," Bil continued, taking a long drag on the cigarette usually hanging from his lower lip, "the public perception of Mother Nature is completely different. The conservation movement has turned her into some helpless, anorexic waif who is dying right before our eyes. Now people want to embrace her, protect her, and save her for future generations. Most professional environmentalists don't know anything about the real Mother Nature. They've never met the mean old bitch from the Old Testament."

I've met the real Mother Nature. Skipper Tonsmeire introduced me to the "mean old bitch." It was the one and only time I've ever been completely alone in the wilderness, and I have no desire to do it again.

Skipper's a character, in the best sense of the word. His business, Tonsmeire Construction, builds, owns, and manages apartment complexes, office buildings, and shopping malls primarily in and around Mobile, Alabama. Besides running his business, Skipper has many hobbies: astronomy, flying, scuba diving, skiing (water and snow), shrimping, fishing (specifically for ling), photography, jogging at least five miles a day, and flirting with Mother Nature. Fortunately for the people of south Alabama, Skipper's main hobby is conservation. He probably spends more time doing that than he does running his own business.

I first met Skipper in 1976 when he called TNC looking for help to save the last major undeveloped tract of land along Alabama's Gulf Coast. Right from the beginning I realized I was dealing with a wonderfully odd duck. Despite all his real estate holdings, Skipper chose to live by himself in a little fish camp on a creek back in the woods. People who knew him, and that included just about everyone in Fairhope, Alabama, considered him something of a recluse. They called him "The Phantom" because they never knew when and where he was going to show up. When he did, they were glad to see him, which was not surprising. Working behind the scenes, Skipper was always creating bike trails, walking trails, organizing the Boys and Girls Clubs, sponsoring Little League teams, saving old trees, rehabbing historic buildings, and doing other things that make Fairhope such a nice place to live.

Skipper's never been comfortable with me as a conservationist. It bothers him that I'm content to spend my time sitting in an office doing deals rather than trudging through the wilds. He thinks I'm too wedded to hot showers and soft beds. When I visit him he tries to toughen me up by making me sleep on a hard little bunk at his fish camp, then go swimming in the creek before breakfast. The temperature makes no difference. For Skipper, the colder the better. As I stand on his dock shivering, he tells me, "Boy, get your Yankee ass in there. It'll get your blood moving, not to mention your spirit."

Skipper loves to run rivers. Every fall he and his four younger brothers organize a float. Inevitably, a couple of brothers can't make it and that's when friends get invited. My invitation came in 1980. The river was the Tatshenshini, one of the most remote in North America. The Tatshenshini starts up in the Yukon, runs southwest through British Columbia, and merges with the Alsek, which eventually empties into southeast Alaska's Dry Bay. I had no desire to visit any of these places. I politely told Skipper that while I was honored to be asked, I was too busy and he should find somebody else. Skipper would hear none of it. I was going to float the Tatshenshini. I was going to experience the wilderness. I was going to spend some quality time with Mother Nature. What he didn't tell me was this Mother Nature was not the young, helpless, anorexic waif the conservation movement had created, but the mean old bitch Bil Gilbert so much admired.

Besides me, the group that met in Juneau on September 10 consisted of Skipper, his brother Pepper, Skipper's friend Pat Ogburn from Mobile, and a Canadian named Loch McSomething. I never did catch Loch's last name, not that it mattered. Where we were going, I'd have no occasion to introduce him to anyone. I did learn that he ran a dive boat in the Grand Caymans. That was how Skipper knew him. Skipper likes to explore some legendary underwater ledge off Grand Cayman Island.

After an all-night ferry ride to Haines and a three-hour drive over a single-lane dirt road into the Yukon Territory, we stopped on a desolate, featureless, windswept plain in the middle of nowhere. I didn't see any river. I didn't see anything. I figured our driver needed to take a pee. "How much further do we have to go?" I asked.

"We're here," said Pepper. "Start unloading."

Here was Dalton Post, a long-abandoned hunting station at the confluence of the Klukshu and Tatshenshini Rivers. I was disappointed. I'd expected Dalton Post to be some quaint frontier town with a general store, wooden sidewalks, and a log saloon, the kind that Sergeant Preston used to frequent for a sarsaparilla. Right then, I was hoping for something a little stronger than a sarsaparilla. I grabbed my duffel and walked down the bank. Then I saw a glacial stream. Even with help from the Klukshu, the Tatshenshini didn't look like much of a river. I couldn't fathom why it would be of much interest to anyone as experienced as the Tonsmeire brothers. "This is it?" I asked.

"Don't worry," Pepper assured me, "the Tat'll give you a thrill before it's over."

After unloading we inflated two rubber rafts, a big one that held four people comfortably and a smaller one that carried most of the gear and could be rowed by one person. We pushed off. The Tonsmeire boys felt obligated to split up. That way, one could look after the guests while the other took care of the equipment. Skipper manned the little raft; Pepper took Pat, Loch, and me in the bigger one.

Over the next few days, the Tatshenshini picked up strength. She left the plain and wound her way through the rugged St. Elias range. We passed Mount Fairweather, the highest peak in Canada. On the fourth day we came out of the mountains into a broad valley. We had been treated to an exceptional morning—clear, hot and sunny. Quaking aspen and yellow birch were shimmering in the sunlight. We all had our shirts off. Skipper even went for a swim before lunch. I put in my toe. It immediately went numb.

The valley was about four miles wide and eight miles long. Pepper, who had floated the Tatshenshini before, mentioned during lunch that we would camp at the bottom of the valley. It would be our last night on the Tatshenshini. When she emerged from the valley, she would be absorbed into the much larger Alsek. It was the Alsek that would take us to Dry Bay, 175 miles northwest of Juneau.

Eight miles didn't seem like much of a run. "How come we're not going all the way to the Alsek?" I asked.

Pepper gave me a knowing look. "You want to be fresh when you leave the Tat. She don't let go easily."

The sun felt good as we cleaned up after lunch. The Tatshenshini looked smooth and serene as she prepared for her meeting with the Alsek. I volunteered to row the little raft for the afternoon. That would give Skipper a chance to be with his brother and friends, and it would give me a chance to get away from Loch. Loch was getting on my nerves. He talked incessantly and, like many Canadians, was openly critical of America. According to Loch, Ford was an idiot, Carter was a little shit peanut farmer, Reagan was a washed-up actor, and America was responsible for all of the world's problems. If that wasn't enough, Loch inevitably lit up a joint after lunch. Sober, Loch was annoying; wrecked, he was intolerable. What I needed was a quiet afternoon by myself, a chance to view the wilderness without having to squint through a blue cloud of marijuana. The little raft would be a welcome escape.

I was still shirtless when we pushed off. Skipper threw me my shirt, vest, and rain gear. "Keep these with you," he said. "They might come in handy." I couldn't see why. Except for the one hanging over Loch, there wasn't a cloud in sight.

We drifted peacefully along for about a mile. I lay back on the oars and soaked up the wilderness. It was very enjoyable. No phones, no pressure, nobody telling me I had to do something. Maybe Skipper was right. Maybe I should spend more time in the wilds. Soon I was pre-occupied with thousands of Canadian geese milling around overhead, waiting for a front that would help carry them south. I marveled at their lack of symmetry. There were no obvious leaders, just total bedlam. This prelude to their fabled V formations looked and sounded more like an Italian traffic jam.

Through the honking, I heard a shout. "Over here! Pull over here!"

I swiveled in my seat. The Tatshenshini was breaking up. The main channel and the big raft were going to the right. I was going to the left. I leaned into the oars with everything I had, but it was too late. Pepper smiled and gave me a little wave good-bye. "See you later," yelled Loch as he sat there puffing away. Within seconds, the big raft floated behind a line of trees. I was alone in the wilderness.

No big deal, I thought. We're probably just going around an island. Pepper knew the river. If there were any problems, he would have told me to pull over. The Tatshenshini had to come back together sooner or later. All I had to do was keep floating.

I reached for my shirt. It was getting cold. The sky suddenly became overcast. A front was coming through. I looked up at the geese. The traffic jams were beginning to unsnarl. Familiar V's started forming as the lead-ers caught the wind. Singles were flying from group to group, attempting to link up with the right flock. I could sympathize with their plight.

A cloud bank descended into the valley. Soon it was raining, lightly at first, then much harder. The temperature plummeted by what must have been thirty degrees. I was thankful to have my vest and rain gear. It soon became evident that we were not going around an island. The Tatshen-shini kept braiding into smaller and smaller strands. I kept bearing to the right, toward the big raft and my only contact with civilization. I should have followed the main current. My channel dwindled to a trickle.

I got out, grabbed the rope, and began to pull the raft over the graveled bottom. It made a terrible grinding noise. I was afraid that I would puncture the skin. What would I do then? I'd left my waders in the big raft. My boots were soaked, my feet cold. My glasses were useless; the rain and my own panting kept them permanently fogged. I had to take them off to see anything, and everything I saw looked like a blurred grizzly. Now I was getting nervous. Two weeks in Maine every summer had not prepared me for this introduction to the real Mother Nature.

I had no idea of the time or how long I'd been separated. The Tonsmeires didn't allow any watches on their trips; to them, watches signified appointments, commitments, schedules, all the things I was used to. The Arctic day was still fourteen hours long, so I had plenty of light, but I was getting tired. Slogging through the gravel as I dragged the raft was taking its toll. My feet were going numb, and my hands were ripped and raw from the rope. Of course, I had no gloves; they too were in the big raft.

Between the rain and my sweat, I was drenched to the skin. I was starting to shiver. I tried to remember what I had read about hypothermia. What would happen if I passed out? I thought about stopping and trying to make a fire, but how would I make a fire when everything was wet? And what would the others do? I had most of the gear. I had to keep going.

Sometime much later the rain stopped. I cleared my glasses and was relieved to see that the valley was narrowing. The raft offered less resistance as the water rose against my boots. I flopped back in and tried to row, but my hands had no feeling. I lay back and shoved them down into my groin.

I must have dozed off for awhile. When I looked up I was at the bottom of the valley. I became euphoric. The Tat was coming back together. I'd made it. I'd met Mother Nature head on, I'd conquered the wilderness. Triumphantly I glided around the final curve. The raft began picking up speed. The river suddenly was swollen from the rain. Ahead lay the gorge. I could hear the roar. I recalled Pepper saying we wanted to be fresh when we left the Tat. Now I understood why. He knew her intimately. He knew we needed all of our strength for this last encounter.

I could see the big raft bobbing in an eddy that formed where the Tatshenshini's two limbs reunited. Skipper was standing in the raft, waving me over. I strained at the oars. I had to get into the vortex before the Tatshenshini came together for her final plunge into the gorge. I wasn't going to make it. I was going to miss Skipper by a couple of yards. "Throw the rope! Throw the rope!" he yelled.

I fumbled in the icy water sloshing in the bottom of the raft. By the time I found the rope, it was too late. I was past him. Skipper was shouting instructions. "Tie down the equipment! Keep your bow downstream! Don't get turned around! We'll be right behind you!" By the look on his face and the urgency in his voice, I knew I was in trouble.

The little raft was being swept into the gorge. I frantically looked for a place to land. There was none. A cliff of blue ice was on one side, solid rock on the other. Giant waves spumed over me. I became frozen with fear. I let go of the oars and hugged the seat. The raft twisted and bent as we hurdled through the rapids. I was sure I was going to be cast into the Tatshenshini. If she got me, she'd never let me go.

It was over in a matter of seconds. I came into the Alsek. I watched as the gray-green Tatshenshini reluctantly gave herself over to her brown, muddy companion. The big raft pulled up next to me. They were all exhilarated. I was still shaking. I'd been alone in the wilderness for eight hours and had no desire to ever do it again.

The next summer, I built a rustic little cabin on a lake in Maine. For two weeks every summer, that's where I go to flirt with my Mother Nature, the anorexic waif. Whenever Skipper tries to get me back out into the wilderness, I tell him to "come on up. We've got an extra bunk, and there's plenty of hot water." He's only come once, and didn't stay long. Too many people, too much noise, too tame. Skipper likes flirting with the real Mother Nature.

Let the Diva Sing

THE BEST WAY TO SELL CONSERVATION IS TO LET MOTHER NATURE SING for her supper. That means putting potential donors out onto the land. A good example was when my wife, Ruth, was processing year-end stock gifts to the Conservancy. A woman called wanting to know how she could donate ten shares of IBM. During their conversation Ruth asked her if she had a particular project she'd like the money to go to. The woman said no, she'd never seen a Conservancy preserve. Ruth asked her where she lived. She said Florida. Ruth said the Conservancy had a lot of projects in Florida. Would she like to visit one? The woman thought that would be nice. Ruth said she'd see what she could do.

It turned out the woman lived near a preserve that was set up to protect the endangered scrub jay. Our Florida people told Ruth that a block of land next to the preserve that was prime habitat for the jay was just about to come on the market, and developers were lining up to bid on it. To save it, the Florida chapter needed to raise $100,000 immediately. At the time, IBM was selling for $100/share so $1,000 would help. They would be happy to take the woman on a tour. The day was beautiful; the woman loved her tour. The deal was sealed when a scrub jay, which is an unusually friendly bird, landed on her shoulder. Instead of ten shares, the woman, who turned out to be an IBM heiress, gave a thousand shares and felt so good about doing it she soon became one of the Conservancy's major donors. You got to love that scrub jay.

Pat used to say, "Bait the hook to suit the fish." If you're trying to save a beach for nesting turtles, take donors there when the turtles are nesting. If it's a stream for spawning salmon, go when the salmon are spawning. If it's habitat for migrating birds, go when the birds are migrating. There are certain spots where at certain times of the year, Mother Nature puts on a real show. Hawk Mountain in Pennsylvania is one such spot. In the fall hundreds of hawks can be seen circling in the updrafts over the mountain. Cape May in New Jersey is another. For a couple of weeks each spring, tens of thousands of horseshoe crabs congregate on the beaches to lay their eggs. These eggs, which are rich in protein, present a much welcome feast to the hundreds of thousands of songbirds that flutter ashore with their gas tanks on empty after a long flight over the Atlantic.

A few species have a migration pattern that Walt Matia, the Conservancy's director of stewardship during the 1970s and now America's premier wildlife sculptor, termed the "bowtie effect." One of the most dramatic bowtie effects belongs to the North American sandhill crane. After wintering along a wide range of the Texas and Mexican Gulf Coast, almost the entire North American population of sandhill cranes (about a half million birds) converges on a shallow stretch of the Platte River just outside of Grand Island, Nebraska. There they fatten up on grubs found in the surrounding fields during the day and roost in the safety of the river at night. Once rested and refueled, the birds fan out again to their breeding grounds across the plains of central Canada and shores of Hudson Bay. Hence, the bowtie effect. According to Walt, there are only a dozen or so bowties in the world and it's imperative that these knots (in this case, the Platte River) are protected. It shouldn't be that difficult. The sight and sound of a half million cranes flying through the dusk to roost on the Platte River was enough to compel many donors to add a few zeros to their checks.

Warning: Like any diva, Mother Nature can be temperamental—and maybe worse. Exposing donors to her whims may be dangerous to your health. Canoes tip; rafts flip; and snakes, alligators, bears, and birds (especially raptors) don't always cooperate. However, if you catch Mother Nature at the right time, she can put on a great show. We got lucky once with the Mellon trustees. While they were considering funding the Rivers of the Deep South program, Pat, Skipper, and I gave them a tour of the Mobile-Tensaw Delta and Mobile Bay. The tour ended on the beach at Gulf Shores. We were standing on a dune in the Bon Secour National Wildlife Refuge. The spring sky was a robin's-egg blue, the sand a sparkling white, the waters of the Gulf a deep green. To the west we were watching a big, red sun slowly sink into the Gulf when Skipper said, "Ya'll might want to turn around."

We did, and there to the east was the tip of a golden-yellow full moon rising from off the water. These solar/lunar exchanges occur on a full moon. There are only thirteen of them a year, but they're a time when Mother Nature is belting out one of her very finest arias. If you can catch this show, you'll be in business. Just ask the Mellon trustees. They committed $15 million on the spot.

Divine Intervention

In December 1982 The Nature Conservancy was confronted with a new and major problem. Thanks to Jane Yarn, the prominent Georgian and longtime member of the Conservancy's National Board of Governors who was responsible for saving Wormsloe and starting the Georgia Natural Heritage Program, we had gotten quite close to the Carter administration. Both President Carter and Secretary of the Interior Cecil Andrus were very supportive of conservation, and, based on their commitment to expand the Nation's Wildlife Refuge System, we had set up a program to aggressively pre-acquire significant natural areas for the U.S. Fish and Wildlife Service. Under this program TNC bought lands identified by the Fish and Wildlife Service and held them until Congress appropriated the money to buy them back. During President Carter's four years in office, we had successfully acquired and resold more than $20 million of prime habitat to the FWS.

When Jimmy Carter was defeated by Ronald Reagan in the fall of 1980, TNC owned an additional $18 million of land that it had purchased on behalf of the FWS. This land was a huge investment for us and we needed to get our money back as quickly as possible. In the spring of 1981, Pat and I met with James Watt, President Reagan's new secretary of the interior.

The purpose of this meeting was to bring the secretary up-to-date on TNC's efforts to pre-acquire significant natural areas for the Fish and Wildlife Service, and to find out when the government was going to repurchase the lands we were holding. We knew Watt was no fan of conservation, but had no idea how much he despised the movement. "What land?" he said when we asked him about the repurchase. "We can't take care of the land we've got. We want to be selling, not buying."

Pat quickly pulled out the "letters of intent" we had from Cecil Andrus and gave them to the secretary. These letters said that if TNC would pre-acquire certain tracts of land, the Department of the Interior would make every effort to buy them back within a year. Watt looked at the letters and laughed. "The Reagan administration has nothing to do with these letters. You're a conservation organization. If the land's so important, you keep it." End of meeting. Rather than just crippling the environmental movement, Watt wanted to annihilate it, and us along with it.

We were in deep trouble. Based on Secretary Andrus's letters of intent, TNC had borrowed the money to buy this land and our bankers were starting to wonder when they were going to get their money back. Fortunately, the career professionals at the Fish and Wildlife Service came up with a plan. Instead of looking for the funding from a general appropriation to the Department of the Interior, they told us to work with legislators who were pro-conservation and have them tack on specific appropriations for our projects to other bills. The plan worked well. By the fall of 1982, we'd worked our debt down to $8 million, but there was one big project that was killing us.

Back in 1979 TNC had spent $3 million to buy 450 acres from the Chesapeake Bay Bridge-Tunnel Authority. This land was right at the end of the bridge-tunnel that ran from Norfolk across the Chesapeake Bay to the Eastern Shore of Virginia. It was immediately adjacent to the Fisherman's Island National Wildlife Refuge, an important staging area on the Eastern Flyway. In addition to migratory waterfowl looking to cross the Chesapeake Bay, passerines like warblers, finches, and orioles used this tract to fatten up while they waited for favorable winds that would carry them across the Atlantic to Spain, Africa, and the Azores. The property was surplus to the bridge-tunnel project and conservation had always been its highest and best use. Then in the late seventies, some developers had come up with an aggressive subdivision plan.

Thanks to the bridge-tunnel, people from Norfolk, Hampton, Portsmouth, and Newport News were flocking across the bay looking for second homes. Prices on the Eastern Shore were soaring and the developers saw this land as prime recreational real estate. The Bay Bridge-Tunnel was losing money and the bond holders were pushing the Bay Bridge-Tunnel Authority to find ways to generate more income. For that reason, the authority didn't look at this land as a significant natural area. They saw it as a way to make money.

Fortunately, the Fish and Wildlife Service had a hook. By law, the Bay Bridge-Tunnel Authority had to offer any surplus property to the U.S. government before it could sell it on the open market. The price had been set by appraisal at $3 million, but when the authority offered the land to the U.S. Fish and Wildlife Service, the service had neither the authorization nor the funds to buy it. That's when Secretary Andrus had sent the Conservancy his "letter of intent."

Working with members of Congress who knew us and were pro-conservation, a bill with a rider authorizing funds for the purchase of the bridge-tunnel tract as an addition to the Fisherman's Island National Wildlife Refuge had passed the House. On Monday, December 12, 1982, that bill was going to the Senate, but we were not optimistic about its passage. Senate protocol said that no addition to a wildlife refuge or park would be made without the consent of the two senators from the state involved. Paul S. Trible Jr. was the newly elected junior senator from Virginia. Senator Trible was a relative unknown from Newport News who'd been swept into office as a Reagan Republican. None of our supporters knew him. When we tried to set up a meeting, his staff wouldn't give us the time of day. With Watt strongly opposed to any more land acquisition, they'd never recommend the project to the senator. As Reagan Republicans, they didn't want their man's conservative reputation tainted by consorting with liberal conservationists, and without Senator Trible's approval, the project would be DOA. As Walt McAllister, the head of land acquisition for the Fish and Wildlife, told us, "It doesn't make any difference how many senators are for it, they're not going to stick something in Trible's backyard unless he supports it. That's the way it works."

On the day before the vote, Ruth and I went to Christ Church in Alexandria to hear the Right Reverend George L. Cadigan preach. George Cadigan was the former bishop of Missouri and the current chaplain at Amherst College. We knew him through Amherst and I'd worked with the bishop on several conservation projects on Lake Kezar in Maine. The bishop had gone to Episcopal School in Alexandria and had maintained a special relationship with Christ Church and its rector. Every year at the rector's request, the bishop came to Christ Church to perform the confirmation service.

Constructed in 1773, Christ Church is one of the oldest Episcopal churches in America. From its knoll above the Potomac, it has dominated the center of Alexandria for well over two centuries. To this day it is still is known as "George Washington's church," but as we drove through Alexandria, I wasn't thinking about the bishop or George Washington's church. I was thinking about Senator Paul Trible. How were we going to get to him before the vote? It would take a miracle.

We'd arranged to meet the bishop in the rectory before the service. After the service he'd be too busy greeting the new confirmees and their families to talk with us, so this would be our only time to visit. As Ruth chatted with the bishop, my mind was still fixed on the bridge-tunnel land. With the vote the next day, I had to figure out a way to get the Conservancy's money back. Eventually, I heard the bishop say, "Come on, I'll take you over to the church. I want to make sure you get to sit in George Washington's pew."

When we walked into the church, the usher recognized the bishop and rushed over to greet him. I froze. The usher was Paul S. Trible Jr., the junior senator from Virginia. "Bishop Cadigan, we're so delighted you could make it," the senator said.

"Thank you so much," the bishop said. I could tell he didn't know who Trible was. "I was wondering if my good friends Dave and Ruth Morine might sit in George Washington's pew?"

"By all means," the senator said, turning to Ruth and me. "If you're ready, I'll be happy to seat you now."

We said goodbye to the bishop and followed Senator Trible down the aisle to George Washington's pew. My head was spinning. I didn't know what to do. This was an unbelievable bit of luck, but how was I going to capitalize on it? Should I grab the senator now and start telling him about the importance of the refuge? No, that would never do. The church was beginning to fill up. He wouldn't have time to listen. I'd have to wait until later. But when? After the service he'd be swarmed by parishioners wanting their young confirmees to shake hands with their senator. It had to be now.

"Here we are," the senator said, lifting the latch to the wooden door on George Washington's pew. All the pews at Christ Church had wooden doors. "Enjoy the service."

"Ahh, Senator," I started to say but immediately was interrupted by a constituent eager to have the senator meet his daughter. We sat down, the organ sounded, the service started, but I hardly noticed the grand processional, the lesson, the psalm, the epistle. All through the confirmation I stared at Senator Trible. How was I going to get to him?

It wasn't until the gradual hymn, "Savior, Like a Shepherd Lead Us," that I realized the bishop was about to speak. I watched as he made his way up the steps that led to Christ Church's historic wineglass pulpit. The hymn ended. There was a rustle as the congregation reclaimed their seats. I was running out of time. I needed a plan.

"Before I begin my sermon," the bishop said, his voice filling the church, "I would like to introduce my good friends Dave and Ruth Morine." He pointed toward George Washington's pew. I could see Senator Trible looking right at us. "Dave heads the land acquisition efforts of a wonderful organization called The Nature Conservancy," the bishop continued. "Thanks to Dave and The Nature Conservancy, thousands of acres of our finest woods and streams and lakes and meadows are being saved for future generations, and it is these lands that support the plants and animals that add so much to our lives. Without organizations like The Nature Conservancy, our world would be a much poorer place, and for that we must give thanks."

The bishop lowered his head in silent prayer. The congregation joined him. I snuck a peek at Senator Trible. He was reverently giving thanks to The Nature Conservancy. Then the bishop delivered his sermon. It was about fly fishing and how being close to nature was being close to God. He couldn't have made a more compelling case for conservation.

When the service ended, Senator Trible made a beeline for Ruth and me. "I'm Paul Trible," he said extending his hand. "I agree with everything the bishop said and I just want you to know that if there's ever anything I can do for The Nature Conservancy, I hope you won't hesitate to call on me."

"As a matter of fact," I said, still stunned by my good fortune, "there is something you can do for us right now. Tomorrow, a bill's going to be introduced in the Senate that would authorize the funding for the acquisition of a very critical piece of land by the U.S. Fish and Wildlife Service. This tract's right at the end of the Bay Bridge-Tunnel. We bought it back in '79 when they had to sell it. Given its natural significance, we feel this is one of the most important projects we've ever undertaken, but we need your support to make it happen."

"I've heard about this project," the senator said. "And don't worry, I'm all for it."

We shook hands and the senator left us to mingle with the parishioners. Ruth and I got in line to say goodbye to the bishop. When we reached him he was quite apologetic. "I hope you didn't mind my introducing you," he said, "but when I looked out and saw all of these young people, I suddenly felt that I should say something about conservation."

"Not at all," I said, thinking of the fun I was going to have with the bishop when I told him how his sermon had raised $3 million for conservation.

The next day, the bill was passed with Senator Trible's blessing. Thanks to divine intervention, the land and TNC had been saved.

〜

Genesis 1:28

"And God blessed them, and God said to them, 'Be fruitful and multiply, and fill the earth and subdue it; and have dominion over the fish of the sea and the birds of the air and over every living thing that moves on the earth.'"

Talk about a recipe for disaster. God, or whoever's running this show, must have been kidding when he came up with that one. "Be fruitful and multiply?" In 1970, the year of the first Earth Day, there were 203,302,031 Americans. In 2010 that figure had jumped to 308,745,538. That's an increase of more than 50 percent in just forty years. This means clogged highways, overcrowded schools, high unemployment, out-of-control medical costs, and whole families homeless and sleeping under bridges. Right now "be fruitful and multiply" doesn't look like such a hot idea. Part of the modern-day conservation movement should be getting those Gideon bibles out of every motel room.

"Have dominion over the fish of the sea and the birds of the air"? That had to be a joke. Two examples come to mind: Atlantic cod and the passenger pigeon. With its mild flavor, low fat content, and dense, flakey white meat, Atlantic cod has long been one of the world's most popular eating fish. The Vikings first started selling cod commercially to Europeans in AD 800. The Portuguese began fishing for them in the fifteenth century. It is widely believed the Basques were harvesting cod from the Grand Banks off Canada well before Columbus discovered America. By the late twentieth century, the stocks of Atlantic cod had been so seriously depleted that there was real concern the fish would be wiped out. Despite many discussions about overfishing and a few actual attempts to control it, the situation has not improved. The stocks of Atlantic cod, once the fish that was the staple of the European and North American diet, are still on edge, but the Atlantic cod is just one canary in the coal mine. Unsustainable fishing continues to destroy ocean ecosystems all over the world. What good has having dominion over the fish of the sea really done for us?

As for the birds of the air, the passenger pigeon was once the most populous bird on the planet. At one point there might have been as many as four billion passenger pigeons flying around North America. In colonial times, flocks a mile wide and three hundred miles long were so dense that they darkened the sky for days at a time. J. J. Audubon recounts lying on the banks of the Ohio River in the 1850s and not seeing the sun for three days as one flock passed overhead. At 1:01 p.m. on September 1, 1914, a mere sixty years after Audubon's sighting, Martha, a resident of the Cincinnati Zoo and the last-known passenger pigeon on this earth, passed away. Since then Martha has been joined by other such notables as Bachman's warbler, the heath hen, the dusky seaside sparrow, and, of course, the settler of all forest disputes, the ivory-billed woodpecker. How's that for having "dominion over the fish of the sea and the birds of the air and every living thing that moves on the earth" when it's led to the extinction of quite a number of species?

While the word *dominion* is open to interpretation, there's no question that dealing with Mother Nature is a spiritual business. On more than one occasion, we were sure a project was going down the crapper when divine intervention interceded. Bishop Cadigan's preaching to Senator Trible was one good example. Another is the Great Dismal Swamp.

In the spring of 1972, Pat called me into his office. He wanted me to join him in a meeting with Bob Tomassetti, the head of real estate for Union Camp Corporation. Union Camp was shutting down its operations in southeastern Virginia and Bob was disposing of a 50,000-acre tract the company owned in the heart of the Great Dismal Swamp. Bob had several parties interested in buying the land, most notably Malcolm McLean, the former farm boy from Maxton, North Carolina, who'd invented the shipping container and become one of the richest men in America. Reaching back to his roots, McLean had just started First Colony Farms and was in the process of buying what would eventually amount to 376,000 acres of forested peat lands in the lower coastal regions around Albemarle Sound. McLean's plan was to convert these forests, which historically had been too boggy to farm, into fields. The Japanese had developed a new machine that was able to do just that. McLean had bought one and had it in the swamp, where it was busily living up to its reputation.

Sox Calder, the president of Union Camp, was a good conservationist and thought these fifty thousand acres in the heart of the swamp would make a wonderful national wildlife refuge. Sox was willing to have Union Camp donate the land to the government if Bob Tomassetti could figure out a way that the donation would not adversely affect Union Camp's stockholders. Walt McAllister, the head of land acquisition for Fish and Wildlife, sent Bob over to see us. Walt was hoping we could work something out.

The plan was simple. Union Camp would have to get the property appraised, and if the appraisal came in at $14 million or above, the after-tax return to the company from donating the land to TNC would approximate the after-tax return Union Camp would get from selling it to First Colony Farms. We would then transfer the property to Fish and Wildlife once it had gotten all the local, state, and federal approvals it needed to create a new wild refuge. The appraisal was the key, but would it be enough?

On Monday, June 19, 1972, Bob Tomassetti called Pat. He had bad news. The appraisal had come in at $12 million. A gift of the land would not match a sale. Union Camp was going to sell the land to First Colony Farms. We were devastated. The thought of this great swamp being cleared and turned into an industrial farm was incomprehensible, but there was no way we could make the deal work. The Great Dismal Swamp had been lost.

On Tuesday, news came that a rare June hurricane named Agnes had made landfall on the Florida Panhandle and was dropping record rains in Georgia. As we watched Agnes veer to the east, it appeared to be taking dead aim at the tidewater section of Virginia. On Wednesday, June 21, it stalled over Albemarle Sound depositing more than a foot of water directly on the Great Dismal Swamp. On Friday, June 23, we got another call from Bob Tomassetti. The Great Dismal Swamp had turned into a huge sponge. The Japanese machine had sunk out of sight and the prospect for turning the great swamp into farmland was more dismal than the swamp itself. The sale with First Colony was off, and Union Camp's board had just approved the gift to The Nature Conservancy.

When you've done everything you can do, and it might not be enough, have faith and hope for Divine Intervention.

Breaking the Ice

SOMETIMES THE BEST PROJECTS ARE SO OBVIOUS YOU DON'T EVEN SEE them. To get to the Gulf of Mexico from Skipper Tonsmeire's little fish camp, we'd jump into his nineteen-foot Aquasport and slowly motor for a mile or so around the sweeping bends of Turkey Branch, then open it up for a half mile down Fish River, cut back to No WAKE speed as we went under the Route 98 Bridge, go full blast for two miles through Weeks Bay, then fifteen miles across Mobile Bay to where it enters the Gulf at Fort Morgan. Being just one link in a uniformly spectacular aquatic chain, we always took Weeks Bay for granted. For most people, this little environmental jewel was just someplace you went through to get somewhere else.

Roughly two miles long and a mile wide, Weeks Bay is formed by salt water seeping up from the Gulf that converges with freshwater flowing down Fish River. It's this mix of fresh and salt water that forms an estuary and creates the exceedingly rich and fertile environment that nourishes a wide variety of marine life. Ecologists have determined the brackish brew found in estuaries produces more food per acre than the best Midwestern farmland and that two-thirds of all the fish caught and eaten by Americans are directly dependent on these natural systems. In other words places like Weeks Bay should never be taken for granted.

In 1981 Weeks Bay was still a relatively undeveloped backwater near the southern end of Mobile Bay's Eastern Shore, but it wasn't going to stay that way for long. A wave of growth flowing east over the causeway from Mobile was putting tremendous developmental pressure on the entire Eastern Shore. Seeing this trend, Pat Ogburn, a friend of Skipper's who'd been on the Tatshenshini with us, had stockpiled 158 acres on Weeks Bay for future development. This tract contained almost all the frontage on the south side of the bay, and Pat figured it wouldn't be long before he could convert it into a very attractive subdivision. Then the economy turned. With interest rates hovering around 18 percent, Pat, like most developers, couldn't afford to be holding land for future development. Looking for a way out, he asked Skipper if TNC would have any interest in buying this piece for conservation.

That was the first time Skipper and I had ever looked at Weeks as a potential project. What we saw was an area that met all of TNC's criteria: it was significant; it was threatened; thanks to Pat, the price was right; Skipper could manage it, at least until we found a permanent home; and getting this first piece definitely would open the door to a much bigger assembly of land. In addition, Weeks Bay fit very nicely into an overall plan we'd gradually been developing for protecting Mobile Bay and the Delta.

This plan had started in 1976 when Skipper first called TNC looking for help to save the largest undeveloped block of land left on the Alabama Gulf Coast. Known as the Perdue tract, this piece consisted of two and half miles of white, sandy, unbroken beach running along the Fort Morgan Peninsula. The beach provided one of the last undisturbed habitats in Alabama for nesting green, loggerhead, and Kemp's Ridley sea turtles. What made this area even more significant was a series of rolling dunes immediately behind the beach that provided a buffer for a unique assortment of interior lowlands. This intact system of beach, dunes, and interior lowlands served as a major landfall and staging area for at least ninety species of migratory birds that made their way across the Gulf each spring and fall. There was nothing else like it on the Alabama coast, and unlike Weeks Bay, nobody, especially a long line of developers, took it for granted. Fortunately, none of them could match Skipper's determination to save it.

The property was owned by the Perdues, one of Mobile's older and finer families. Back in the fifties when Skipper was coming of age, he'd dated Ashley Perdue. Through Ashley, Skipper had gotten to know the property intimately and it held many pleasant memories for him. It was these memories, along with the land's great natural significance, that drove him to save it. As Bil Gilbert once noted, my commitment to conservation was based on my desire to recapture life in the fifties at Jordan's Camps.

Skipper had much the same feeling for the Perdue tract, only thanks to Ashley, his desire was even stronger. With Skipper working the deal, TNC was able to acquire the land from the Perdues, and in 1980 it became the nucleus for the Bon Secour National Wildlife Refuge, a 6,700-acre natural gem created by Congress "to provide habitat for nongame birds migrating south in the fall and north in the spring over the Gulf."

Having established a beachhead, Skipper and I started looking north. Thanks again to 18 percent interest rates, a tract containing close to four miles of untouched shoreline in the southeast corner of Mobile Bay became available. This parcel lay between Weeks Bay and the new Bon Secour NWR, so we took some of the Mellon trustee's Rivers of the Deep South money and bought it. Using this parcel as a connector, our plan was to make Weeks Bay a component of the Bon Secour Refuge, only there was a problem: James Watt. Once again Reagan's secretary of the interior was making life tough for us. When we approached Walt McAllister about the possibility of Fish and Wildlife adding Weeks Bay to the refuge, he told us, "No way. Watt will kill it."

Then I got an idea. In 1972 Congress passed the Coastal Zone Management Act. Part of this act was something called the National Estuarine Sanctuary Program. This relatively obscure program was designed to make 50 percent matching grants to coastal states for acquiring estuarine areas. Of the seven sanctuaries already established, TNC had played an active role in creating two: South Slough in Oregon and Elkhorn Slough in California. In both cases the process was long, tedious and required going to lots of meetings and filling out tons of paperwork. With so many other sources of funding available under the Carter administration, we'd forgotten about the Estuarine Sanctuary Program. What made it attractive now was that it was administered by NOAA, not the Department of the Interior, which meant Watt had nothing to do with the funding. If we wanted to save Weeks Bay, making it an estuarine sanctuary looked like our best bet.

That wasn't going to be easy. The act creating the program envisioned only twenty sanctuaries nationwide and Apalachicola Bay already had been designated as one. Just two hundred miles east of Mobile,

Apalachicola Bay, with its world-famous oysters and considerable size, was an outstanding example of an estuary and why they're important. Getting another area approved along this part of the Gulf would be difficult, especially since, from a political standpoint, Weeks Bay didn't have much going for it. Besides being small and unknown, it was in Alabama. Under the Estuarine Sanctuary Program, states were responsible for both managing the sanctuaries and coming up with 50 percent of the funding needed to run them. Historically, Alabama had done little to support conservation.

On the bright side, one of the people responsible for evaluating potential estuarine sanctuaries was Jim McFarland, and Jim was family. Before going to work at NOAA, Jim had been manager of TNC's Virginia Coast Reserve. I set up a meeting with Jim and asked Mike Dennis to come along. Mike had just moved down from Boston to become TNC's general counsel, but he'd worked closely with Jim when he was in the Eastern Regional office. Having Mike with me would make it tougher for Jim to say no.

In early February 1981 we met with Jim in Washington. He was cordial but not encouraging and voiced all the reservations we'd expected: Weeks Bay was small, NOAA already had a world-class sanctuary in Apalachicola, what were the odds of Alabama coming up with 50 percent funding? "Look," Jim said, "we'd love to do some projects with TNC, but can't you guys come up with something better than Weeks Bay?"

"We're looking at other stuff," I said, "but I think you might be selling Weeks Bay short. It's a real neat area and fits nicely into a much larger effort we were working on in Alabama. Won't you at least come down and see it?"

Jim looked like someone who'd just been invited to a distant cousin's wedding in West Virginia, but he was family, so he dutifully accepted. That was the opening we needed. If we could get Jim out on the bay, Skipper could sell him. Skipper could sell almost anything to anybody. Just ask Ashley.

I called him right after the meeting. "Our guy at NOAA's agreed to come down and have a look. I've scheduled him for the full moon. This will be our only shot so pull out all the stops. Oh, and do me a favor, turn on the hot water."

I couldn't have picked a worse day. When Jim and an associate pulled into Turkey Branch, the temperature was hovering right at freezing. Skipper, Mike, and I watched as they carefully parked their little rent-a-car front end facing out. All true government employees park with their front facing out. They figure that when they get to work, they're parking on the government's time, but when they're leaving, it's on their own. As Jim and his buddy got out, we could see they weren't dressed for a boat ride: black Thom McAn shoes; gray double-knit slacks; white wash-and-wear short-sleeve shirts; clip-on ties; and blue double-knit blazers. They started shivering immediately. Skipper quickly got them into the camp and turned up the woodstove full blast.

Over steaming cups of herbal tea and honey, Skipper spread a map of Weeks Bay out on the counter. As Jim and his associate Pete sipped their tea, Skipper walked them through the area we'd be seeing from the boat. Then he unrolled a huge NASA photo showing the Alabama Gulf Coast, Mobile Bay, and the Mobile/Tensaw Delta. "This here's the big picture," he said, pointing to the top of the photo. "The Tombigbee and Alabama Rivers meet up here, about forty miles north of Mobile, formin the Mobile/Tensaw Delta, the best bottomland hardwood forest left in North America. The delta catches and cleans all this here water comin down from north Alabama and Mississippi and then releases it into the bay. It's the timin of these releases that cause a Jubilee. That's when the oxygen level of the water gits so low that fish, crabs, and everything else start swimming up onshore. They got this big bell in Fairhope that they start ringin and people start runnin to the bay with baskets. It's really sometinhin and it only happens two places in the world, here and some-place in Japan."

Skipper took a sip of his tea while he let that fact brew for a moment, then continued. "The bay flows into the Gulf, and we're fixin to protect as much of the big picture as we can, but look here." He pointed to Weeks Bay. "Weeks Bay's a perfect microcosm of the bigger system. If we could turn it into a sanctuary, we'd have us a teachin tool for how to manage all of Mobile Bay. Ain't that what these NOAA sanctuaries are supposed to be doin, teachin people the importance of estuaries and how to manage them?"

Jim and Pete nodded, but not enthusiastically. They were far from sold. Skipper wasn't worried. He'd do that on the boat, only I was beginning to have second thoughts about going out in the boat. A cold wind kept rattling the windows of the fish camp. Clearly, a bad day was getting worse. Maybe we should just drive Jim and Pete up to the top of the Route 98 Bridge and show them the bay from there, but Skipper was undaunted. He opened a closet and started throwing out parkas, down vests, Nepali yak hats, gloves, mittens, and anything else that might keep a body warm. Once he had us all outfitted, we settled into the Aquasport and began slowly winding our way down Turkey Branch.

This ride was unlike any I'd ever experienced before. Usually there were turtles sunning on logs, great blue herons fishing in the shallows, a family of screech owls hooting at us from their nest inside the trunk of a dead tree. Today there was nothing. Jim and Pete huddled in the bow as a persistent raw, damp cold wrapped itself around us. Mike and I kept comparing the weather to the Virginia Eastern Shore, telling Jim he must be feeling right at home. Jim said nothing. Skipper kept pointing out sites that usually were lush and verdant. Now they looked drab and dark. Out on Fish River the sky was a gunmetal gray and getting darker. Gusts of wind from the northeast kept kicking up a spray that stung our faces like needles.

Skipper pushed on. At the Route 98 Bridge, he stopped to show Jim and Pete the largest live oak in Alabama. Even with its winter foliage still hanging on, it looked old and cold. On the far side of Weeks Bay, he pointed out an Indian mound and explained how Native Americans had camped there for thousands of years feasting on a bounty of oysters and shrimp produced by the estuary's rich waters. From under the hoods of their zipped-up parkas, Jim and Pete sat and shivered.

Skipper had planned the trip perfectly. Just when the sun should have been setting in the west, a full moon would have been rising in the east, but instead of a spellbinding solar/lunar exchange, all we saw was a black wall of sleet and rain rushing over the open water right at us. "Damn, let's get out of here," Jim said. Nobody argued with him.

By the time we got back to camp, a thin layer of ice had formed over Turkey Branch. It cracked under the bow as Skipper guided the Aquasport up to the dock. Not wanting to waste any time, I got up, grabbed the bow line, and prepared to jump out. As Skipper cut the engine, I put one foot on the gunnel and the other up onto the dock. As I pushed off, rather than me going up, the Aquasport went out. The next thing I knew, I was falling backwards into the water. "Ahhhhhh!!" I could feel the ice splinter as Turkey Branch swallowed me up. "Damn, it's cold!" I screamed, fighting my way back to the surface.

"Quick, give me your glasses and wallet," Mike said, leaning over the side, trying not to laugh.

"Hell, man," Skipper said, "if I'd known you was going swimmin, I wouldn't have bothered turnin on the hot water. Git over to that ladder there and pull your sorry ass out."

As I came up the ladder, I could see Jim and Pete rolling around in the front of the boat. They couldn't stop laughing. Watching me fall into Turkey Branch had made their day. If nothing else, I'd broken the ice.

When I got out of a long, hot shower, Jim, Pete, Mike, and Skipper were gathered around the kitchen counter. The map of Weeks Bay was spread out over the top. On it were two big bowls. One was full of steamed shrimp, the other grilled oysters. A couple of bottles of wine were sitting next to them. Everyone was relaxed, happy, enjoying the feast. In between bites and sips, Jim and Pete were peppering Skipper with questions. How many acres did he envision the total sanctuary? What state agencies would be involved? Who were the key players? What were the odds of the state coming up with the funding? Would the town of Fairhope accept and support the sanctuary? Who could they get to do all the research necessary to prepare the proposal? As Jim sucked down the last oyster, he said, "What the hell, watching Dave go into Turkey Branch has given me a warm feeling for this place. If you guys want to take a shot, we'll recommend it."

In February 1986, after five long years of endless meetings, studies, papers, and proposals, Weeks Bay was officially designated as the nation's sixteenth national estuarine sanctuary. Thousands of hours had been volunteered by professional scientists and local citizens who recognized the importance of the area and the benefits that would flow to the community from having a national estuarine sanctuary in Fairhope. The political effort was led by Congressman Jack Edwards in Washington, the public effort in Alabama by John Borom, a well-known and much-respected professor of biology and marine sciences at Faulkner State University in Fairhope. Behind the scenes Skipper built a private effort. This overwhelming political, public, and private support for the sanctuary has never ebbed. Today, nobody takes Weeks Bay for granted. It has become a focal point of the community and the whole area. Entire families participate in programs and activities like the John L. Borom Coastal Alabama BirdFest, Kids' Fishing Day, and the Annual Weeks Bay Photography Contest. The state's 50 percent of the funding has never been a problem. People in Fairhope and all along the Alabama Gulf Coast have made it clear they want the Weeks Bay National Estuarine Sanctuary to be a permanent part of their lives and will do whatever it takes to keep it going. We just had to break the ice.

❧

Home Cookin'

WHILE I WAS AT THE TNC, PART OF OUR MANTRA WAS "WE DON'T LOBBY and we don't litigate." That slogan played well with our corporate donors and distanced us from most of the other conservation organizations, but it was only partially true. We definitely didn't litigate. The only time we ever went to court was to settle boundary disputes, and we could count those on one hand, but we did lobby, at least in a limited fashion. Once we got into pre-acquiring land for governmental agencies, we had to do whatever we could to make sure those agencies got the funding they needed to buy the land back. While we maintained we didn't lobby, we spent a good part of our time up on Capitol Hill or in state legislatures meeting with senators and representatives regarding certain projects.

What we learned from these experiences was that it's important to *always* have a local constituent, someone who has given a senator or representative their vote, with you. We could present the details of a project and how the funding would work, but it was the local constituent who made the case of why the project was important to the community and why it had to be funded.

One of my favorite stops on Capitol Hill was when Skipper Tonsmeire and I would go to see Representative Jack Edwards. As head of the House Armed Forces Committee, Jack Edwards was a very powerful man. He'd been in Congress for eighteen years and was greatly respected on both sides of the aisle, yet for all of his power, Jack Edwards was a very down-home guy. When Skipper and I walked into the congressman's office, we might as well have been back in Mobile. "Why Skipper," some very Southern and very attractive young woman would say, "what brings you to the big city?"

Skipper would ask her how her daddy and momma were doing and tell her how he'd seen her brother the other day out fishing for ling. And so it went until we were ushered into the congressman's inner sanctum. "Skipper," the congressman would say, coming around his big desk to greet us. "It's so good to see you. What's in that cooler you're toting?"

The congressman already knew. Anytime Skipper came to Washington, he'd bring a cooler filled with oysters, shrimp, crabs, and an assortment of fresh fish straight from the Gulf. "Oh, I just thought bein stuck up here, you and your staff might enjoy a taste from home," Skipper would say, putting the cooler down on the congressman's beautiful State of Alabama rug. "These here oysters were sleepin in Weeks Bay last night."

There'd be more discussion of people and things going on back home until finally the congressman would say, "Skipper, what can I do for you boys today?"

Skipper would then describe the project we were working on and have me explain the details to the congressman. By this time I'd notice the congressman looking at the cooler and getting nervous it might start leaking onto his rug. "So, sir," Skipper would conclude, "the Conservancy's willin to put up the $2 million we need to buy the land, but what Dave here needs to get the project approved by his board is some type of guarantee the fundin will be available so the Fish and Wildlife Service can buy it back."

"Hang on," the congressman would say, still nervously looking at the cooler on his rug. "Let me run down the corridor and see Sid."

Congressman Sid Yates was the head of House Appropriations and arguably the most powerful man in Congress. Not a nickel got spent by the federal government unless Sid approved it. A few minutes later the congressman would be back. "Sid says it's OK. See Nancy and she'll give you whatever Dave needs for his board." Nancy Tippens was one of the congressman's key aides. Nancy knew where every dollar in the federal budget was hidden. Then, as we headed for the door, the congressman would add, "Oh, and Skipper, take that cooler out with you, and ask Nancy to put them oysters on ice. We sure do appreciate you bringin them up."

If you're looking to create political appetite for a project, bring along someone who knows how to grease the pan. You can't beat "home cookin'."

The Intern

ONE OF THE NATURE CONSERVANCY'S BEST-KEPT SECRETS WAS ITS intern program. We started this program back in the late seventies, at the same time we kicked off our first capital campaign. Every summer the Conservancy would select a handful of students and scatter them over our biggest and best preserves. By no coincidence, all of these students had two things in common: they were the offspring of our major donors, the very people who we hoped would contribute generously to the capital campaign, and they were unpaid. The stated objective of the Conservancy's intern program was to introduce the next generation of conservationists to the business of conservation. The application process was quite simple. A major donor would call and suggest that it might be nice if his or her kid could work on a Conservancy preserve for the summer. The selection process was even simpler. We'd say, "Gee, that sounds like a swell idea."

There was always a sigh of relief when Labor Day came and the kids went back to school. So long as no one got kicked by a horse, lost in the woods, or bitten by a snake, we considered the summer a success. If the kids happened to learn something about nature and the business of conservation, so much the better. But once the school bells rang, our job was done.

That's why I was somewhat surprised when Pat came into my office on a frigid mid-January morning and announced, "We have a new intern."

I recognized the name immediately. It was the son of one of our major donors, a prime prospect for the capital campaign. "You name it, he's got it," I said. "Where would he like to go? The Hamptons, Santa Cruz Island, Maine, Montana, Alaska? Any one of them would make a great summer vacation."

"This isn't for the summer," Pat said. "Junior's applying for our winter program."

"Winter program?" I said. "We don't have a winter program."

"We do now."

"Then I guess it has to be the Seven Sacred Pools on Maui. That's the warmest preserve we have in January."

"Junior doesn't want to go to a preserve," Pat said. "He wants to work here, at the national office. He's a senior in prep school and is doing an independent study over winter break. He's going to write a paper on conservation."

"Sounds like a perfect job for the president," I said. "You can give him the big picture."

"No, no," Pat said. "His father wants him to learn about land acquisition. You know how Senior likes his money to go to projects."

That was true. Over the years I'd gotten to know Senior, and he, like us, felt that the best way to save land was to step up and buy it. "OK," I said, "I'll take care of Junior. When's he coming, and for how long?"

"Two weeks, and he's here now. I'll send him right in." I had to give Pat credit. He was always a couple of steps ahead of me.

Junior seemed like a nice kid, but after chatting with him for a while, I detected that his main interest in coming to Washington wasn't to learn about conservation. A group of students from St. Paul's, his prep school, were spending their winter break working on Capitol Hill. Junior was sharing a house with them in the nicest part of Georgetown. The house belonged to some alum who was in the diplomatic corps and had just been assigned overseas so Junior and his friends had the place to themselves. With this setup, I didn't expect to see much of him. I figured most of his "independent study" would be taking place at night over in Georgetown, but when he showed up at the office, I'd keep him busy.

I took Junior back to the file room and set him up at a little desk in the corner. "The best way to learn how we save land," I told him, "is to study the project files. If you follow the paper trail, you can see how we put a project together."

I dug out the files of some projects that Senior had helped fund, gave them to Junior, and told him I'd be back in a couple of hours to take him to lunch. I figured he would shut the door and sack out for a while, but when I came back, there he was, deep into the files studiously taking notes. At lunch he asked me some good questions about a big tract of land we'd just acquired in Alabama. How were we going to manage it? Would it be open to the public, and if so, how were we going to balance public use with conservation? I began to think that maybe I could teach Junior something about land acquisition after all.

We were in the process of transferring this tract to the U.S. Fish and Wildlife Service, and in two days I was going to a public hearing in Mobile that would address the very questions Junior was asking. "There's a hearing in Mobile on Wednesday regarding this project," I said. "I have to go down for it. Why don't you come along?"

The trip to Mobile went perfectly. First we toured the property with some local volunteers, then we went to the public hearing. The room was packed with conservationists, hunters, fishermen, community leaders, business leaders, and professionals from the both the State Game and Fish Department and the U.S. Fish and Wildlife Service. After much testimony and lots of give and take, we finally hammered out a management plan that seemed acceptable to all the different parties. It was a great example of what it takes to save a piece of land, and I was pleased to see that Junior was taking notes the whole time.

As we were driving back to the airport, I pulled into a gas station. I figured here was a chance to impress Junior with how tight we were with his father's money. "Always return a rental car with a full tank," I told him. "Otherwise, they'll charge you an extra 50 cents a gallon." It had started to rain while we were at the hearing, and now it was coming down in buckets. "OK," I said, "why don't you hop out and fill 'er up?"

Junior looked at the rain, then at the gas gauge, then at me. "I'm not going out there," he said, reaching into his pocket. He pulled out a couple of bucks and slapped them on the dashboard. "Here, this'll cover the difference." Junior was no dope.

When we got back to the office, there was a message from John Clark.

John Clark was a senior fellow at the Conservation Foundation who was working on a land-use plan for Franklin County, Florida. The focus of John's plan was Apalachicola Bay, one of the most significant estuaries in North America. The bay is formed where the Apalachicola River flows into the Gulf of Mexico and is separated from the Gulf by three barrier islands: St. Vincent, St. George, and Dog Island. St. Vincent was totally protected as national wildlife refuge. St. George was almost all developed, and Dog Island was hanging in the balance. The west half of Dog had been subdivided in the fifties and was spotted with second homes, but the east half was completely wild. According to John's message, a developer from Miami had just offered $2 million for the 1200 acres that made up the east half, and the owner was ready to sell.

"The developer wants to put up a thousand condominiums," John told me when I called him. "If that happens, the whole bay could be destroyed. Fortunately, there's a group of homeowners who want to turn the east half into a nature preserve. They need some help so I told them I'd set up a meeting with you."

"When?" I said.

"Time is of the essence. How about Friday afternoon in Tallahassee?"

As long as I had to go to Florida, I figured I might as well take Junior with me. He had seen why one project worked, now he could see why one wouldn't, and I knew from experience that Dog Island wouldn't work. "Any time you've got an island with people on it," I told Junior as we were driving from the Tallahassee airport to our meeting, "you've got a problem. Nobody wants to give money to save land with people on it, and if these homeowners had any money, they wouldn't be calling us. No money means no land, so as a favor to John, we'll listen to what they have to say, but I can tell you right now, this project is DOA."

The group from Dog Island was a strange one. There was Leroy Collins, the former governor of Florida; Cass Vickers, a member of the state senate; Sam Neal, the mayor of Tallahassee; Clay Spencer, a wealthy businessman from New Orleans; Larry Huntsman, a local dropout; and just plain Alexander, a long-haired hippy who was writing the great American novel. While we were shaking hands, I noticed

Governor Collins looking quizzically at Junior trying to figure out what he was doing there.

"Oh, this is Junior, my intern," I announced. "He goes to St. Paul's up in New Hampshire. He's writing a paper on conservation for his senior project so I'm showing him how The Nature Conservancy saves land."

The governor arched his eyebrows. "St. Paul's is a good school, and you're a fine-looking young man," he said. "I'm sure you'll learn a lot traveling with Mr. Morine."

"Yes, sir," Junior said. "He's already shown me a lot."

Governor Collins naturally assumed charge of the meeting. He said that if the Conservancy could beat the developer to the punch, he and his people would figure out a way to raise the money. "Dave," the governor concluded, "between federal funds, state funds, and private money, I'm sure we can come up with the two million. The money's there, we just need time get it, and once you see the island, I'm sure you'll want to help us save it."

This was a tough one. These guys had a lot of clout, and the Conservancy was very active in Florida. It wouldn't be good to just say no. That could hurt us with other projects we were doing with the state, and who knew, with their clout, maybe they could raise the funds. "Gee, I don't know, Governor," I said. "Two million's a lot of money and if we want to protect the bay, maybe we'd be better off spending it trying to save the river."

"I'll tell you what," the governor said. "Clay, Larry, and Alexander are going back to the island tonight. Why don't you go with them and they can show you the land tomorrow morning. That way, you'll be in a better position to make a decision."

Junior wasn't happy. "What's going on?" he said as we were walking out to the car. "I'm not going to that island. I've got to get back to D.C." Undoubtedly, this being Friday night, there was a party at the house in Georgetown.

"The governor asked us to go," I said. "What could I say, especially with the mayor of Tallahassee and a state senator sitting there? You just can't say no to people like that without even seeing the land. That's not the way this business works."

"You said we were just going for the day," Junior whined. "I didn't pack my toothbrush. And where are we going to stay? With that hippy?"

"No, no, we'll stay with the guy from New Orleans. He looks like he's got some dough. I'm sure he has a nice place. Relax, I'll have you home by tomorrow night."

We followed Clay, Larry, and Alexander sixty miles south to the little fishing town of Carrabelle. It was pitch dark by the time we pulled into the marina. A cold wind was whipping off the Gulf, the dampness cutting through to our bones. Clay and Alexander headed across the street to the Piggly Wiggly for beer while Larry puttered around readying a small sailboat. Junior looked at the boat and peered nervously out into the darkness. "Is that the boat we're going on?" he whispered. "Do you think these guys know what they're doing?"

The crossing was long, dark, cold, and scary. Despite the cold, I consumed a six-pack during the trip. Both Junior and I were very relieved when the boat left the chop of the bay and chugged into the snug little harbor on Dog Island. As we approached the dock, a single light rattling in the wind cast eerie shadows on the old wooden piles. A half dozen modest boats creaked and groaned in their slips. The pines whistled, calling in the darkness to people who weren't there. Dog Island was one spooky place, a little like Cape Fear.

We unpacked the boat and walked up to a fleet of rusted cars parked haphazardly under the pines. From what I could see, Dog Island looked like a throwback to the fifties. "We'll see you at eight tomorrow morning at my house," Clay said to Larry and Alexander. "And bring the maps so we can show them the land." As the only permanent residents of Dog Island, he correctly assumed that Larry and Alexander had no other pressing engagements.

We walked over to an old Willys, and Clay told Junior and me to get in. I climbed into the front and Junior got in the back. When Clay turned the key, there was a loud rumble indicating that the Willys had parted with its muffler. Through the rotted floorboards, I watched the oyster shell road zip by below us and heard Junior start coughing from the sandstorm that came swirling in through the open back. After about two miles Clay turned into the dunes and pulled in under a cottage that was set high on pilings. When he turned off the key, the rumble from the exhaust was replaced by the roar of the surf. The house faced directly to the Gulf.

Inside, it was freezing. Clay began turning on lights and pulled out a couple of small portable space heaters. He took one and led us to a bedroom in the front. A cold, hard wind was beating against the windows making them rattle, its draft blowing up through the floorboards. "If you don't mind sharing," Clay said, "this room warms up pretty well with a heater."

"No, that'll be fine," I said, "Please, plug it in."

Junior studied the room but didn't say anything. There were two single beds. I threw my coat on the one next to the outer wall. I figured that bed would be the colder, and I wanted Junior to be as warm and comfortable as possible.

"Here's the bathroom," Clay said, opening a door at the foot of Junior's bed, "but watch it. This bed sticks out a little. Make sure you don't trip over it going to the head." After a bowl of soup and a few more beers, it was time for bed. When Junior crawled in, I noticed he still had all his clothes on. The room had heated up so I figured he was staying dressed just in case he had to make a fast escape. Being stuck on a deserted island with the surf pounding and the wind howling was not Junior's idea of a good time. I stripped down to my boxer shorts and climbed in under a stack of blankets. Thanks to all the beer, I went right to sleep.

When I woke up I had no idea where I was. All I knew was that I had to take a pee, and I had to take it bad. Then, the wind and surf reminded me that I was on Dog Island. I looked around, and in the darkness I could just make out the door to the bathroom. I slid quietly out of my bed and inched toward it. I was just about there when I tripped over the corner of Junior's bed. "Whoa," I yelled, losing my balance and falling into the bed. The next thing I knew, I was lying right on top of Junior.

He woke up with a start. "Hey! What the hell's going on here?"

"It's OK," I said. "It's just me."

Junior was not reassured. He started flailing around in the dark, trying to push me off him. I started turning, trying to roll off, but we were wedged between the wall and the bed, and the more we twisted and turned, the more tied up we got in the covers. When the lights went on, we were wrapped together in a ball. It didn't look good, me lying in bed with my young intern.

"My God!" Clay said, eyeing the situation.

"No, no, it's not what you think," I said. "I got up to take a pee and tripped over the end of the bed." Neither Junior nor Clay seemed too sure.

"Well, if you're going to be getting up," Clay said, "maybe you'd better sleep in another room."

"Yeah," Junior said, still eyeing me suspiciously.

On Monday, back in the office, Junior called and told me that he wouldn't be coming in. He said that he'd finished his research and was going to spend the week writing his paper at the home in Georgetown. If he had any questions, he'd call.

A few days later, Pat came in to see me. He was all smiles. "Good news," he said. "I just talked to Senior and he's prepared to make a substantial gift to the Capital Campaign. Apparently, Junior told him about some very exciting projects. Senior especially liked hearing about Dog Island. Haw, haw."

"Well," I said, "you tell Senior to add a lot of zeros to his check because despite my little mishap with Junior, Dog Island is something we ought to do. If we don't buy this land, it'll really mess up the bay."

"Sounds good to me," Pat said. "Anything else?"

"Just one thing. From now on, let's have no more interns at the national office, unless, of course, you want to take care of them."

So ended The Nature Conservancy's winter intern program.

❧

Doggone It

DOGS CAN BE TROUBLE. ON TNC PRESERVES THEY CHASE FAUNA AND defecate on flora, but that's not the worst of it. Where they really create a problem is when they ingratiate themselves with a major donor.

Competing for funding with the arts, education, medicine, even religion, is difficult, but we can do that. What we can't do is compete against some warm, cuddly, devoted bundle of affection who has won the heart of a potential patron. Don't laugh. Dogs are territorial. They can sense when someone has designs on the hand that feeds them and they then become very protective. They know when they've got a good thing, and they don't like other freeloaders mooching their Milkbones.

One of the Conservancy's classic dog stories happened in 1976 when Pat was summoned to Tennessee. Day Lohman, the new state director, needed help. For years, this particular state program had been existing on a shoestring. Conservationists, like dogs, are territorial. They don't like to share donors and we'd never been able to find a Volunteer who could pick up the program. Now Day was on the threshold of a major breakthrough. She'd identified a wealthy, well-connected widow who could help solidify The Nature Conservancy's presence in Tennessee.

The widow had agreed to host a black-tie dinner for the Conservancy. The "who's who" in the state had been invited. Pat was the guest of honor. All he had to do was sell the widow and her friends on the Conservancy, and no one was better at selling the Conservancy than Pat. He was quick, funny, had just the right amount of irreverence, and he loved raising money. This dinner party was right down his alley: good food, good drink, and a cornucopia of well-heeled donors. He borrowed my tux (I was the only staff member with a tux, at least one that would fit Pat), shined his shoes, and polished his speech. In the time-honored Southern tradition, the affair was being held at the wealthy widow's home, an old plantation nestled along the banks of the Tennessee River. The guests were ferried from the parking lot up the magnolia-lined driveway by horse and carriage. They were greeted by a distinguished, gray-haired butler. He'd usher them across the portico, through the massive Doric columns, and into the living room where mint juleps were served in silver goblets. Pat was resplendent in my tux. All the guests were genuinely pleased to meet him. Only Calhoun, the widow's much-beloved Airedale, seemed piqued by his presence.

Calhoun was used to being the center of attention and resented the fuss the widow was making over Pat. Calhoun sat neglected in the corner while the widow bustled Pat around, chattering gaily about flora and fauna. Pat could feel Calhoun's jealous glare all through cocktails, but what did he care? Calhoun didn't write the checks. Things were going so well that Pat, always a gracious winner, stooped to slip Calhoun an occasional pig in a blanket. As the chimes sounded and the guests began to file into the dining room, Pat stood back politely with the widow. They would be the last to enter. Pat would seat the widow, and after grace she would propose a toast to The Nature Conservancy. Pat would be asked to say a few words just before the soup. Nothing fancy, nothing formal, just a friend talking to other friends about conservation.

As the last guest gulped his drink and tottered by, Pat offered the widow his arm. She took it, smiled, and turned toward the dining room. It was then that Calhoun struck. He got Pat on the left buttock. It was a quick, piercing bite, clean and deep. Pat yelped and grabbed his buns.

He wheeled to look at Calhoun. Calhoun was sitting there, happily wagging his tail. "Is something wrong?" the widow inquired.

Pat wanted to say, "Your g-d dog just bit me in the ass," but being the consummate professional, he caught himself. It was clear that if Pat accused Calhoun, it would embarrass the widow, and that would be it for the Conservancy. He could feel the blood oozing into my trousers. "No, no," he said, re-offering the widow his arm, "just a little cramp."

Pat clenched his cheeks, swallowed his pride, and proceeded to give the speech that permanently established the Tennessee state program. Every now and then you've got to take one for the team.

Lt. Colonel William Barrett Travis

In the mid-1970s The Nature Conservancy planned to start a major program in Texas. I knew setting aside acreage in Texas for conservation wasn't going to be easy. Residents of the Lone Star State at that time didn't cotton to conservationists, especially ones promoting the acquisition of land by the government. Texans, most notably wealthy Texans, felt land should be private and they didn't want anybody telling them how to use it. Still, there were a lot of Texans, particularly bird hunters, who understood the importance of conservation and practiced it on their own properties.

Such being the case, we decided that the best way to get the program going was to find one influential Texan and sell him our brand of conservation. My job was to find that Texan. It only took me a couple of calls to identify my man. T.H. was from San Antonio and was big, even by Texas standards. He'd inherited one fortune and made another. He generously supported groups like Ducks Unlimited, Boone and Crockett, and Safari International, and nothing concerning conservation in Texas was undertaken without his approval. T.H. was not a member of The Nature Conservancy.

When I called and asked for a meeting with T.H., he seemed receptive but reserved. He'd heard of TNC from some of his business buddies, and he liked the fact that we didn't litigate and lobby, but what he really wanted to know was whether we were sportsmen. "You ain't opposed to huntin are ya?" T.H. said, testing me.

"Oh, no," I said, "we all like to hunt and fish."

"Great," he said. "Y'all come down and we'll git us some snows."

"That would be great," I said.

"We'll go up to Eagle Lake," he said. "Goose capital of the world. Yew ain't never seen nuthin like it."

Right before Christmas I flew to Houston. T.H. met me at the airport. He was wearing big boots, a big hat, a big belt buckle and was smoking a big cigar. His big Bronco was parked right out front. It was filled to the roof with camouflage clothes, gun cases, boxes of shells, and racks of decoys. Under all the equipment was a big dog cage. The door was open. As soon as I got in, a young, enthusiastic yellow Lab jumped out of the cage into my lap. It started lapping my face. "This here's Lt. Colonel William Barrett Travis," T.H. said. "I'm jest breakin him in. Had his daddy for twelve years. Best retriever in alla Texas. Had to put'm down last year, but this here dawg's gonna be even better."

It was obvious T.H. had high hopes for this pup. His namesake, Lt. Colonel William Barrett Travis, had commanded the Alamo, and giving a dog his name immediately equated it with greatness. "Remember the Alamo!" I said scratching Trav's ears. "You can't beat a good dog."

"Ain't that the truth," T.H. said, flooring the big Bronco as we barreled out of the airport.

As we rambled through a hundred miles of south Texas ranchland, I tried to steer the conversation toward conservation, but T.H. didn't want to talk about conservation. He wanted to talk about Travis. According to T.H., Travis had the best nose, most brains, softest mouth, and biggest heart of any retriever in all of Texas. "Ol' Trav here, he's gonna be a champ," T.H. said proudly. "Smart as a whip and there ain't nuthin he can't find."

"Good for you, Trav," I said wiping a glob of drool off my Brooks Brothers blazer. It didn't take me a hundred miles to figure out that being nice to Travis would help the Conservancy get a program going in Texas. If Travis liked me, T.H. would too.

We pulled into Eagle Lake right at dusk. Eagle Lake, Texas, was a one-horse town about a hundred miles west of Houston. The only hitching post was in front of the "Farris 1912," a quaint old brick building smack in the middle of town. In its brochure the Farris 1912 described itself as "A Step Back in Time, the Queen of Early Texas Hotels." It was a good description. As we walked in, men in big boots, big hats, and big belt buckles were sitting around smoking big cigars. There were no women registered at the Farris 1912.

T.H. knew everyone. After a big country dinner, we settled in to one of the Farris 1912's public lounges for some big drinks and some big Texas stories. Every story revolved around hunting, and from the sound of them, they'd all gotten better with time. When the stories turned to dogs, T.H. droned on and on about Travis. I could tell by the yawns that Travis did not yet command the same respect as his father. "T.H., that dawg's just a pup," said a roly-poly little Texan with a big diamond ring on his pinky finger. "Now his daddy, he was a retriever, but this dog, he ain't shown us nuthin yet. He's gotta earn them braggin rights." The other men at the Farris 1912 nodded in unanimous agreement. T.H. was not pleased.

"Ya'll be singin a different tune by this time tomorrow," he said, stomping off to bed.

Beautiful! I thought tossing down another big drink. This could be the break I was looking for. If I could help make Travis a star, we'd be set in Texas, but to do that, I was going to have to prove myself in the field. I was going to have to pop a few birds, and that could be a problem. Between bagging the limit at Long Point and hanging around with the boys down South, I'd done some bird hunting, but it turned out I wasn't much of a shot. What they figured out was that I shot from the right but was left-eye dominant, which meant I was never quite on a bird. There were ways of correcting that, but they all required hours at the range and I wasn't into that. Plus, I didn't really mind missing a lot of birds. Watching them fly away always made me feel more like a conservationist.

It was 4:30 in the morning when we piled into the big Bronco. There was no sign of daylight. I hadn't been able to eat my big country breakfast. My head was killing me. I had a Texas-size hangover, but luckily I'd not forgotten Travis. Knowing the importance of our budding friendship, I'd stuffed my pockets with patties of spicy sausage.

T.H. was in great shape and his mood had improved dramatically now that Trav was set to shut up his detractors at the Farris 1912. As we rattled through the darkness splashing through puddles and dodging around potholes that pocked the gravel roads, T.H. chattered on about the history of Eagle Lake. "This here land used to be the Garwood and Eagle Lake prairies. In the late forties and early fifties, Jimmy Reel, a rice buyer and a helluva hunter from Arkansas, convinced these landowners to spot their fields with ponds." My stomach heaved as the big Bronco skidded through a mud hole the size of a horse and I grabbed Travis, who was crawling all over me trying to get at the spicy sausage, to keep him from falling to the floor.

"Good catch," T.H. said to me, patting Trav on the head, then continued, "Jimmy figured if we had some water, all this rice would attract a lotta geese, and he was right. Within ten years we was winterin over a million snows, and Eagle Lake had become the undisputed goose huntin capital of the world."

"Very interesting," I said, surreptitiously slipping a spicy pattie to Trav, who was quickly becoming my new best friend.

To the east a faint glow was spreading over the horizon when we slid to a stop. T.H. popped the tailgate and hauled out a huge canvas bag and two gun cases. "Yew grab the guns, Ah'll take the gear," he said, slinging the bag over his shoulder. "OK, Trav, it's time for you to show those morons back at the Farris who's boss." Travis ignored T.H. and stuck his nose under my vest. "Ah cain't b'lieve it," T.H. said, genuinely amazed, "Trav's takin a likin to a conservationist. Hail, that's like lickin Santa Anna's boots. Haw, Haw."

We started to slosh through the furrows of rice. A couple of inches of standing water separated each furrow from the next. Gobs of mud clung to my boots. We hadn't gone ten yards before my feet felt like cinder blocks and my mouth was dry. Pain pulsated through my head with each step. Those big Texas drinks were taking their toll. We finally stopped next to a little pond. The day was arriving overcast and unseasonably warm. I put down the gun cases and unzipped my vest. Rice fields stretched as far as the eye could see in every direction. I was about to collapse when T.H. said, "We'll set up here. That way, we might git some ducks comin into the pond as well as geese feedin in the fields. Trav likes'm both. Ain't that right, boy?"

Travis didn't hear him. He was still busy sniffing my pockets searching for more spicy sausage. When T.H. wasn't looking, I slipped him another patty. It was gone in a gulp.

T.H. dumped out the bag onto the ground. Much to my surprise, it was loaded with diapers rather than decoys. He pulled out two white surgical gowns from the pile. "Here, put this on," he said, handing me one. Where was the traditional camouflage? T.H. had to be joking, trying to make this Yankee conservationist look like a fool, but he sure was going to great lengths. He put on his gown, picked up an armload of diapers, and headed into the field.

"Diapers? What are they for?" I asked.

"Decoys," he said. "Ain't nuthin that decoys snows better than these here diapers."

I knew that Texans were strange, but this was unbelievable. Diapers for decoys? White gowns as camouflage? This had to be some kind of practical joke, only I began to realize T.H. was dead serious. "Follow me and spread these out," he ordered. "Them geese are gonna be flyin right quick and we're gonna knock down a bunch of 'em." He stopped and petted Travis. "Ain't that right, Trav. Them boys at the Farris are gonna be eatin crow tonight."

T.H. started dropping diapers in the field. I squished along after him. Believe me, spreading diapers as decoys is no easy job. There were hundreds of them, and each one had to be opened up and spread just right. Sweat fogged my glasses and dripped off my nose. My legs started to feel like jelly. I tripped over my gown. All the while Travis kept hounding me for more spicy sausage. "Daggone it," said T.H., "I ain't never seen a dawg take to anybody like that." Still bent over in agony, I patted Travis on the head and snuck him yet another patty. He swallowed it in one bite, his big brown eyes begging for more.

I was so exhausted from spreading the diapers that it took me a moment to hear the honking. Geese, thousands of them, started to get up. A solid wall of birds formed like a cloud and began rolling over the fields toward us. The sound of their honking soon covered the plains. "Let's go," T.H. yelled. He threw down the last of his diapers and sprinted back to where we'd left the guns. I stood there, numbed by the sight and sound. I'd never seen or heard so many birds. "Come on," T.H. shouted, "here they come." A rush of adrenalin gave me a second wind. I plowed through the furrows after him.

"Here," he said unbuckling the gun cases and handing me a beautiful Browning over-and-under. "Yew shoot the twelve. Ah'll shoot mah ten." His ten-gauge was the biggest gun I'd ever seen. It looked like a cannon. "Ah'll tell ya when to shoot. First bird's all yours."

I lay down and loaded my gun. T.H. and Travis nestled in behind me. Travis had forgotten all about the spicy sausage. The geese now had his full attention. Like a true champion, his mind was riveted on retrieving. T.H. produced a goose call and started honking. Much to my surprise, a couple dozen birds immediately spun away from the main flock and decoyed right to the diapers. Travis whimpered as he watched them coming in. "Steady, boy, steady," T.H. crooned. Honk, honk, honk. "Steady." Honk, honk. The geese set their wings and were about to land right on top of us. "NOW!!" T.H. shouted.

I sat up, aimed and pulled the trigger. Nothing. "Damn," I said, fumbling with the safety.

"Shoot! Shoot!" yelled T.H. The birds wheeled and started flying back across the fields. I clicked off the safety, raised my gun and fired. At the sound of the shot, Travis burst past me. "Whoa! Whoa!" screamed T.H., knowing I'd missed. Travis ignored him. He splashed across the furrows, faithfully expecting a bird to fall. He must have run half a mile before he stopped and watched the geese fly out of sight. I could understand how he was confused. The geese had practically landed on our heads. How could any of them not fallen?

T.H. was red faced from blowing his whistle. "Back, Trav, Back! Come on back, boy," he kept hollering. When Travis finally returned, he was caked with mud. Saliva slobbered from his empty mouth. He didn't look like much of a star. He flopped into my lap, obviously expecting at least one patty for all his trouble. "Damn, that Trav's got a big heart," T.H. marveled. "Ah'da peed on ya leg if ya'd done that ta me."

"I got mixed up with the safety," I said. "I've never shot this model before."

"Never mind," T.H. said scanning the sky. "Quick, git down. Here come some teal."

I looked up and saw a flock of blue-winged teal high in the sky. Suddenly, they dropped and strafed the pond. The *whoosh* they made as they swept over us sounded like a jet. Then they turned back into the wind, their blue wings glistening in the morning sun. Once again I was mesmerized. I'd never seen such precision. It was like watching the Blue Angels.

"Shoot! Dammit, Shoot!" T.H. yelled. I rolled up into a sitting position and fired wildly at the formation. Travis was off at the sound of my gun. He plunged into the pond. I prayed at least one bird would fall. None did.

Tweet! Tweet! "Back, Trav! Back!" Tweet! Tweet! Lt. Colonel William B. Travis would have been proud of his namesake. Young Trav paddled on. He wasn't about to admit defeat. "There's no bird, daggone it!" T.H. screamed. "Travis! Come back, boy! That damn Yankee missed again!"

Travis's tongue was dragging as he struggled up the bank. It had been a long swim. He stopped next to me, shook himself and plopped his head into my lap. "Ah swear, ah cain't b'lieve this," T.H. said. "That has to be the most forgivin dawg. His daddy would've peed on your leg."

"These birds fly faster than the ones I'm used to," I said. "I haven't been giving them enough of a lead."

"Well git set," T.H. said. "Here come some more geese." Honk, honk. Travis looked up and started to whine. The sky was white with geese. The whole flock turned and decoyed to our diapers. There were hundreds of them. Even I couldn't miss.

Kabooooom! T.H.'s big ten roared. I was so startled by the sound I dropped my gun. Two geese immediately folded and tumbled to the ground. I could see T.H.'s hubris on the rise as Travis instinctively marked both birds. He fetched one, then flawlessly went back and picked up the other. It was a perfect retrieve, one that had all the bragging rights any man could ask for.

T.H. beamed with pride as Travis pranced past me with the second bird. Travis didn't even give me a glance. My spicy sausage couldn't compete with the natural taste of warm goose. This dog was a born retriever, a guaranteed star.

"Ah'm sorry, son," T.H. said, removing the second bird from Travis's smiling mouth, "but Ah had ta shoot. Yew was wreckin mah dawg."

After my dismal showing, I never went back to Texas. We hired a good ol' boy to run our Texas program. He was not an MBA, but he was a crack shot who did an outstanding job selling our brand of conservation to the sportsmen of Texas. He went hunting with T.H. on a regular basis and claimed I was a legend at the Farris 1912; that I played the lead role in one of T.H.'s best "dawg" stories. He said T.H. still can't figure out what a champion like Trav ever saw in a crummy shot like me. Maybe someday I'll call and tell him about the sausage. That would sure add some spice to his story.

Compatible Bedfellows

Sportsmen in the Deep South are, in their own way, America's best conservationists. Thanks to their religious pursuit of hunting and fishing, they live close to the land and have a good understanding of nature. This respect for the out-of-doors, like their love of God, country, and football, is something dutifully passed on from generation to generation. But unlike God, country, and football, hunting and fishing rely on land, lots of land. To pass on this way of life, sportsmen need to protect large areas of wildlife habitat. Superb areas for hunting and fishing were something the sportsmen in the Deep South had always taken for granted. Back in the 1970s, they didn't see the changes coming their way. They'd forgotten Gerald O'Hara's advice to his daughter Scarlet: "Land is the only thing in the world that amounts to anything, for 'tis the only thing in the world that lasts. 'Tis the only thing worth working for, fighting for, dying for, and don't you be forgetting it."

Before the Pascagoula project and the Rivers of the Deep South program, sportsmen along the Gulf viewed conservationists as fuzzy-faced liberals, maybe even communists, who were trying to socialize America. Worse yet, they were mostly Yankees. Once the sportsmen of the South got into saving land themselves, they discovered we weren't quite as bad as they thought and began to realize that what we had been preaching actually made some sense. They could see that their land and the lifestyle it supported were threatened. They knew that if they were going to pass on a hunting and fishing ethic, they were going to have to start protecting it, and they did.

The hook-and-bullet crowd, as Bil Gilbert likes to call them, have played an important role in land conservation. During the 1970s and '80s, TNC did numerous projects with Ducks Unlimited, Quail Unlimited, Trout Unlimited, Boone and Crockett, and American Fisheries. Some of our biggest and best projects came from working with hunt clubs. For example, most of the land that's protected in Albemarle Sound along the North Carolina–Virginia line came from four hunt clubs: Swan, Monkey Island, Currituck, and Pine Island. Farther to the south 50,000 acres of prime marshland was given to TNC by the Santee Hunt Club. Then there was Mike Wright's project with Long Point up on Lake Erie in Canada. The list goes on, but the point is hunters and fishermen make good conservationists. Their focus may be on protecting habitat for a single species like ducks, quail, trout, dove, turkey, or deer, but in saving habitat for one, they're saving it for all.

The most emphatic example I ever saw of this "one for all" attitude was embodied in Toddie Lee Wynne. Toddie Lee was the epitome of a big-time Texas oil man. His silver hair, string tie held together with a big turquoise clasp, big silver belt buckle, Tony Lama boots, gracious home in Dallas, bourbon in one hand and a young, beautiful, very social wife on the other made him the real deal. Toddie Lee had the big hat and the cows, and he was about to get the money to buy more. In the late 1980s we were buying the 11,502 acres from him on Matagorda Island for a cool $13.6 million. To seal the deal, Andy Samson and Chuck Cook, a couple of gifted good ol' boys who ran our Texas Program; Mike Dennis, our general counsel; and I were going out to the island to meet with Toddie Lee at his hunting lodge. To get there, we had to go by boat through the Aransas NWR. On the way over, we counted 17 of the 116 whooping cranes left on this Earth.

Later that evening we were standing around the bar talking about seeing the cranes, and how buying Toddie Lee's piece of Matagorda would play a key role in protecting their winter habitat, when Toddie Lee said, "Boys, let me tell you somethin. There ain't but four species of birds worth saving in Texas: doves, ducks, quail, and turkey. And ya know why? 'Cause they're good eatin, that's why."

That was conservation in Texas. When saving land, there's no such thing as one size fits all. It's the result, not the reason, that counts, "and don't you be forgettin it."

Beebe Tours

WHAT MAKES SPENCER BEEBE ONE OF THE WORLD'S GREAT CONSERVA-
tionists is that in addition to being a tremendous fund-raiser, he actually
knows something about nature. Plus, it doesn't hurt that he looks a lot
like the Sundance Kid. As such, Spencer does not fund-raise by writing
proposals and putting together slide shows. He sells his projects by taking potential donors out into the field where he can show them firsthand
what he's trying to save. The problem is Spencer's not always attuned to
a donor's physical comforts. Go into the field with him and you're likely
to find yourself well off the beaten track and up close and personal with
things that could kill you: bears, snakes, gators, piranha, or most often, a
very angry set of rapids. Robert Redford can vouch for that. When Beebe
took Redford down the Snake River seeking support for TNC's Birds
of Prey preserve, the Sundance Kid got bounced out of the raft into the
rapids. As every movie buff well knows, Sundance can't swim. Fortunately,
Redford can, and did.

Spencer started with TNC in the summer of 1974. He'd just graduated
from the Yale School of Forestry and was searching for a job in conservation. We had an opening in our Northwest field office and Spencer applied.
Spencer was from Portland, looked right, acted right, and knew all the right
people, but would he feel awkward asking friends and family for gifts of
land and money? We offered Spencer the job provided he could raise his
$11,000 starting salary. As it turned out, he had no qualms. He raised the
entire amount almost overnight. In fact, Spencer took great umbrage if any
of his friends or family refused him, which is why very few ever did.

It soon became obvious that in addition to being a good fund-raiser,
Spencer had a rare gift for doing deals. This gift can't be taught; it's

something you're born with. It's part of your DNA. Drop someone with the gift naked out of an airplane anywhere in the world, and at the next project review meeting, they'll be sitting there at the table with a project that's bigger and better than anyone else's. In all my years in land conservation, I've only known a dozen or so people with the gift, and Spencer definitely is one of them.

Spencer, like many of us, started off with a river. Rivers are a good place to get your feet wet. They're significant, threatened, and always lead to something bigger. That means you're three for five before you even step up to the plate. Spencer's river—the Sandy—was a six-mile stretch of cliffs, falls, and forested flats twenty miles east of Portland. Soon after he started, Sandy River projects began showing up at every board meeting. They all had a certain eloquence: clean and neat, with the money in hand.

From the Sandy, Spencer moved to Silver Creek in Idaho. Silver Creek is where Ernest Hemingway lived and fished, and thanks to "Papa" it is recognized as one of the great trout streams in America. Saving Silver Creek meant raising $600,000 to buy two miles of creek, stopping the overgrazing along the creek by adjacent ranchers, and closing down a very prominent fishing club. Working with Henry Little, who was in charge of TNC's Western Regional Office in San Francisco and gifted in his own right, Spencer bought the land, convinced the local ranchers to fence off their fields, and managed to piss off the entire membership of the prominent fishing club by terminating its lease, not that either Henry or Spencer ever doubted their decision. They were both superb fly fisherman who knew closing the club was a key part of preserving the creek.

After Silver Creek Spencer was becoming recognized within TNC not only as a rising star, but also as something of a loose cannon. He moved fast and his penchant for big projects and uncanny ability to woo donors made some people within TNC very nervous, most notably Dr. Bob. Dr. Bob was aghast we'd spent so much time and money protecting a creek for rainbow trout, which were hardly endangered. Still, saving Silver Creek had put TNC on the map in Idaho and much of the mountain west.

While most of us paid lip service to Dr. Bob's ever-evolving system for classifying and quantifying biotic diversity, Spencer openly ignored it.

He went by his gut, and, loose cannon or not, kept hitting big, important projects like Pine Butte Swamp in Montana and Sycan Marsh in south-central Oregon. These two projects sealed his reputation as a star who didn't let Dr. Bob's system get in the way of a good deal.

In 1979 Mike Wright resigned as the director of TNC's International Program to accept a position with the World Wildlife Fund. It was a good move for Mike. TNC's strong focus on saving land within the United States meant Mike never had much support for expanding TNC's International Program. Many of us at TNC viewed international conservation as a bunch of Ivy Leaguers jetting around in white pith helmets and pressed khakis telling our "little brown brothers" in Central and South America how they should be saving their natural resources.

Still, there was a growing interest in international conservation among TNC's board, which by then included a handful of CEOs of international corporations, so we needed to find a new international director. The most logical candidate was Spencer. After graduating from Williams he'd spent four years in the Peace Corps working primarily in Central America. He'd maintained many of his contacts from those days, and after six years in the Northwest producing a steady stream of world-class projects, he was ready for a new challenge. In 1980 Spencer stuffed his wife Janie, their young three kids, and Buffalo, their golden retriever, into their Volkswagen bus and headed east.

From the very start, Spencer took a different approach to international conservation. Rather than sending Ivy Leaguers south, he started bringing our "little brown brothers and sisters" north. This particular group of Latinos and Latinas were smart, funny, bilingual, loaded with doctorial degrees, and loved to party. Pat's old Friday afternoon happy hour soon was reincarnated as salsa music and rumba dancing at the International Program offices. Spencer's plan for these very talented *compadres* in conservation was to see how TNC operated in America, figure out what might work in their own countries, and then go back to start their own programs.

The *compadres* liked coming to project review meetings. With all the yelling, arm waving, posturing, and critiquing, there was a Latin flair to

them, but for the most part, Spencer's gang wouldn't be doing land acquisition. In Latin America, especially Mexico, TNC's motto, "Land Conservation Through Private Action," wouldn't work. Private ownership of land
was very limited. Land-use decisions were made mostly by governments.
According to Spencer, if TNC was going to have an impact on conservation south of the border, it was going to have to develop new techniques
based primarily on governmental and community-based initiatives.

After two years of experimenting in Mexico and Bolivia, Spencer
decided that what TNC's International Program really needed was a
national model. He chose Costa Rica. From a natural standpoint, Costa
Rica's vast array of deciduous forests, swamp forests, rain forests, cloud
forests, *holillo* forests, riparian forests, oak groves, mangrove swamps, her-
baceous swamps, *paramos,* and coral reefs, made this little Central American country about the size of West Virginia an ecological Eden. From a
practical standpoint, Costa Rica had an ideal year-round climate, beautiful beaches, a democratic government, no standing army, friendly *ticos,*
cheap booze, and plenty of good Cuban cigars. Most important, it had a
nascent conservation movement led by Alvaro Ugalde.

Alvaro Ugalde was the director of Costa Rica's *Servicio de Parques
Nacionalis,* politically very well connected, and like Avery Wood in Mississippi, wanted to do something big. As a trained biologist, Alvaro fully
recognized the importance of protecting Costa Rica's vast array of biotic
diversity and felt the most effective way to do that was by highlighting
its economic importance. While Avery pushed creating a system of wildlife management areas to protect Mississippi's game and fish "bidness,"
Alvaro claimed a world-class system of national parks would make Costa
Rica the leader in ecotourism. Now what he needed was a way to prove it,
and Spencer had just the answer. He proposed TNC raise $6 million to
expand three existing parks and create three new ones along Costa Rica's
spectacular Pacific coast. Alvaro jumped at the offer. "Drinking rum and
Coca-Cola, working for the Yankee dollar," was sweet music to his ears.

With a plan in place, Spencer started inviting his major donors to the
international program to go on a ten-day boat trip down the west coast of
Costa Rica. They all said yes. When it came to fund-raising, Pat warned,

"Never put all your eggs in one basket." Now Spencer had all his eggs in one boat. Realizing he might have gone a bit overboard, he asked Ruth and me if we'd come along. Ruth spoke Spanish and was very good with older donors. I could help evaluate the projects and, if things got off track, provide some comic relief.

The group that met in Miami on January 31, 1983, was definitely the A-team. Along with Spencer and his wife Janie, there was Chuck Hedlund, former head of international operations for Exxon, and his wife, Helen Marie; Joe Van Vleck and his wife, Louise Moore, heiress to the Dixie Cup fortune; Jean Vollum, whose husband, Howard, had created the electronics titan Tektronix, and their son Danny; Sophie Engelhard, middle daughter of Charles Engelhard, the world-famous industrialist who Ian Fleming used as the model for *Dr. No*; Frances Beinecke, a member of the Yale Beineckes and a driving force behind the National Resources Defense Council; Dolly Leonhardt, the perfume queen from Texas, and her daughter Tudy; Eliot Porter, the Ansel Adams of color photography; John Craighead, the grizzly and raptor expert, and his wife Margaret; and Ernesto Barriga, a tropical rain forest ecologist from Colombia. At our "Welcome Aboard" dinner at the Gran Hotel on Cultural Square in the heart of downtown San Jose, Alvaro Ugalde was the guest of honor. Alvaro set up a big map detailing the west coast of Costa Rica and sailed us through our trip from Santa Rosa Park on the north to Corcovado in the south. Then Chuck Headland, as chairman of TNC's International Committee, advised us all to get a good night's sleep, as the bus for Puntarenas, where we'd meet the boat, would be leaving right after breakfast the next morning. It was all very exciting.

At breakfast, however, there was bad news. We were going to have to postpone the trip for a day. The boat had been impounded by the Nicaraguan authorities. Its papers weren't in order, but Alvaro assured us not to worry. He had planned an exciting excursion to Irazú Volcano National Park, locally known as "nature's deadly powder keg." Situated about an hour by bus from San Jose, Irazú stood at 11,260 feet above sea level and had a paved road leading right to the summit. We all piled onto the bus. The fact that the road was paved was the best thing that could be said about it. Our little bus wound around and around up Mount Irazú. By the time we got to the top, Helen Marie Hedlund was suffering from a severe case of vertigo. The only way we could get her back down was to stretch her out on the floor of the bus, and even then she was terribly ill. Watching poor Helen Marie rolling around on the floor made us all queasy. When we finally made it back to the hotel, Helen Marie was put to bed while the rest of us headed for the bar.

The next day there was more bad news. The boat was still stuck in Nicaragua, but again Alvaro assured us not to worry. He had planned another exciting trip. This time we were going to visit a community-run coffee plantation. The words "exciting" and "coffee plantation" should never be used in the same sentence. Despite an enlightened talk by Alvaro on how these small rolling fields represented the best of both development and conservation, the donors were getting restless. This was not the expedition they'd signed on for.

Back at the Gran Hotel, Tudy, who'd slept through the trip to the coffee plantation, sashayed into the bar wearing next to nothing. Her tight T-shirt, short shorts, and spiked heels were highlighted by gold earrings, a gold necklace, gold bracelets, and above her right heel, a gold anklet. Tudy announced she was going to take a walk to San Jose's central market place. Would anyone care to come along? Ernesto, the courtly Colombian, volunteered. I grabbed Danny Vollum, who at six-foot-two and a very solid 220 pounds could run interference, and said that we too would like to visit the market. Strolling through the streets of San Jose, Tudy could have passed for a young Jayne Mansfield walking down Rodeo Drive. People couldn't take their eyes off her. Inside the market it was dark, crowded, and full of little alleys and cubby holes. Even though the *ticos* were reputed to be friendly, Tudy was so hot and the gold so alluring we hadn't gone twenty feet before two police officers stopped us. They were polite but firm. They told Ernesto that Tudy was creating such a commotion they couldn't guarantee our safety. They would drive us back to the Gran hotel. A disappointed buzz rippled through the crowd as we hustled Tudy into the police car. When we reached the hotel, we were greeted by a favorable omen. A bush in the plaza had caught fire. Flames were shooting twenty feet into the air. Sure enough, when we entered the bar, our crew was in high spirits. The boat had been released from Nicaragua. We would be leaving first thing in the morning for Puntarenas.

Due to a blown tire, it was late afternoon the next day before our bus pulled up to the pier in Puntarenas. Scanning the harbor, the donors expected to see a sleek, stylish luxury liner with comfortable cabins, individual bathrooms, and a crew dressed in short-sleeve shirts with epaulets, neatly pressed Bermuda shorts, and white knee socks. After all, they were the A-team. But the only boat bobbing in the harbor was an old tub badly in need of a paint job. Surely this couldn't be our boat. It was.

While working on projects around the Sea of Cortez the previous year, Spencer had met Tim Means, the owner/operator of Baja Expeditions. Tim was an avid conservationist who strongly supported Spencer's program, so rather than looking for a boat in Costa Rica, Spencer asked Tim to send down his boat, the *Don Jose,* a fifty-footer Tim had built himself. Ruth and I were sharing a cabin with Spencer and Janie. It was so cramped, hot, and uncomfortable we lugged our mattresses up onto the deck. Most everyone else did the same. If the cabins were bad, the bathrooms were worse. There were only two for all of us and they were like something you'd find on a tuna boat: small, dark, with showers that didn't drain properly. There was always three or four inches of used soapy water sloshing around the floor. The *Don Jose* had been designed for day trips around the Sea of Cortez, not a ten-day cruise down the west coast of Costa Rica, but to Spencer a boat was a boat and the price was right. It never occurred to him the A-team might expect more.

The one saving grace was a well-stocked bar manned by a comely German lass who made a mean margarita. We gathered on the upper deck, drinks in hand, to watch a magnificent tropical sun set into the Pacific. Suddenly there was a tremendous roar from the engines. Immediately, we all were engulfed by a plume of gritty, noxious diesel soot. We drained our drinks, wiped ourselves off with our "Bienvenidos al Don Jose" cocktail napkins, and headed back to the bar.

All that night we motored north. The following morning, Spencer announced we were going to get back on schedule by making a twenty-four-hour power run north to Santa Rosa Park on the Nicaraguan border. That announcement, along with the cabins and bathrooms, caused a mini-mutiny. Chuck took Spencer aside and told him nobody wanted to be stuck on the boat all day. Eliot Porter had pictures to take, the serious birders wanted to get into the rain forests, and everybody wanted to walk the glorious white, sandy beaches. Spencer relented. We were approaching Cabo Velas, one of the areas proposed for a new park. We could stop there, but before anybody went ashore, Spencer wanted to make sure the Zodiacs wouldn't have trouble landing in the surf.

Once we'd anchored, Spencer and one member of our Mexican crew got into a Zodiac and motored toward shore. Due to some miscommunication, Eliot and another crew member came whizzing by them. The next thing we knew, there was eighty-year-old Eliot rolling around in the surf. By the time Spencer fished him out, poor Eliot was bruised, but not broken, or so we thought. While we were patching Eliot up, Jean Vollum decided to go for a swim. The next thing we knew, there was Jean with a big smile trolling past the *Don Jose*. The crew had tied a rope around her waist and was towing her behind the Zodiac. We all shuddered, Jean looked like giant bait just waiting to be snapped up by a great white shark.

The next morning, there was more bad news. Eliot, who before becoming one of the world's great photographers had received a medical degree from Harvard, informed us that during his roll in the surf, he'd twisted his intestine into a knot and now was suffering from a full blockage. He would have to get to a hospital immediately. Via ship to shore, Alvaro arranged for a small plane to meet him and Eliot in Nosara. It would fly them to San Jose, where Alvaro would get Eliot priority seating on a flight to the States. Chuck Hedlund carefully laid Eliot's mattress in the bottom of the Zodiac to ease his ride. As it pulled away, we all were surprised to see Alvaro lying on the mattress while Elliot bounced along on the hard metal seat up front. This trip was turning into a full-blown disaster.

Sophie Engelhard had brought along a diary. After five days she hadn't written a word. Sophie had a great sense of humor and, despite all of our mishaps, seemed to be having a good time so I asked her if she'd like me to fill in her diary for her. After all, what was staff for? "It's about time," she said. "Just make sure I sound smart and interesting. If it's any good, I'll read it to the group during cocktails."

The diary turned into a compilation of whimsical fantasies lampooning all of our trials and tribulations. Tudy being crowned *Senorita San Jose* and given a police escort. Louise, the Dixie Cup heiress, raving about the luxurious accommodations of a Beebe Tour. Jean becoming demoralized because, unlike Tudy, she'd failed to attract a single shark. Ernesto lecturing on tropical rain forests from twenty miles at sea. Frances, having vowed never to get into one of the showers, was now best friends with Dolly, the perfume queen. And, of course, Alvaro taking tender care of Eliot by offering to share his mattress. Sophie's reading that night turned out to be a big hit. After a few margaritas it was easy to laugh at ourselves.

The highlight of the trip came two days later. A group of us were in the Zodiacs watching the birds on Cabo Blanco, a big rock island just off Cabo Velas that had turned white from bird droppings. Ernesto, who pronounced all his *y*'s like *j*'s, was just showing us all another "jello bird" when Chuck Hedland looked back and saw the *Don Jose* being boarded by a ragtag group in a PT boat with a big gun on the front. At first we feared they were pirates. Then Chuck refocused his 10 x 50, $1,195 Leica binoculars and saw it was the Costa Rican navy. We rushed back to the rescue. Interestingly, the navy was staffed mostly by Asians, all of whom were transfixed by Tudy, who was sunbathing on the rear deck.

With Alvaro gone, we were left to fend for ourselves. It didn't go well. The navy was arresting us for harassing the birds on Cabo Blanco, a protected reserve. Their captain said he was taking command of the *Dos Jose* and bringing us into Cabo Velas. Spencer kept telling them in his patchy Spanish that we were working with the government and kept dropping names from the *Presidente* on down. After checking all of our passports, the navy captain demanded to meet with our captain.

That was going to be interesting. Since we traveled at night, our captain slept all day. Except for Spencer, none of us had ever seen him. A little Mexican with a pot belly emerged from the wheelhouse. He was wearing a clean white T-shirt, but shreds of toilet paper were stuck all over his face. Obviously, in his haste to get cleaned up, his razor had run amuck. Still, with his head held high and his pride intact, our captain ceremoniously walked the plank over to the navy boat. Unlike Nicaragua, this time his papers were in order and we were released with a respectful salute and a stern warning to stay out of restricted areas.

Chuck had seen enough. Forget trying to make it all way down to Corcovado. Instead, we'd spend the last two days swimming, hiking, and birding at Manuel Antonio, one of the most beautiful beaches in all of Central America, and the crown jewel in Costa Rica's emerging national parks system. Spencer was crushed. Corcovado, a world-class tropical rain forest on the Osa peninsula just north of Panama, was known for its big wild cats, and big cats were tremendous fund-raisers.

Staying at Manuel Antonio proved to be the right decision. While everything for the first eight days had gone wrong, the last two days at Manual Antonio made it all right. We swam, lay on the beach, hiked, and saw enough birds, beetles, butterflies, monkeys, sloths, and boa con-strictors to make any donor happy. Back at the Gran Hotel for our fare-well dinner, Chuck announced that Eliot was alive and well at a hospital in Houston. Then he turned to Alvaro and told him that due to what we'd seen of Costa Rica over the last ten days, The Nature Conservancy's International Program was prepared to commit $6 million to what we hoped under his leadership would become the world's strongest system of national parks and protected areas.

Alvaro met that challenge, and then some. Since our trip, Costa Rica has created a world-class system of national parks that serve as a model for other developing countries. In addition, this system of parks and reserves has made Costa Rica the conservation capital of the world. Today, Costa Rica is the most popular spot for conventions, conferences, and other gatherings regarding international conservation and ecotour-ism. It was Beebe Tours that laid the foundation for this success. As Yvon Chouinard, the founder of Patagonia, once noted, "The adventure doesn't start until something goes wrong." We had a great adventure and to com-memorate it, Jean Vollum made up little silver pins in the shape of oak leaves that read, "Beebe Tours: I Survived." Once again, the loose cannon had hit the mark.

—◆—

Dancing with John D.

WHEN AN INDIVIDUAL MAKES A DONATION, IT'S A DIRECT TRANSFER OF wealth. The donor instantly becomes poorer. This fact tends to limit major gifts from individuals. Foundations, on the other hand, have to give it away. It's what they do. So when raising money, it's much easier and more fun dealing with foundations.

Back in the 1970s and '80s, foundations were TNC's best source of funding. Unlike today when all the major foundations are run by professional staffs, back then we usually were dealing directly with members of the families who'd set up the foundations. Many of them were on TNC's board. If we wanted a grant from the Dayton Foundation, we went to see Wally Dayton. If it was the Rockefeller Foundation, Mrs. Rockefeller; the Surdna Foundation, John Andrus (which is Surdna spelled backwards); the R. K. Mellon Foundation, the Mellon boys; the Hewlett Packard Foundation, Bill Hewlett and David Packard: the Goodhill Foundation, Ms. Catherine Ordway; the Charles Engelhard Foundation, Sophie Engelhard. Their foundations had to give money to somebody so why not TNC? They knew us, they liked what we were doing, and most important, they were no poorer for doing it. Giving money to TNC for land conservation was fun and made them feel good.

Not that it was always that easy. When Pat became president of TNC, his favorite book became the *Foundation Directory*. He carried it around with him everywhere he went. Whenever he had a free moment on a plane, train, or even in the men's room, he'd be poring over it. That's how Pat discovered the John D. and Catherine T. MacArthur Foundation.

In the late 1960s John D. MacArthur was the sole owner of the nation's largest privately owned insurance company and one of the wealthiest people in America. Around that time, John D.'s lawyers must have advised him to set up the foundation to shield his billion-plus dollars from estate taxes. Today, everybody knows about the MacArthur Foundation, but when John D. was alive, it remained pretty much below the radar. In the insurance business you make your money by collecting premiums, not paying out claims, and foundation or no foundation, paying out money did not come easily to John D. Rumor had it he was as tight as a frog's behind, but Pat had discovered a way he thought we could get to him.

About the time he set up his foundation, John D. had retired from the insurance business, bought the Colonnades Beach Hotel in Palm Beach, moved to Florida, which has no estate tax, and set out buying more than 100,000 acres of land all across the Sunshine State. Pat figured some of that 100,000 acres had to be wetlands. Heck, most of Florida was a wetland. If any of this property was in the foundation, which seemed likely, we could show John D. how he could meet the foundation's disbursement requirements by giving appreciated land rather than cash to TNC, and for this, he would be eternally grateful. Pat set up a meeting in Florida and asked me to come along.

We were meeting at the Colonnades. Ever the frugal Scotsman, John D. ran his businesses, including the foundation, from a table in the hotel's coffee shop. When we came in, he eyed us suspiciously. Once we were settled, he asked if we would like a cup of coffee. We said that would be nice, then Pat launched into his plan. John D.'s face immediately lit up, especially when we told him that the value of land given to conservation is not lost; that we'd discovered it seeps over to properties around it, which in this case would be his. With that John D. pulled out a stack of maps and for the next hour we went over his holdings piece by piece. The one question he kept asking over and over was, "What do you think it's worth?"

When John D. excused himself to take a call, Pat turned to me and said, "Pick up your stuff. We're getting out of here."

"Why?"

"Because this old fox's not going to give us anything. He's just looking for a free appraisal."

When he came back, Pat told John D. it had been a pleasure meeting him, but we had to catch a plane. Knowing Pat was on to him, John D. gave us a wry smile and granted that catching our plane was important. Then, as we got up to leave, he said, "Say, aren't you boys forgetting something?"

We looked around, wondering what we could have left, whereupon he handed us the bill for two cups of coffee. You had to love the guy.

Up until recently, foundations have been the province of the very rich, but that's not true anymore. As the baby boomers hit retirement, there has been a huge increase in small family foundations. In addition, seeing a niche that needed to be filled, Fidelity, Vanguard, and most of the other major money managers have set up charitable gift funds that give even relatively regular people a vehicle for charitable giving much like a foundation. If you're working for a nonprofit, chances are you know somebody who either has a charitable foundation or is on the board of one. If you have a good project, use your contacts to find a foundation and then get the trustees out on the land to watch the sun set during a full moon. They'll never regret it, and neither will you. There are a lot of worthy causes, but you can't beat saving land.

One final note: Pat ended up having the last laugh on John D. MacArthur. In 1985 in recognition for all his work on behalf of land conservation, the McArthur Foundation gave Pat one of its "genius grants." John D., whose policy had been cashed on January 6, 1978, would have enjoyed that. Watching those two dance around in the Colonnades coffee shop, Pat angling for a grant and John D. sniffing out a free appraisal, was like watching the mating dance of two whooping cranes. They were of the same rare breed. Pat was John D.'s type of genius.

The Coachella Solution

By the spring of 1981, Jim Watt, President Ronald Reagan's secretary of the interior, had made it quite clear he was no fan of the environmental movement and would do everything in his power to kill it. The irony was that this attitude soon made Watt the greatest fund-raiser in the history of conservation. Concerned Americans, conservatives and liberals alike, began digging deep into their wallets to help save land, and nobody dug deeper than the Richard King Mellon Foundation. From their little offices hidden away in the Alleghenies, the Mellons kept pouring millions upon millions into the protection of wildlife habitat.

The largest recipient of these funds was The Nature Conservancy. Over a ten-year period, the R. K. Mellon Foundation gave TNC $55 million for land acquisition. These gifts came with four conditions: First, all projects had to be approved by the foundation. Second, all money had to be used to buy land. Third, all deals had to be leveraged. And fourth, all funds had to be rolled over. These conditions made the foundation's project approval process tougher than our own, but that was OK. The five trustees who ran the foundation were much bigger thinkers than we were and had a far better understanding of how to make money work.

We first saw this with the Rivers of the Deep South program. Our original proposal was for a million dollars of seed money for each of the five rivers we'd identified. By leveraging and rolling over this $5 million, we figured we could create five new wildlife refuges that would save 150,000 acres of bottomland hardwoods. That would have been the biggest land conservation program TNC had ever undertaken, but by the time the trustees got through with our proposal, it had turned into a $15 million grant that was going to save 450,000 acres. Drew Mathieson, the family's chief financial officer and a trustee of the foundation, once told me, "The reason we give TNC so much money is so you can afford to fail, and knowing that, you never will."

In late 1982 Pat came to see me. Based on the success of the Rivers program and Watt's cutbacks in federal funding, the trustees wanted to up the ante. They were prepared to give TNC $5 million a year for five years to create a national wetlands program, only there was a catch: it would be nice if one of the projects was around Palm Springs. That came as no surprise. Whenever possible, the trustees liked to create a major preserve in communities where members of the family had a home. That way, they'd have a constant reminder of what their grants were saving and in this case, one of the boys had just bought a condominium in a new development outside of Palm Springs. "With Watt cutting all funding for land acquisition," Pat said, "this grant would help TNC get through his time as secretary, so see if you could find a project somewhere around Palm Springs."

"Pat," I said, knowing his limited knowledge of the natural world, "what the trustees are proposing is a wetlands program. In case you haven't noticed, Palm Springs is in the middle of a desert."

"Necessity is the mother of invention," Pat said. "There must be something out there."

I called Steve McCormick, the director of TNC's California state program. Steve had graduated from Berkeley in 1972 with a law degree, but quickly decided he didn't want to be a lawyer. Instead, he became TNC's director of stewardship for California. Steve was a good fit. As a San Francisco native and a pretty good amateur botanist, he looked right, acted right, and had no qualms about asking people for land and money. As an unexpected bonus, we soon discovered that although it was somewhat muted by his legal training, Steve, like Spencer, also had the gift for doing deals. Within five years he'd become the California state director and was putting together major projects like Santa Rosa Bighorn Sheep, Kern River, and Dozier Vernal Pools. In addition, Steve had recruited a state board that in terms of work, wisdom, and wealth rivaled, some would say even surpassed, the national board.

When I told Steve about the Mellon trustees' desire to create a national wetlands program, he started rattling off rivers: McCloud, Consumes, Kern, Sacramento, and, of course, all of the wetlands around San Francisco Bay. I told him I was sure we could look at those areas, but was there any chance he could come up with something around Palm Springs? There was a long silence on the other end of the line. Finally, understanding that my knowledge of the natural world was about two birds and a tree above Pat's, Steve said, "You realize, of course, it's a desert."

"That's what I told Pat," I said, "but one of the Mellon boys just bought a place outside of Palm Springs and Pat thinks it would give the proposal some extra weight if we had a project out there. Take a look around and see what you can come up with."

In 1980, at the urging of local environmentalists and anti-growth advocates, the U.S. Fish and Wildlife Service had listed the Coachella Valley fringe-toed lizard as a threatened species. This cute little reptile had evolved adaptations that made it uniquely suited for living in the harsh desert habitat of the Coachella Valley, an area that includes Palm Springs. With its shovel-shaped head and flat body, the lizard could avoid the scorching midday heat of the desert sun by burrowing itself under the fine sand of the ever-shifting dunes. Once in the sand, a countersunk lower jaw, eyelids that overlap and blink in two directions, flaps over its ears, and nostrils that worked like valves prevented sand from getting into any of its orifices and lungs. Back on the surface, elongated scales over the lizard's hind feet served as snowshoes that kept it from sinking into the sand as it sprinted away from any number of predators. Hence the name, "fringe-toed lizard."

Despite all of these adaptations, the little lizard was having a rough time of it. Coachella Valley was one of the fastest-growing areas in America, and by 1980, 220 of the lizard's original range of 270 square miles had been developed. Due to the sand fences, trees, and shrubs that acted as wind breaks for these developments, of the 50 square miles that remained undeveloped, only 19 continued to receive the fine "blow-wind" sand that formed the dunes critical to the lizard's survival. Compounding the problem, much of the remaining undeveloped land had been stockpiled by developers who'd bought it just before the lizard had been declared "threatened" under the Endangered Species Act. These developers had been caught completely off guard. Before the lizard was listed, getting approval from the county for their development plans had been a slam dunk. Now, everything was on hold. With the meter running on loans they'd taken to purchase these properties, their development plans were quickly becoming financially infeasible. Something had to happen. The "French toast lizard," as they'd come to call it, was killing them.

"It's a war out there," Steve said, after he'd gotten the lay of the land. "The developers are ready to go to court, the environmentalists say they'll do whatever it takes to make sure the restrictions on development under the Endangered Species Act are enforced, and the local, state, and federal agencies are caught in the middle. They can't do anything. It's a huge problem, and now they want TNC to solve it."

"What are you going to do?" I asked him.

"I've set up a steering committee consisting of all the interested parties and told them The Nature Conservancy could design a preserve that would provide suitable habitat for the lizard, but if we did that, they'd all have to work to make the preserve a reality. Everyone likes the concept of creating one preserve and the Riverside County Board of Supervisors, who control all development in the valley, just passed a resolution supporting the creation of a preserve. But I've got to tell you, with these people, talking about creating a preserve is one thing, actually doing it is something else. So now what?"

"Try to find a project somewhere within the proposed preserve that could stand on its own," I told him, "and we'll take it to the trustees for a seed grant. If they approve it, at least we'll have some skin in the game and that might give us some traction. Who knows, maybe all these people are desperate enough where you can pull them all together. If not, we've got a nice preserve outside of Palm Springs that'll keep the Mellons happy."

The San Andreas Fault has one redeeming feature: some of the Southwest's most impressive desert oases are found where groundwater flows to the surface along the fracture. Set in the Indio Hills just to the east of Palm Springs, Thousand Palms Oasis is one such spot. The oasis was owned by an old desert rat named Paul Wilhelm. On March 18, 1905, Paul's father traded a new buckboard wagon and two handsome mules for the property. According to Paul, on their way to record the deed, Al Thornburg, the previous owner, said to Paul's father, "Maybe I let the oasis go too freely; maybe it will amount to something one day." To which Paul's father replied, "Whatever it will become, it is too beautiful to belong to one man. Perhaps one day it will be a park where everyone can enjoy its cool refreshments and its peace and quiet."

That day had come. Due to Paul's strong desire to honor his father's wish, Steve was able to secure options on the oasis and two adjacent properties. The total was 2,383 acres at a cost of $2 million. At least we had a "wetland" we could bring to the trustees, but we were still a long way from solving the lizard problem. While Steve was working with Paul on tying up the Thousand Palms Oasis, TNC's biologists had concluded that to create a preserve that would protect the lizard, we'd have to acquire all of the remaining 19 square miles of habitat. "The cost of that land's going to be around $25 million," Steve said. "And nobody—not the environmentalists, not the governmental agencies, and certainly not the developers—has bought into that. What's our next step?"

"It's showtime!" I said. "I'm sending out the movie guys."

The movie guys were Jon Huberth, an independent filmmaker, and his partner Nick Doob, an Oscar-winning cameraman. When we got into the Rivers of the Deep South, I'd hired Huberth and Doob to produce a twenty-minute documentary I could use to help sell the program. While the film was good, the making of it was even better. What we discovered was if we put people in front of a camera and let them talk long enough, eventually they would say something we could use to help make our case. Even if everything they said was negative, skillful editing and the right camera angles could make it sound positive. Better yet, when people who thought they said one thing actually saw themselves on the big screen saying something else, they didn't seem to mind. In fact, since it made them look positive, enlightened, and bright, they came to believe that's what they really meant.

The twenty-minute film Huberth and Doob produced for the Coachella Valley was called *An Oasis in Time*. It premiered on November 30,

1983, at the Palm Springs Civic Center. The trustees of the Richard King Mellon Foundation, which had approved TNC's purchase of the oasis and had made a $2 million seed grant to the Coachella Valley Preserve, were in attendance, as were the press from all eight locales within Riverside County, representatives from all the governmental agencies, environmentalists, developers, civic leaders, and a standing-room-only crowd of concerned citizens. Steve and I had helped edit the film and thought everything sounded all right, but we had no idea how it was going to play in Palm Springs. Although everyone on Steve's steering committee had professed support for the preserve, this was the first time many of them would be exposed to its 19-square-mile size and upwards of $25 million cost. When those figures hit the screen, there was a good chance the roof of the Civic Center might blow off, and TNC, along with the Mellon trustees, would be run out of town.

The film opened with Paul Wilhelm standing next to a babbling brook in the cool shade of Thousand Palms Oasis. While songbirds chirped in the background, Paul told the story of how his dad had traded for the oasis, how his family had always loved the quiet and peace of the desert, and how pleased he was that this special place now was the centerpiece for the new preserve. Then came Paul's nephew Ric, a bearded semi-hermit Huberth and Doob had found wandering around the desert. Ric, in very lay terms, explained the ecology of the valley and got a big laugh when he flicked his eyes and wiggled his body imitating how the fringe-toed lizard used its adaptations to deal with the sand.

Ric's appearance in the film was followed by representatives from all the different factions: environmentalists, developers, and the governmental agencies. Due to Huberth's editing and Doob's camera wizardry, every one of them strongly endorsed the preserve and pledged their support. Notwithstanding the context in which it might have been said, the common consensus onscreen was, "If this preserve is not created now, by the coming of the next century, all of the land in the valley will be developed."

Then there was Steve. While lacking Spencer Beebe's Robert Redford good looks, Steve possessed an exceptional on-camera presence. He appeared calm, confident, and very reassuring. He started by taking the heat off the much-maligned little creature by explaining how this preserve wasn't just about saving the fringe-toed lizard, it was about protecting a natural system, one that benefited any number of species, including man. "The Endangered Species Act protects species," Steve said. "It doesn't protect habitat. That's what we do. At The Nature Conservancy we design and create preserves that protect entire natural systems. For that reason, we are the ones most qualified to create this preserve, and working with all of you, we will create it."

There was no mention that we'd never tackled a land assembly this complex or raised $25 million for one project, or that creating this preserve would be the conservation equivalent of putting a man on the moon. Steve made it sound like just another day at the office. He could have been the spokesman for NASA. Sure it seems impossible, but don't worry, TNC can do it. We're going to get you there, and we're going to bring you back home. Coachella, we have liftoff.

Rather than wrangling, name calling, and the general animosity that had marked most public meetings about Coachella Valley over the last two years, *An Oasis in Time* was met with a standing ovation. At that point we were committed, and it was no casual commitment. Even though all thirty-five members of the steering committee had professed support for the preserve, it turned out they all had different objectives. But then the devil is always in the details, and although it took him four years and the wisdom of Solomon, Steve was able to deliver on his promise. He got them there and brought them home.

By 1986, after dozens of long and difficult negotiations with individual landowners, Steve had put together a 13,000-acre preserve that started in the upper watershed, ran down the washes, flowed through Thousand Palms Oasis, and settled in the valley floor, where the finely ground-up sand was constantly shifting into blow-wind dunes. To pay for all of this land, Steve had raised $2 million from private donors in California, which was used to roll over the Mellon's initial $2 million seed grant; $10 million from the U.S. Fish and Wildlife Service, $5 million of which was a special congressional appropriation for protection of the fringe-toed lizard (Watt was gone by then and Palm Springs was Reagan country); $5 million from the Bureau of Land Management, which Steve was able to secure through a series of very complex land exchanges with Ed Hastie, the head of BLM for California; $1 million from the California State Wildlife Conservation Board; and, much to everyone's amazement, including their own, $7 million from the developers in Riverside County.

This $7 million came from the mitigation fees every developer had to pay in order to get their projects approved. In short, for every acre of development that was approved anywhere in Riverside County, a $600 fee had to be paid into a fund for the creation of the preserve. Rumor had it you could hear the developers squealing "that damned French toast lizard!" all the way to the planning board, but in the end, they all came out smiling. In fact, everybody came out smiling. They all got what they wanted: environmentalists, developers, and governmental agencies. As a bonus, since everyone had some skin in the game, the Coachella Preserve didn't have to wait three generations to be fully accepted as a vital part of the community. It achieved that status on day one. As one of the county supervisors noted at the dedication ceremony, "In fifty years this preserve is going to be Riverside County's Central Park."

What TNC got was a perfect model. After fifteen years we'd finally figured out all the pieces that had to fit together to create a major preserve. It was such a good model, in fact, that I sent Huberth and Doob out to make a follow-up film. In it they had all of the players explain just what they had done, why they had done it, and what they had learned from doing it. We called the film *The Coachella Solution,* and with that model, we honestly felt there was no natural area in America we couldn't save. What made it more exciting was that now we had the means to do it. We had the people. As part of the National Wetlands Program, all of our state offices had identified areas they wanted to protect. We had the money. We'd been able to roll over Mellon's Rivers of the Deep South grant and were in the process of rolling over the National Wetlands grant so soon we'd be sitting on $40 million for land acquisition. We had the projects, and even Dr. Bob was smiling. Finally, the state offices were using the data generated by his natural heritage programs as the basis for designing preserves. We were loaded, locked, and ready to fire. What could possibly go wrong?

One Piece at a Time

ONE OF THE THINGS THAT MADE THE COACHELLA SOLUTION UNIQUE was that we publicly laid out our total plan for the preserve ahead of time. Normally, we wouldn't do that. When putting together a large, complicated assembly like Coachella, it's smarter to let the preserve evolve on its own over time. With Coachella, we didn't have a choice. The fringe-toed lizard was a big public problem that required an immediate, publicly acceptable solution. Still, it was a huge gamble packing everyone who'd be directly affected into the Civic Center and showing them our entire plan. If one person had jumped up and shouted, "You're not taking my land," things easily could have gotten out of hand.

Usually, it's better to focus on one piece at a time. In the "bundle of sticks" that make up the ownership of a piece of land, there's always a few sticks missing, bent, or broken. Publicly presenting all the properties in an assembly at one time means having to address all of these individual problems at once, and doing that is a good way to derail a project before it ever gets started. Plus, presenting a grand plan can upset people. They see a big map on the wall colored green and they get nervous. Who's going to pay for it? Who's going to manage it? How is it going to be used? If part of that green is land they own, they get particularly nervous. Often their first reaction is "over my dead body." Even if they are willing sellers, you can end up bidding against yourself, because once they know you're committed to acquiring their land, each of them will want a better deal than the next guy. That's human nature.

Working one piece at a time lets people get used to the process of creating a preserve, and more important, it gives them a chance to become part of it. Instead of you going to them, you want them coming to you. It's always easier to work out a deal if adding a parcel of land to the preserve is the owner's idea, not yours.

Starting with the Mianus River Gorge, TNC has done a lot of assemblies. One of the best was the Big Bend in Florida. Edging the extreme northeast corner of the Gulf of Mexico, this combination of state parks, national wildlife refuges, water management district preserved lands, and state wildlife management areas has protected the heart of 200 miles of coastline that has been called the wildest land left in the Sunshine State. Dick Ludington, TNC's representative in Florida during most of the 1970s and 1980s, was a gifted deal maker and the person most responsible for protecting the Big Bend. If Dick had gone to a public meeting in the early 1970s , hung a map on the wall, and said, "Here's my plan for protecting more than 300,000 acres along these 200 miles of coast," he and TNC would have been laughed out of the state. Instead, Dick locked his map away in a drawer and started pecking away.

In 1986 when Governor Bob Graham signed Florida's $250 million "Save Our Coasts" program into law, the director of natural resources came to Dick and said, "You know, I just realized if the state could acquire that 65,000 acres Procter and Gamble owns along the Big Bend, we'd have a sixty-mile link between the St. Marks NWR in the north and the Suwannee River NWR to the south."

Dick responded, "Let's do it." Thanks to some rollover funds from the Mellon's National Wetlands Program and a generous bargain sale from Procter and Gamble, he did it. At that point Dick took his map out of the drawer. After fifteen years the land was all green. He had colored in the map, one piece at a time.

An Imperfect Storm

IN THE FALL OF 1986, BILL BLAIR, THE VERY PATRICIAN, VERY DIPLOMATIC, and very laid-back president of TNC, announced his retirement. Bill had been the perfect follow-up to Pat Noonan. Having just finished his two-year term as chairman of the board, Bill knew TNC inside and out and wasn't inclined to make any big changes. As president, Bill's major contribution was to keep the peace. With a Princeton diploma, a long and distinguished career at the State Department, and family roots that could be traced back to Blair House, he possessed the civility needed to balance TNC's raucous, no-holds-barred, often argumentative management style. With Bill in the room, flying too far off the handle or holding a grudge would appear impolite. Maintaining this undercurrent of civility was important.

To replace Bill, the board once again turned to one of its own, Frank Boren. The staff was elated. Frank was a deal guy, a big-time real estate lawyer from L.A. who'd been responsible for building the Conservancy's program in Southern California. Frank was just completing a ten-year term on TNC's national board and seemed like a natural successor to Bill. With Steve's Coachella Solution, the Mellon's $40 million, the state reps raring to go, and Dr. Bob's forty-three state natural heritage programs pumping out data, Frank would be the ideal person to drive TNC to the next level. Then, the wheels fell off the bus.

For six years, Spencer Beebe had been busily building TNC's International Program. Some of the staff felt it was getting out of control. So, what else was new? Spencer was Spencer, the loose cannon who always managed to hit something big. The best way to manage Spencer was not to manage him, let him do his thing and trade up on his success. Why change now? With Spencer flying the International Program, the rest of us could stay grounded and focus on land conservation in the United States. Unfortunately, too many people perceived Spencer as a threat, notably Dr. Bob.

Dr. Bob was convinced Spencer was jeopardizing his mission for creating a worldwide system for classifying and quantifying the earth's biotic diversity. With forty-three state natural heritage programs up and running, Dr. Bob was getting ready to take his show international, only Spencer didn't buy into the Doc's system. He felt Dr. Bob's insistence on using his scientific methodology precisely the same everywhere wouldn't work internationally. It was too slow, too tedious, and too expensive. "Central America isn't like Ohio," Spencer would say. "There are more species of plants and animals in any one of these countries than there are in all of North America."

To prove his point, Spencer cited a recent census researchers at the Smithsonian's Tropical Research Institute had just completed in Panama. Instead of scouring the forest floor for species, these researchers decided to see what was up in the canopy. They took a white sheet, spread it out under a tree, climbed up to the top, and started shaking. When they came down, there were more than 3,500 beetles, bugs, caterpillars, worms, and all types of other things lying on the sheet, many of which had never been cataloged before. For that reason, Spencer adopted the same "protect it now and sort it out later" attitude that drove TNC in the early days. Dr. Bob hadn't liked it then, and he liked it even less now.

The issue was joined, and Frank was caught in the middle. Staff members began battling among themselves, and board members started taking sides. Frank wanted one big happy family. What he got was quickly turning into the Hatfields and McCoys. On January 27, 1987, Spencer, along with just about the whole international staff and five very influential board members, resigned from TNC. On January 30, they created a new organization, Conservation International. With it, Frank's presidency and TNC suffered a serious blow to both its morale and fund-raising.

To help heal the wound, Frank decided spending some time with Peter Drucker, whom *Businessweek* magazine had labeled "The Man Who

Invented Management," would be therapeutic and booked the senior staff into a two-day seminar at Claremont College in California. Drucker lived up to his billing. He was smart, funny, and relaxed. He started by insisting we call him Peter. Then, after we'd all introduced ourselves and defined our roles within the Conservancy, he asked if we had any specific problems we'd like to address.

One problem we were having was the relationship between the state offices and the national office. Unlike the International Program, where the problem was procedure, here it was mostly about money. As TNC kept growing, arguments over who got what were becoming more and more contentious. Who had first call on individual donors? Who had first call on major foundations? If a member left an undesignated bequest, where did the money go? The first question for Peter was, "How do we resolve this conflict?"

"Vell," Peter said in his thick Austrian accent, "you haf presented a ferry difficult but not uncommon problem. The Catholic Church first faced this same dilemma in the year 400 AD and after trying for sixteen hundred years, has yet to figure it out, so please, do not expect an answer to this qvestion this morning."

We spent the next two days not trying to solve particular problems, but discussing the broad concepts of managing a nonprofit organization like TNC after a major rift. Drucker's historical knowledge, insights, and ability to see the big picture were enhanced by a never-ending supply of anecdotes about major companies like Coca-Cola and AT&T and business leaders like Welch and Gerstner. At the very end of our last session, Frank asked, "Peter, if you could name the one thing that's most important in running a successful organization, what would it be?"

Without hesitation, Peter Drucker, the man who invented management, confirmed something we'd always known but recently seemed to have forgotten: "Be nice to people," he said.

When we got back from California, Frank suffered another wound, this one self-inflicted. In an attempt to avert any conflicts with the field offices, he decided to fill several key positions at the national office with people from the field. The problem was, he didn't get the best people—he got the biggest complainers. It was like the pope bringing in disgruntled parish priests to run the Vatican. When they made mistakes—and they made a lot of mistakes—instead of asking for help, they went around blaming Frank, which only heightened tensions both at the national office and in the field.

With Spencer gone and Pat no longer directly connected with TNC, we were missing our two best fund-raisers. This fact was not lost on Frank. He became obsessed with finding new sources of funding, or "green juice" as he called it. Given his background in commercial real estate, he thought an easy way to raise money for TNC would be to buy our own headquarters building. At the time, it seemed like a good idea. Dr. Bob was bringing in a legion of computer jocks to run his inventories, and with the regional and state offices expanding, we were adding more and more support staff nationally. Having our own building would save on rent, or so we thought.

During his first year Frank found a building. TNC bought it but then discovered that our major donors had no interest in giving to a building. They liked buying land. Paying for the building ended up knocking a bundle out of the funds we'd put aside for land acquisition, and that was just the start. The time and expense it took to refurbish, move in, and manage the building put a huge drain on the national office. For the first time ever, TNC finished in the red. All the while, Frank kept searching for new sources of green juice.

In the early 1980s American Express announced it would take the lead in raising the funds needed to refurbish the Statue of Liberty. To do that, they came up with a new idea. Every time somebody used their card, American Express would donate a penny to restoring the statue. This campaign proved to be an outstanding success. New card holders soared by 45 percent, card usage increased by 28 percent, and millions of dollars were raised. American Express labeled their idea "cause-related marketing." This concept was quickly adopted by numerous other companies and charitable causes.

By the late 1980s, TNC had around 500 corporate members. To be a corporate member, a company had to give a minimum of $1,000 a year to TNC. The terms of the donation were simple. If a corporation made a gift to TNC, we'd publicly acknowledge the company as a supporter and the company was free to publicly mention it was a member. You give, we get, we both do our own thing. After cause-related marketing came into vogue, things got complicated. Corporations constantly wanted to tie their giving to certain products. We thought about it and decided it was a bad idea. Take for example International Paper. It was a wonderful company that supported TNC with both gifts of land and money. We praised them for their support, they praised us for our work, everything was clear and straightforward. If we tied IP's donations to a product, that would all change. We'd be part of their business, they'd be part of ours. How could TNC oppose an IP clear cut if we were benefiting from it? Plus, if we entered into a cause-related marketing agreement with one company, we'd be under pressure to do the same for all our other corporate members: oil companies, chemical companies, mining companies, waste-management companies, you name it. That would never pass Charlie Deaton's stink test. Better to remain as pure as Caesar's wife.

Frank didn't see it that way. In his ongoing quest for green juice, he was out squeezing every fruit on the tree. It was then that a senior partner at McKinsey & Co, the big international consulting firm, offered him what appeared to be a shiny apple. The McKinsey man personally owned a well-known seed company. Working on behalf of the seed company (not McKinsey), when he proposed a cause-related marketing deal with TNC, Frank bit. What could be cleaner than squeezing green juice from a packet of seeds?

Now that we were into cause-related marketing, the McKinsey man persuaded Frank to let McKinsey do a pro bono study of TNC. While TNC was a great organization, he was sure an outside look by McKinsey could turn up exciting new opportunities. Turning up new opportunities was just what Frank wanted to hear. Soon the entire organization was being overrun with young, newly minted MBAs demanding to know what everybody did and how they did it.

First it was the breakup with Spencer, then the disgruntled parish priests, then the building bust, and now the pretentious kids from

McKinsey. Going to work wasn't fun anymore. TNC had lost its focus. Whatever happened to saving land? Something had to change. On Wednesday, December 21, 1988, it did.

After spending the first semester of her junior year at Boston College studying in Austria, Karen Noonan, Pat and Nancy's oldest daughter, was flying home on Pan Am 103.. We'd always said we were saving all this land for future generations. For those of us who'd been building TNC through the 1970s and '80s, one of the leaders of that next generation was Karen. We'd watched her grow from a quick, funny, cute little kid into a quick, funny, beautiful young woman. Now she was gone. What was the use? I'd had it. I needed to get away from TNC for a while.

Fortunately, we had a relief valve. Back in the late 1970s, Henry Little had pushed himself to the edge by taking on the Big Creek Redwoods, Santa Cruz Island, and Silver Creek projects all at the same time. With those three major projects completed, we figured it might be good for Henry to take a six-month sabbatical and explore the possibility of TNC opening an office in Hawaii. That set the precedent. If you'd been with TNC for at least seven years and needed a change of scenery, you could take a paid leave of absence for six months and do something different. I told Frank I needed a break; that I wanted to write up some stories about how TNC had grown during the '70s and '80s.

Frank wasn't happy. He, along with his disgruntled parish priests, wanted me to give up running land acquisition and explore new opportunities in marketing. "Find out who we want to reach. What action we want to generate. What results we seek. What we can say about our current supporters. Where are our potential additional supporters?" They sounded like the McKinsey kids, plus, it was a terrible idea. I wasn't a fund-raiser, not like Spencer and Pat. Any money I raised for TNC was tied directly to projects. Without a land deal, I'd be just another organ grinder's monkey standing on the corner, tipping my hat and waving a tin cup, but Frank and his priests didn't want to hear that. I told them we'd discuss it when I got back from my break.

I was in Maine working on my history of TNC when McKinsey's pro bono study was presented to the board. After reading it Frank was gone and McKinsey's executive search firm was hired to find a replacement. When I got my hands on a copy of the study, it was clear to see why. Titled "Building on Preeminence," the study contained sixty-five pages of charts, arrows, bullets, graphs, and broad general statements of what was wrong with TNC. It zeroed in on the problem between the national office and the field offices. The conclusion was that this problem could be solved by having headquarters "assume a more active value-adding role by providing stronger leadership and pursuing national and cross-border business opportunities."

My conclusion was that McKinsey had never met with Drucker nor did he know anything about the history of the Catholic Church. His Holiness would have paid big bucks if he'd known the solution to the Church's sixteen-hundred-year-old problem was this simple. To me, the study looked like a hatchet job. After an introduction about how TNC was an "impressive organization" staffed by a "highly talented, dedicated group of professionals," it proceeded to tear the entire organization apart department by department. At the end of each section, there was something called "Representative Quotes." These quotes were taken from the fifty staff members McKinsey interviewed. There were eighty-nine separate quotes. They made up more than half the study. All were anonymous and all were negative, especially when it came to Frank and his leadership. "It's a ship without a captain," "TNC has suffered from a lack of leadership," "Headquarters is going through an identity crisis," "Frank has a vision . . . but has not been able to convey it."

For good measure, the study took some gratuitous shots at Pat. "Pat has dampened all our efforts to solicit corporate associate memberships from Fortune 1000 companies," "No one will stand up to Pat," "Pat is becoming a competitor." You'd think fifty people working for TNC, many of whom were longtime employees and knew Frank and Pat very well, would have had at least one nice thing to say about them, like how they'd both played major roles in building the organization and were totally committed to the cause of conservation. And why were all these quotes anonymous? Nobody I knew at TNC ever hesitated to express their opinions on the record.

The list of names for president that began circulating was a who's who of the environmental movement, luminaries like Russ Train, Mo Udall, Bill Riley, Doug Wheeler, and Tom Lovejoy. There was one exception: John Sawhill. Who the hell was John Sawhill? We soon found out. He was the senior partner at McKinsey in charge of energy. The word on the street was he was angling to become the secretary of energy in George Herbert Walker Bush's second term and that two years as the president of a major conservation organization would look good on his résumé. Whether that was true or not, who knows, but in the fall of 1988, John Sawhill was chosen as TNC's next president.

I first met Sawhill in June of 1990, when I came back from my break. I was refreshed, refocused, and even minus the money we'd dumped into the building, was convinced we still had the resources necessary to take TNC to the next level. With the Coachella solution, Dr. Bob's state inventories, and the Mellon money, I felt that by going back and rounding out many of TNC's existing preserves, we could create a nationwide network of natural areas that would in fact have a real impact on preserving America's natural diversity.

When I walked into Sawhill's office, it became clear right away his management style was different from Pat's, Bill Blair's, or Frank's. Sawhill was not family and didn't want to be. There was no "Dave, nice to meet you" or "It's good to have you back." John Sawhill was all business. "So," he said, "where do you see the Conservancy going?"

It was a simple question and I had a simple answer. While I explained how we had all the pieces necessary to go back and round out many of our preserves, Sawhill just sat there and listened. He asked no questions and gave no indication whether he agreed or disagreed. When I was through, he said, "I've been wondering, why does The Nature Conservancy have eleven hundred preserves?"

"Because that's what we do, John, we protect significant natural areas."

"But they're loss leaders," he said, "We lose money on every one of them. Surely we don't need eleven hundred preserves to promote the Conservancy. If we want to have an impact on conservation, what we need is a million members."

At the time, TNC had around 100,000 members, but they were by far the best supporters any organization could ask for. About the only way our members left was by dying, and even then they kept giving by remembering us in their wills. To get anywhere near a million members, we'd have to move very heavily into direct mail. We'd tried that in the early eighties and had not been very happy with the results. For TNC, it felt like a Ponzi scheme. Donations from new members were used to pay for the next mailings, which meant we had to keep getting more and more new members. To do that, we needed more mailing lists and to do that we had to start trading the names of our old faithful donors. As the lists got less selective, the returns went down while our costs kept going up. Worse yet, our most loyal members were now being inundated with direct mail from other groups, and that annoyed the hell out of them.

In addition to being expensive, direct mail brought in people with totally different agendas: population control, recycling, clean air, animal rights. What made our current members so loyal and generous was that most of them were connected to one of our preserves. They had their hands in the dirt. They cut trails, led tours, did bird counts. They were not only members, they were stewards, and if they ever wondered what The Nature Conservancy did or where their money was going, all they had to do was go out for a walk on their preserve. They supported TNC because they were part of it. Many of these new members were just looking for a free gift.

Going for a million members would transform TNC into a different organization, one whose mission no longer would be "Land Conservation Through Private Action" but "Land Conservation Through Aggressive Marketing." World Wildlife, National Wildlife, Audubon, Defenders of Wildlife, National Parks and Conservation, the Wilderness Society; in fact, all of the major groups were into marketing, but we'd always resisted going in that direction. Why waste our time and energy selling trinkets when we should be out saving land? But there was no sense worrying about that now. Sawhill had just started. Saving land was infectious. Once he got his feet on the ground, maybe he'd see that. In the meantime we still had the Coachella solution, Dr. Bob's data, what was left of the

Mellon money, and a bunch of people in the field who were fully committed to land preservation. It was time to get back to work.

I had no sooner gotten back to my office when I got a call from Charlie Haffner. Charlie was from Chicago and had served on TNC's National Board from 1974 until 1984. As the treasurer of R.R. Donnelley & Sons, the big global printing company, Charlie had connections all through the Midwest. "What the hell are you guys doing?" Charlie said.

"Doing about what?"

"About this Gray Ranch down in New Mexico?"

"Charlie, I've been on sabbatical for six months. I don't know anything about Gray Ranch."

"Well, I'm going to tell you about it," and he did. According to Charlie, TNC was getting ready to buy a 300,000-acre ranch in southwest New Mexico for $18 million, or roughly $60 an acre. A lot of the other ranches in that area were owned by influential families in Chicago and throughout the Midwest, many of whom were big supporters of TNC. Their concern, and the reason for Charlie's call, was that these families had the land appraised for estate purposes at $15 an acre. At that price they could afford to keep the ranches intact and pass them on to the next generation. At $60 an acre, they wouldn't be able to pay the estate taxes and all of these great ranches would have to be broken up and sold off. "These people are all good conservationists," Charlie said. "They love this part of the country and want to keep it the way it is, but if you guys set a price of $60 an acre, which, by the way, is way more than the land is worth, you're going to destroy everything. And I don't have to tell you, if that happens, these people aren't going to be very happy with the Conservancy."

I told Charlie I heard what he was saying and I'd look into it. What I found out was that Gray Ranch was in fact one of the last great ranches left in the Southwest. It currently was owned by a wealthy Mexican who'd been trying to sell it for a couple of years, and as Charlie Haffner noted, it was way overpriced. Originally, it had been one of the three ranches owned by Senator George Hearst, father of the newspaper magnate William Randolph Hearst, and his partner J. B. Hagen. In the 1890s these three ranches made up the largest cattle operation in the United States and Gray still carried the famous "Diamond A" brand. Given its size and elevations ranging from 5,100 to 8,500 feet, biologically it was quite diverse, but no more so than a lot of land already in public ownership. According to a report prepared by the New Mexico Department of Agriculture, "Any one of New Mexico's five national forests has greater diversity than Gray Ranch."

In 1988 the U.S. Fish and Wildlife Service had proposed buying the ranch and turning it into the Animus National Wildlife Refuge, so I called Walt McAllister, the head of land acquisition for the Fish and Wildlife Service. I'd worked with Walt for fifteen years and he, along with Vern Lindholm, his counterpart at the U.S. Forest Service, probably had done the most for adding significant natural areas to the public domain since Teddy Roosevelt and Gifford Pinchot. Walt knew everything there was to know about Gray Ranch, and none of it was good. Fish and Wildlife had thought about buying it, but their appraisal had come in at $12 million, which was way below the owner's asking price. In addition to price, managing the ranch for anything other than cattle would be prohibitively expensive, especially since it had a forty-mile-long unprotected and unpatrolled border with Mexico. Manual Lujan, George Herbert Walker Bush's secretary of the interior, was from New Mexico. He too knew all about Gray Ranch and wanted nothing to do with it. All the surrounding ranchers, many of whom were Charlie Haffner's politically well-connected cronies from the Midwest, were adamant that the ranch remain in private ownership. "Dave," Walt told me, "if you guys get involved, I'll tell you one thing—don't come looking to Fish and Wildlife to bail you out."

I'd heard enough. Gray Ranch wasn't significant, wasn't threatened, wasn't priced right, couldn't be managed, and would lead TNC into nothing but trouble. Just when I concluded that TNC didn't need any more reasons for not doing this deal, I got one, a call from an old friend who worked at American Express Bank. During the last couple of years, TNC had established an interesting relationship with the bank. When Spencer Beebe founded Conservation International, he was looking for new sources of money and discovered that Latin American governments were having trouble servicing their foreign debt. The big banks were stuck with a lot of this debt and a market had evolved where the paper was being sold for as little as 10 cents on the dollar. Spencer worked out a deal where Conservation International would buy some of these loans, then go back to the country and let them pay off the loan with land. He called it "debt-for-nature" and within a year, all the major conservation groups were doing it.

TNC was working on these debt-for-nature swaps with American Express Bank. One of the bank's clients was the owner of Gray Ranch. My friend said that TNC had asked the bank if they could help deal with the owner. He was calling to tell me that, of course, the bank could act as an intermediary, but he didn't think it was a good idea. "Look," he said, "I get the impression your people think we can work some type of deal with this guy, but I can tell you right now, that's not going to happen. He's sharp, he's tough, and he's a great trader. He's not going to listen to anything we have to say, and if it turns out to be a lousy deal for you, you're going to blame us. We've got a nice relationship going with TNC. Why wreck it by putting us in the middle? Oh, and by the way, you didn't hear it from me, but the guy you've got handling this deal doesn't know shit from shinola."

The person handling it was another one of Frank's parish priests. I went to see him. I told him why Gray Ranch didn't meet any of the five criteria we used to judge a project. In addition, the asking price was way too high, there was no leverage, and there'd be no rollover, at least as long as Lujan was the secretary of the interior. I told him about Charlie Haffner's call, and about the American Express Bank call, and how we didn't want to be anyplace near Gray Ranch. It was like talking to the wall. "Don't worry," he said, "I just met with the senior senator from New Mexico and he told me he'd support the Fish and Wildlife buying the ranch."

"Look," I said, "we've never worked with this senator before. He's never done anything for conservation. All his constituents are opposed to the project. He's not going to go against Lujan, and in all likelihood, the owner is one of his major contributors."

"What you fail to understand," he said, "is that the owner told me he's got an offer from the Japanese, and unless we act now, he's going to sell the ranch to them."

"If you believe that," I said, "I've got a bridge I want to sell you."

I walked out and made an appointment to see Sawhill. Unlike the old TNC, you couldn't just walk in to see the president anymore. I guess that was part of being a good manager. At that meeting I ran through all the facts. Once again, Sawhill just sat and listened, asked no questions, and gave no indication whether he agreed or disagreed with anything. When I was through, he said, "You know, this would be the largest single private conservation acquisition in the history of the United States."

"John," I said, "you talk about TNC's preserves being loss leaders. Well, let me tell you, what you're looking at in Gray Ranch is the largest single loss leader in the history of American conservation. You're paying too much, there's no leverage, there's no rollover, and the management costs will eat us alive. Gray Ranch is a lousy deal. Unless you've got twenty-five million bucks I don't know about, it's not something we can afford to do. Believe me, this is not how you want to start your presidency."

That was Friday afternoon. On Saturday morning I got a call at home from Cliff Messinger. Cliff was the chairman of TNC's national board. He'd made some money fixing up troubled companies in the Rust Belt and had been on the board of TNC's Wisconsin chapter. He'd never been on the Project Review Committee so I didn't know him well. "Dave," Cliff said in his methodical Midwest manner, "John told me you're opposed to the Gray Ranch deal."

"I am," I said, and went through my litany. "Frankly, Cliff," I concluded, "I don't see how it'll ever get through the project review process."

"It'll be fine," Cliff said. "John really wants to do it and I've polled the executive committee of the board. We're all behind him."

"Which means?" I said.

"Either you're in or you're out."

"I'll let you know on Monday morning."

I called Drew Mathieson, the chief financial officer for the Mellons. Over the years we'd been working with the Mellon Foundation, I'd gotten close to Drew and he'd always given me good advice, both professionally and personally. After I'd explained the situation, all he said was, "Dave, it's over. It's time for you to get out of there."

On Monday morning I tendered my resignation. After eighteen years my career with TNC was over. Sometimes you have to pay the price for being right, which brings to mind my favorite epitaph:

> *Here lies the body of William Jay*
> *Who died defending his right-of-way.*
> *He was right, dead right, as he sped along*
> *But he's just as dead as if he were wrong.*

The Harvard Syndrome

THE LAST TIME I LOOKED, HARVARD UNIVERSITY HAD AN ENDOWMENT in excess of $39,000,000,000. That's right, $39 billion, as in thirty-nine thousand million. That's more than the GNP of half the countries in the world. So why would anybody give Harvard $100 or $1,000 or $10,000 or $100,000, or even $1,000,000 for that matter? Isn't Harvard all about being smart? Wouldn't it be smarter to give that money to some group that actually needed it and could use it to help further a worthy cause? Giving money to Harvard just doesn't make sense, but then why would Patty Hearst rob a bank?

The answer is what I call the Harvard syndrome. Much like the Stockholm syndrome, people who give to Harvard are captives of the institution. According to Frank Ochberg, who is widely credited with coming up with the psychiatric definition for Stockholm syndrome, "They've developed a primitive gratitude for the gift of life." Big donors express this gratitude to Harvard by endowing chairs and giving money for new buildings with their names on them. Little donors take comfort with the crimson block H decal they can stick on a window of their car to let people know they're smart. The same can be said for people who are longtime members of the major conservation organizations. They've become captives. They believe these groups are giving them the gift of life by saving the world. Big donors give to capital campaigns with catchy names like Resources for Action and the Land Preservation Fund, which in reality are just endowments. Little donors receive a decal of a great blue heron or a panda or an oakleaf, or whatever's the natural equivalent of the block H they can stick on their car to let people know they're doing good.

Nonprofits are supposed to be conduits for directing support to a cause. During the last twenty years, the major conservation organizations have taken on too much overhead. Maintaining them is eating up most of the money meant for conservation, and the cause has fallen victim to the Harvard syndrome. Good, well-meaning people are giving to the major organizations based solely on their aura. That's not as bad as robbing a bank, but it is robbing the cause of conservation. If you're smart, you'll want to know where your donation is going.

Before you make your decision on what to give and to whom, you might want to find out how much the president of the organization is making. All through the 1970s it was understood that working for a non-profit meant you weren't going to make as much as you might working for industry. The tradeoff was "feel good, but don't do as well." Back then I'd tell kids who wanted to work for conservation, "Look, in one respect we're a lot like Wall Street: we both steal from widows and orphans. The difference is when you're working for a nonprofit, you give that money to the cause. When you're working on Wall Street, you keep it for yourself."

That attitude changed when Jay Hair, a former professor of zoology at North Carolina State University, became president of the National Wildlife Foundation. In 1981 I was asked to represent TNC at one of the lunches Jay regularly hosted for conservation leaders at snazzy D.C. restaurants. I asked him, "Don't you think this is a little pricey for nonprofits?"

Jay responded, "Businessmen don't respect us unless we can meet them on their own level." Based on this theory, one of his first acts as president of NWF was to sell a very valuable preserve that had been given to the organization and use the proceeds to build a fancy new headquarters in downtown D.C. At the top of the building, he incorporated a penthouse for himself. He also insisted on having his own car and driver. His salary compared quite favorably with that of many CEOs and was by far the highest for any president of a conservation group.

While Jay honestly believed in his theory, at TNC we knew it was all wrong. We were a charity. Our corporate members liked the fact that we had modest offices over the river from D.C., always flew coach, hosted brown-bag lunches in our crummy little conference room, and didn't get paid a whole lot. Jay, for all his good intentions, changed "feel good, but don't do as well" to "do well by doing good." It's this philosophy that has gotten the major conservation organizations up to their necks in overhead.

Another indicator that maintaining a conservation organization has become more important than its mission is when it buys its own building. Churches, hospitals, educational institutions, museums, and animal shelters need their own buildings, but conservation organizations don't. Any conservation organization with its own building should sell it, rent a good class C building in a reasonable location, and use the money from the sale to go out and save some land.

Direct mail is another red flag. Four mailings are all that's necessary to inform the public about what the group is doing. One of those should be an annual report to members that contains all of the organization's financials, lists its accomplishments for the year, includes a membership renewal envelope, and can be recycled to your dentist's waiting room. The other two or three should be newsletters that provide updates on projects, not lists of gloom and doom. These too should include an envelope for donations to help fund actual projects. Finally, in each mailing there should be information about how to leave a bequest in your will to the organization. If a group has done a good job supporting the cause during your lifetime, it deserves a going-away present. Other than these three or four mailings, throw everything else away, especially if the group's offering you a gift. You're supposed to be giving to a cause, not paying for tote bags, water bottles, and personalized address labels.

A sure sign that an organization has lost its focus is when it starts selling trinkets. For some major groups, selling trinkets has become a large part of what they do. If you want T-shirts, tote bags, mugs, hats, pillows, sheets, lamps, quilts, and other trinkets embossed with wildlife, you don't need to buy it from some conservation group. Orvis, Cabela's, L.L. Bean, Patagonia, Eddie Bauer, and lots of other real companies sell these things, and many of them have made a major commitment to conservation.

Patagonia's catalog is probably one of the best conservation magazines published today, and Yvon Chouinard, the founder of Patagonia, is one of the world's great conservationists. Thanks to Yvon, Patagonia has committed 1 percent of gross sales—not net profit but actual gross sales—to the preservation and restoration of the natural environment. With his buddies Kristine and Doug Tompkins, Yvon is creating a world-class preserve in southern Chile. The 750,000-acre Patagonia National Park is an all-volunteer effort, so if you really want to be sure 100 percent of your donation is going to a project, send it to *Conservacion Patagonica*. Better yet, you can go down and work on the preserve. According to Kristine Tompkins, "All willing hands are welcome."

What more could a real conservationist ask for? Here's an invitation to be held captive in Chile by a world-class preserve and show "your primitive gratitude for the gift of life" by clearing out old sheep fences twelve hours a day. Under the Patagonia syndrome you'd be abetting a worthy cause. Unlike Patty Hearst, you probably wouldn't get brainwashed and end up robbing a bank, and unlike the Harvard alumnus, you probably wouldn't be paying a hundred dollars for a 20-cent decal.

Back to the Future

IN 2003 RAMSAY PEARD, AN OLD BUDDY OF MINE FROM BUSINESS SCHOOL, invited me to canoe the Connecticut River with him. I said, "Sure, but under one condition: no camping. I'm too old to be sleeping on the ground, cooking over an open fire, and crapping in the woods—and so are you."

"But where will we stay?" he said.

"We'll be like Blanche DuBois in *A Streetcar Named Desire*. We'll rely on the kindness of strangers." And that's what we did. For the entire month of June 2003, we wound our way down the Connecticut staying with different strangers every night.

What I learned from that trip is that we've beaten the hell out of the Connecticut, like we have most of our major rivers. The place where a river gets to show who's boss is at its falls. There you realize it has the power to kill you. The once mighty Connecticut doesn't have falls anymore. They've been eliminated by sixteen major dams. We've stolen all the river's power. For the most part the Connecticut's nothing more than a series of lakes, and they're polluted. Years of dumping industrial waste, sewage, and storm runoff into the river have made large parts of this great river unsuitable for drinking, swimming, and even fishing.

One of the strangers we stayed with on our trip was Dr. Charles Cunningham, a retired pathologist living in Springfield, Vermont. By the time we got to Springfield, the icy spring waters of the Connecticut were starting to warm up and I was thinking if it got hot, I might want to go for a swim. Knowing much of the lower Connecticut was polluted, I asked the Doc if it was all right to swim along this section of the river. "Do you like swimming in treated or untreated crap?" he said. "The storm drains and sewer plants in towns like West Lebanon and Springfield use the same lines for water runoff and sewage. When the weather's dry, the sewerage is treated. When it rains, they divert everything directly into the river. They're working to straighten it out, but treated or untreated, crap is still crap."

The day was sunny and hot. When Ramsay and I stopped for a break, I stripped down to my shorts and lay back on a big rock next to a quiet eddy in the river. The rock had absorbed much of the morning heat, so before long I felt like a piece of bacon sizzling in the pan. The cool, clear waters rolling by looked tempting and I was about to roll off the rock into the river when the Doc's words flashed to my mind, "treated or untreated, crap's still crap."

That put an end to my swim, but it was the start of an epiphany. Lying on that rock, I realized my definition of a truly civilized society is one where any kid, at any time, anywhere can jump into any river and go for a swim. That's not true for 40 percent of America's rivers. Why is it that the richest, most powerful nation in the world won't clean up its rivers? Why is it we think it's OK for our rivers to be polluted? Sure, cleaning them up is a big job, but it's not a difficult one. We have the technology. What we're lacking is the willpower.

On May 25, 1961, John F. Kennedy announced before a special joint session of Congress that by the start of the next decade, 1970, America would land a man on the moon. Given that commitment, on July 20, 1969, Neil Armstrong stepped onto the moon. America had done something that nine years earlier had seemed impossible. I happen to be writing this on Earth Day 2011, just a half century after Kennedy's man-on-the-moon speech. Wouldn't it be nice if today Barack Obama stood up before a joint session of Congress and announced by the start of the next decade, 2020, any kid, any time, anywhere in America could jump into any river and go for a swim? Compared to going to the moon, it would be easy, only it's not going to happen. The last thing the president is thinking about today is cleaning up our rivers. Why should he? We've never made it a priority. Congress doesn't care and for the most part, Americans don't care. As a society, we're content with using our rivers as sewers. So who's complaining?

Back in the early 1970s when I was working on preserving the Pascagoula, I got a call from Charlie Deaton, a member of the Wildlife Heritage Committee and the head of House Appropriations for the Mississippi legislature. The legislature was getting ready to vote on the $15 million appropriation for the purchase of the Pascagoula hardwoods, and Charlie had a job for me. "Morine," he said, "the garden clubs of Mississippi are holdin their annual meeting in Laurel next week and I've got you booked as the guest speaker."

"Me?" I said, totally surprised. "What am I going to say to the garden clubs? I don't know anything about flowers."

"This ain't about flowers," Charlie said. "It's about the $15 million we're tryin to get from the legislature. When it comes to conservation, these gals wield a lot of power."

"What will I tell them?" I said.

"Tell 'em just what you've been tellin us, that these are the best bottomland hardwoods left in the state, that we need more public lands for huntin and fishin, that livin close to the land is who we are, that we gotta start spendin some money protectin our natural resources or we're gonna end up lookin like New Jersey."

I didn't know much about the garden clubs and couldn't imagine these women would have any interest in anything I had to say, but if Charlie said I had to go, I had to go. He was the guy carrying the ball in the legislature.

I was wrong about the garden clubs. They were very interested and ended up grilling me with dozens of questions, all of them right on point. Still, when I left I didn't know what I'd accomplished. The Mississippi legislature was an all-boys club. There wasn't one woman in it. The night the bill passed, Charlie and Avery Wood called me from the governor's office. It was three in the morning. They told me that the opposition had tried to kill it by not bringing the bill up for a vote before midnight, the time when the session officially ended. That was how the legislature killed a lot of bills in Mississippi. They just wouldn't bring them up before the session ended. That way they could go home and say they were all for it, but they couldn't get to it . . . sorry, maybe next year.

For preserving the Pascagoula there was no next year, so Charlie had stationed Avery up in the balcony right over the big Roman-numeraled clock that marks time in the Mississippi legislature. When the clock was about to strike XII, Avery leaned over and turned the hands back an hour, which apparently was an old but seldom used trick in the legislature. "When those boys saw that," Charlie said, "they knew they were cooked. Thanks to your talk at the garden clubs, if they went home without that bill passing, they'd be sleeping out in the garage."

Since that time, I've had great respect for garden clubs, and for good reason. The Garden Clubs of America and the National Federation of Garden Clubs together have more than 200,000 members. These women are well organized, politically and socially connected, have a keen understanding of how natural systems work, and are concerned about the environment. What more could the conservation movement want? If the garden clubs made cleaning up our rivers a major issue, they could help give America the willpower it needs. For that reason, whenever I have a chance, I like to speak to garden clubs.

In November of 2010 Katchen Coley, the grande dame of conservation in Middletown, Connecticut, invited me to speak at her club. Katchen was one of the strangers who took Ramsay and me in during our trip down the Connecticut. The project for Katchen's club for the coming year was to look at the Nutmeg State's water, open space, and forest resources and see what could be done to protect them. *Two Coots in a Canoe*, the book I'd written that described our trip down the Connecticut, had just come out. In it I mention how towns that have embraced the river are cleaner, nicer, more prosperous, and the people happier than those that have turned their back on it. The example I use is a tale of two cities: Springfield, Massachusetts, and Hartford, Connecticut.

Just thirty miles apart, both sit on the Connecticut River. Springfield, though it tried, failed to make the river part of the community. Now, for all practical purposes, Springfield is financially and naturally bankrupt. Hartford, on the other hand, has done a magnificent job incorporating the river into the city, and it is vibrant and thriving. Anchored by a beautiful public boathouse, a well-designed and immaculately maintained river park has set the tone for the entire community. Instead of looking across the river at a sewage-treatment plant and a trash dump like Springfield, Hartford looks at crisp, clean, condominiums buffered by more parkland. The boathouse, with its many programs for getting people of all ages and backgrounds onto the river, has become the keystone to Hartford's quality of life. Take it out, and all the other recent gains Hartford has made as a livable city would collapse.

Over the years, snappy corporate slogans like "We bring good things to life" have convinced people that technology is what determines our quality of life. While that's true up to a point, it leaves out the most important part. Maintaining and improving our quality of life starts with two things: clean air and clean water. That's what brings things to life. Without clean air and water, all technology in the world would mean nothing.

Look at the Gulf of Mexico. I always thought the refuges I helped create along the Gulf Coast would be my legacy to this earth. BP's Deepwater Horizon technical bust blew up that thought. The spill has destroyed much of these refuges and the life they supported. Knowing we have yet to see the full impact of this disaster, and probably won't for years to come, most people along the Gulf are in some stage of depression. They feel that their world has been soiled, that it's a lesser place, that their quality of life will never be the same, and they're right. Then there's the nuclear disaster in Japan. What would they give for clean air and water? And so it goes.

I gave Katchen's club my spiel on how rivers are the lifeblood of our planet and natural systems the keystones to our quality of life. A group from the club was scheduled to meet with members of the Connecticut legislature the following day so when the discussion turned to questions and answers, what the members wanted to know was what Connecticut should be doing to protect its water resources. Like all states, Connecticut was facing serious cutbacks and it was a foregone conclusion that funding for conservation would be severely cut. Why were these very smart and very powerful women willing to accept that? Why weren't they mad as hell and ready to do something about it? Why aren't we all mad as hell and ready to do something about it?

People claim we don't have the money. Of course we have the money, it's just going to other things, some of them important, some of them not so important, but all of them with a constituency that's made them a priority. With $50,000, we were able to help protect seven key areas along the Connecticut River. Think what we could do with a billion dollars, the cost of one day of waging all our wars. That would be a million dollars for 1,000 rivers. If we leveraged that money like we know how and rolled it over like we know how, we could have kids rolling off rocks into clean rivers all over America.

I told Katchen's club they had to make cleaning up Connecticut's rivers a priority. They had to convince the legislature that there was nothing more important it could be doing. They had to start serving up some "Home Cookin'," and if that didn't work, let it be known that any legislator who failed to recognize the need for cleaning up Connecticut's rivers would be sleeping in the garage. If the Mississippi legislature could be convinced to appropriate $15 million to protect the Pascagoula River back in 1974, why couldn't the Connecticut legislature be convinced to come up with $50 million in 2011? Rather than cutting the funding for conservation, they should be increasing it.

Land conservation through private action should be the catalyst. With local land trusts, we have the organizations. With foundations, we have the seed funds. Now's the time for conservation to return to being a movement led primarily by volunteers. It's time to recapture the spirit behind TNC's first and best project, the Mianus River Gorge. If the cause of conservation wants to move ahead, it has to go back to its roots, back to the future.

A friend of mine, Doug Swift, is the president of a little fishing club on the Brodhead, a small stream that runs into the Delaware River just north of the Water Gap. As part of his duties as president, Doug was asked to join the board of the Brodhead Watershed Association, a local group of volunteers whose mission is to protect the stream. Once on the board, Doug asked me if I'd look at the watershed and see if I had any ideas on what the association should be doing to protect it. After driving around with him for a day, I told Doug, "You've got to start acquiring more land along the stream, but whatever you do, don't go public with some big, detailed plan for protecting the watershed. Do that and you'll spend the next twenty years going to meetings listening to people tell you why you can't do it. Instead, start protecting one piece at a time, and they all don't have to fit together. Eventually, the big picture will develop on its own. You'll be sitting there one day and some government official will look at the map and say, 'Hey, you know what, if we just connect these pieces, we can save the whole watershed.' Bingo, that's when you've got it."

Doug mentioned there was a piece abutting the fishing club that was coming up for auction. "Look," I said, "it's time you all got into the game. The club should buy this piece, then give a conservation easement over it to the local land trust. It'll be fun. You'll like it. These auctions can get pretty intense."

Doug was used to intense situations. Before leaving to go to medical school and then on to become the anesthesiologist on Temple University's elite heart transplant team, Doug was the starting outside linebacker for the Miami Dolphins. During his six years with the Dolphins, Doug won two Super Bowl rings and set the defenses that led to Miami's perfect 14–0 season. He called me from the auction. "We got it!" he said, "and let me tell you, this feels as good as winning the Super Bowl."

So, how do you get your feet wet? Go find a spring or a bog. It'll flow into a stream. The stream will meet up with a river. The river eventually will reach the sea. Somewhere along that chain, there'll be a little conservation organization run primarily by volunteers trying to protect it. Join them, then pick a spot where you can look out, make sure it meets the five criteria for a project, figure out where you are on the screw, get yourself into some trouble, find a foundation, wait for a full moon, let Mother Nature sing, have some fun, save some land, and all the while, be nice to people. You'll feel like you just won the Super Bowl, and we'll all be better for it.

Dumbo's Feather

Since leaving The Nature Conservancy, I've kept a hand in conservation by volunteering for local land trusts. I like working for these little organizations because they're mostly volunteer efforts and the volunteers are more interested in saving land than they are in building big organizations. They're frugal and focused, but the one thing I've noticed about these little groups is even when they have all the pieces of a project put together, they're scared to make the commitment. They keep finding things wrong and I keep telling them, "Look, you can't get yourself out of trouble until you get into it, so pull the trigger."

I call this my "Dumbo's Feather" phenomenon. These fledging groups can fly, but they don't know they can fly. What you have to do is build up their confidence, and there's no better way to do that than by giving them lots of advice and a little money for a specific project. That's the magic feather. Once you've pushed them out of the nest, they start flapping their ears and bingo, they're flying. Better yet, once they get that confidence, it keeps building on itself. After a while some of them are soaring.

During our trip down the Connecticut, Ramsay and I came across Whitty Sanford, associate director of the Connecticut River Watershed Council. Whitty knew of me from my time with the Conservancy and through some volunteer work I'd done with a land trust in the Pioneer Valley. Whitty asked me if, when we came down the river, I'd mind meeting with a few of the sixty-one land trusts that were working on projects along the Connecticut. Whitty thought I might be able to give them some advice. I said I'd be happy to do that but thought we might be able to do even better. Maybe we could give them a Dumbo's Feather.

Most people think of Dan Lufkin, a founding partner of the investment firm Donaldson, Lufkin & Jenrette, as one of America's great businessmen, but Dan's a lot more than that. He's one of America's great conservationists. Besides giving both his time and money most generously to any number of conservation groups, Dan was the first director of

Connecticut's Department of Natural Resources. During the four years he served in that position, Dan completely turned around the Nutmeg State's attitude of taking its natural resources for granted and in doing so, set the standard for state conservation efforts in America.

I first met Dan in 1975 when he joined the board of The Nature Conservancy. Over the next ten years, he used his work, wisdom, and wealth to help TNC undertake some of the biggest and most important land conservation projects in America. Dan was always opening bigger and better doors for us. Having Dan in our corner gave us the confidence we needed to make TNC the most successful private land conservation organization in the world.

About the time we were preparing to canoe the Connecticut, I heard that Dan had gone on the board of a new foundation and was directing much of its giving to land conservation, so I wrote him a letter. I told him that since leaving TNC I'd stayed active in conservation by volunteering for little local land trusts and how most of them could fly, but didn't know they could fly until somebody gave them a Dumbo's Feather. Then I described our trip down the Connecticut and how I'd be looking at projects that some of the sixty-one land trusts along the river were working on. I ended my letter with, "I'm sure what they need more than anything else is confidence, the kind you gave us when you came on the board of the Conservancy."

A couple of days later, Dan called. He said he was making me the foundation's one-month, unpaid project manager for the Connecticut River and had approved a $50,000 grant we could use as "feathers" to seed projects along the river. We ended up making seven grants, and in each case the group working on the project flapped its ears and took off. All seven projects were successful, but one in particular stood out.

The Upper Valley Land Trust, along with numerous other groups, was trying to protect an upland hardwood forest that contained the headwaters for both the Waits River and the First Branch of the White River. Located in the towns of Washington and Corinth, Vermont, this forest marks the divide between the Connecticut and St. Lawrence watersheds. From it, the First Branch of the White winds its way north into the St.

Lawrence while the Waits flows east into the Connecticut. Carl Demrow, who'd been designing and constructing trails for the Appalachian Mountain Club, was the main impetus behind the project. After he'd shown us around, it was obvious the project met all five of TNC's criteria, but that Carl was going to need a push to get started. A little advice and a $10,000 seed grant got him flying. Since then the project has blossomed into a public/private effort that has conserved thirty separate parcels totaling more than 5,000 acres, and they're not through yet. Local groups along the two rivers are beginning to realize the job won't be done until their conservation efforts reach the St. Lawrence to the north and the Connecticut to the east.

What these grants prove is that we can clean up our rivers, that local land trusts can do major projects, that seed grants can push them into action, and that confidence can build on itself. The challenge now is to find enough good projects undertaken by enough frugal and focused organizations that can be pushed enough by seed grants to start a movement that will, over time, save our rivers. The projects, the people, and the money are all there.

Fly Dumbo, fly.

Epilogue: Going Feral

ON THE EVENING I RESIGNED FROM THE NATURE CONSERVANCY, RUTH and I were scheduled to attend a cocktail party in Washington, D.C., at the home of John and Barbara Franklin. Barbara had been Frank Boren's executive assistant at the Conservancy, and John, who'd been a couple of years ahead of me at Amherst, ran the Washington office of Russell Reynolds Associates, a leading executive search firm with thirty-nine offices worldwide. The reason for the party was that Russell Reynolds, the firm's founder and John's boss, was coming to D.C. and the Franklins were eager to present him with a full house. I had no desire to go to a big Washington party, but Ruth insisted. To stand the Franklins up at the last minute would be very rude.

The reception was quite a to-do. The house was packed, the tables groaned with fancy foods and fine wines, and A-list names were holding court in every corner. While I recognized a lot of people, I knew almost no one, and since the first question at these things is usually, "And what do you do," I was quite content to hunker down next to the bar and mind my own business. I was sampling one of John's fine wines when he came up to me. "Dave," he said, "I heard you just left the Conservancy. Why don't you come in and see me tomorrow? I'd be interested in knowing what you plan to do."

As I was explaining to John how I hadn't really made any plans and wanted to take a while to think about things, Russell Reynolds, the big man himself, came over and joined us. After introducing me, John said to Russ, "Dave, here, was vice president for land acquisition at The Nature Conservancy for eighteen years. He's worked with all the big landowners like IP, St. Regis, Union Camp, Champion International.

He's just left the Conservancy and I was telling him he should come in and see us."

"By all means," Russ said, quickly sizing me up. "It's important you get right back on the horse. Otherwise, they'll forget who you are."

I didn't feel like getting right back on the horse, and what could Russell Reynolds possibly have in their stable that would fit me? Nonetheless, I needed a mount so it would be crazy not to give it a shot. "I'll see you tomorrow," I said.

The next morning I strode confidently into the well-appointed offices of Russell Reynolds Associates. The address on the brass plaque next to the door read 1701 Pennsylvania Avenue. From there, John Franklin could fold my curriculum vitae into a paper airplane and literally sail it over to the White House. A well-coifed, stylishly dressed woman was sitting at the reception desk. She immediately informed John I was there. She then ushered me down a corridor lined with expensive art and into his opulent office. John stopped whatever he was doing, got up from behind his big desk, and enthusiastically shook my hand. "Dave, I'm so pleased you came in. Russ and I had a chance to talk about you last night and we're truly excited about the opportunities we see for you."

Opportunities for me? I couldn't believe it, but John sounded like he really meant it.

"Why, thank you, I said. "I'm excited to be here." And by now I meant it.

Once we were comfortably settled into a couple of matching wing chairs, I reached into my breast pocket, pulled out my freshly typed curriculum vitae, and proffered it over the glossy wood coffee table to John. He glanced over it. "Great," he said, laying it aside. "I'd forgotten you got your MBA from Darden. Now, why don't you just tell me about yourself?"

For the next hour, that's what I did. I summarized my career at the Conservancy. I told John about some of the deals we'd done, how we'd been able to save countess islands, prairies, wetlands, and forests from development. I told him why these areas were important, how we had to be willing to take a stand when they were threatened, how we had to balance the use of our natural resources. I even sprinkled in a few quotes from Aldo Leopold's *A Sand County Almanac* and Rachel Carson's *Silent Spring*. I could tell I was at the top of my game: interesting, well informed, topical, and funny. John looked stunned, like he couldn't believe what he was hearing, especially when I finished with my coup de grace, Thoreau's "any man more right than his neighbors makes up a majority of one." That was it. There was nothing left to say.

I sat back, took a sip from my coffee, and waited for John to overwhelm me with limitless opportunities. Instead, all he said was, "My God, I was thinking we could get you a job as the spokesperson for some major corporation like Exxon or DuPont or IP, but that's impossible. You no longer think like an MBA. You actually believe all this stuff. You've gone feral."

So much for getting back on the horse. I've been walking ever since. Not that there's anything wrong with that.